AN INFORMAL HISTORY
OF THE GERMAN LANGUAGE

THE LANGUAGE LIBRARY

EDITED BY ERIC PARTRIDGE AND SIMEON POTTER

W. B. Lockwood

AN INFORMAL HISTORY OF THE GERMAN LANGUAGE

with chapters on Dutch and Afrikaans,
Frisian and Yiddish

ANDRE DEUTSCH

First published by W. Heffer & Son 1965
This edition 1976 by André Deutsch Limited
105 Great Russell Street London wc1

Printed in Great Britain by
Wm. Clowes & Sons Limited
London, Beccles and Colchester

ISBN 0 233 96797 4

To my helpers
E. and V.

CONTENTS

LIST OF MAPS

PREFACE

This book is addressed to anyone interested in the German language. It presupposes a knowledge of the rudiments of Modern German, but otherwise no more than a little linguistic curiosity and an elementary knowledge of grammatical concepts.

Just as historians differ about what properly constitutes history, so philologists may argue about what is fundamental in the history of a language. At any rate it is clear that the historian of language, like the general historian, can do no more than offer selections from an infinite material. In the present work I have chosen matter which seems to me useful for those beginning the historical study of the language. I have often had at the back of my mind the undergraduate who fights shy of the philological side of language study because of the apparently forbidding character of the standard handbooks.

There is much more to German than the modern High German Standard. The historical study of German embraces the language at all stages of its evolution and in all its manifestations, both written and spoken. It is therefore concerned with dialect and with the relationship between the written and the spoken word, a matter of some practical importance to those learning the language. German in its wider sense includes not only High German and its varieties, one of which, Yiddish, is now in every sense an independent language. It includes also Low German, to which Dutch and Afrikaans belong. All these things are touched upon in this book. At certain points on the northern periphery of the main German-speaking area the first language of many of the inhabitants is Frisian. Although not defined as a form of German, Frisian is nevertheless so closely related that it seemed inappropriate to omit it in an account like the present.

The Bibliographies are meant to be helpful indications.

I take this opportunity of publicly thanking the Administrators of the Ernest Cassel Trust for support given longer ago than I dare to recall now.

I am most grateful to Dr. S. A. Birnbaum for a number of suggestions in connection with the chapter on Yiddish and to Dra. T. Feitsma and Professor P. Gerbenzon who gave me advice on Frisian matters. I also wish to thank Gwyneth Wall for a good deal of careful technical assistance.

W. B. LOCKWOOD

PREFACE TO THE SECOND EDITION

A reissue of the book provided an opportunity for correcting various items in the original text. Statistics and bibliographies have been brought up to date.

I am much indebted to Professor Simeon Potter for support in the preparation of this second edition.

W.B.L.

THE OLD PERIOD

1

ANTECEDENTS AND EARLY RECORDS

German is a member of the Germanic group of languages, in older writings often referred to as the Teutonic group. The group is conventionally divided into three sub-groups, the members of each sub-group being more closely related to each other than to the members of the other sub-groups. The sub-groups are termed East, North and West Germanic. The first is now extinct. It comprises the languages of tribes which became prominent in Eastern Europe at the time of the decline of the Roman Empire, but with one exception little is known of these languages. The exception is Gothic, preserved in large fragments of a translation of the Bible made about A.D. 350; it is written in a peculiar alphabet based upon Greek. Gothic is the oldest example of a Germanic language and, as we would therefore suppose, shows many archaic features not found in other Germanic languages.

North Germanic consists of the Scandinavian languages; these are today Swedish, Danish, Norwegian, Faroese and Icelandic. The first three are very similar to each other, but the two island languages are more divergent. They are also more archaic, Icelandic especially being in its grammatical structure hardly different from Old Norse, the medieval ancestral form of the modern Scandinavian languages. Old Norse is a copiously documented language. It was the vehicle of a rich literature, notably of history, sagas and poetry. It was written for the most part in Iceland, hence the term Old Icelandic is often used for the language of such texts. The oldest literary works in Old Norse go back to the 9th century, but there are a few inscriptions on stone as much as four or five centuries older. The literary works are written in the Latin alphabet, but the inscriptions are in Runic.

The West Germanic languages are German (in the wider sense, including Dutch), Frisian and English. Owing to its

1

isolation and especially owing to the mass influx of French elements after the Norman Conquest, English has become very much unlike the related continental languages, while these, remaining in intimate contact, have developed along similar lines. The oldest texts in a West Germanic language are found in Old English documents composed in the 7th century.

PRIMITIVE GERMANIC

The ancestor of all these languages is called Primitive Germanic. By the nature of the case, this could not be an exactly uniform language. It was rather a cluster of closely related, mutually comprehensible dialects. When it first comes into our ken towards the beginning of the Christian era it was spoken in Southern Scandinavia and North Germany. This language was never written since its speakers were all illiterate, but a few words from it are known since they were recorded by contemporary Roman and Greek writers. Thus a Germanic word for javelin appears in Latin texts as *gaesum*, in Greek as *gaison*. It has been established by theoretical deduction that the Germanic original was **gaisan*. The names of various Germanic notables were recorded by the historians. Julius Caesar mentions a certain *Chariovaldus*. This name can be analysed as *Chario-* 'army' and *vald-* 'leader', which in modern German would give *Heerwalt*. The name was common in Scandinavia, its Old Norse form being *Haraldr*. Brought to Britain by Norse settlers in the Viking Age, it is still in use as *Harold*.

From the time when we first get to know about Primitive Germanic its unity was already being considerably disturbed. A great expansion of Germanic tribes in all directions was breaking the old ties. The tribal dialects became more differentiated as once neighbouring tribes moved away from each other. New dialects arose through the isolation of migrating groups or the splitting up of others. Others again arose through new combinations of tribesmen. These movements took the Germanic speakers south as far as the Alps, into the Central European plain and down into the Balkans, eastwards into what is now Poland and Russia and on to the Black Sea. Then those in the east turned westwards again. Germanic tribesmen conquered Italy and sacked Rome. They founded kingdoms in

Southern Gaul and in Spain. One large group, the Vandals, crossed the Straits of Gibraltar and established themselves in North Africa. Such migrations as these, restless, backwards and forwards, criss-cross, continued in full vigour until the 7th century.

By way of illustration we outline the wanderings of one such tribe. The Burgundians are called an East Germanic tribe. Migrating from Sweden via the island of Bornholm, to which they gave the name (< Old Norse *Borgundarholmr* 'Island of the Burgundians'), they crossed to the southern shore of the Baltic probably during the first century B.C. and advanced inland to settle between the Vistula and Oder. Other migrating Germanic tribes moved through this region, but the Burgundians as such appear to have remained there until the beginning of the 5th century. Their neighbours to the west were West Germanic tribes, to the east Baltic and Slavonic tribes. Yielding perhaps to the pressure of the latter, they migrated westward at the beginning of the 5th century. Some of them remained in Thuringia and later came under Hunnish influence. Others reached the Middle Rhine and there established a kingdom in 406. This was destroyed by the Huns in 437 and the Burgundian king, *Gundihari*—King Gunther of the Lay of the Nibelungs—and his royal entourage were slain. The remnant of these Burgundians took refuge in Gaul. They set up a kingdom in the south-east and gave their name to the region, hence French *Bourgogne*, Burgundy. They were later reinforced by Burgundians from Thuringia and maintained their independence until overthrown by the Franks in 534. They are thought to have preserved their Germanic speech until the 7th century or shortly afterwards, when they were finally romanised. We have cited the case of the Burgundians, not because their migrations were particularly striking or romantic, but because they are fairly well documented in the writings of the ancient historians. Furthermore, some of their movements can be traced archaeologically. It is known, for instance, that the Burgundians of Thuringia adopted the Hunnish practice of deforming the skull in infancy. It is thus easy to identify one of their cemeteries.

What would the Burgundian language be like by the time they had reached the end of their wanderings? We can never give a full answer since all that remains are personal names and a few words in the French dialect of Bourgogne, identified as originally Burgundian. But we can imagine the essential trends. The language is traditionally termed East Germanic because the Burgundians themselves were undoubtedly an East Germanic tribe, that is to say, a tribe of Scandinavian origin which had settled or at least passed through the Vistula-Oder region. The speech of the Burgundians must thus originally have had more in common with the Scandinavian dialects than with those of Germany. But as a result of some centuries of contact with West Germanic peoples, the Burgundians will have been irresistibly drawn into the West Germanic orbit, though not without their having contributed something to WGmc. too.

Against such a background we must consider the conventional designations East, West and North Germanic. The terms have some practical convenience, but it may be emphasised that they are not to be understood as primary sub-divisions of Primitive Germanic in the sense that PGmc. first split up into the Proto-EGmc., Proto-WGmc. and Proto-NGmc. languages and that from these are then derived the actually recorded languages. This opinion has, however, been frequently expressed; it was indeed for long part of the doctrine. But the facts do not really warrant such a postulate. It is more reasonable to see North Germanic as the product of local evolution after the 'East' Germanic peoples had left Scandinavia. The earliest records of West Germanic languages are from the 7th and 8th centuries. Certainly the languages at this period are strikingly similar, but the similarities can be due to the languages having co-existed for so many centuries, latterly under the domination of the Franks. We can infer little about the situation at the end of the Primitive Germanic period from documents as late as the 7th and 8th centuries. When the various features of WGmc. are compared with NGmc. and EGmc., it is seen that some are shared with the north, but not the east, others with the east, but not the north. In addition WGmc. has several peculiarities not found in either NGmc. or EGmc. What makes comparative work more difficult is the nature of the early records. In NGmc., the records are not plentiful until much later than the first considerable documents in WGmc. The composition of the oldest literary work in Norse will barely antedate the 10th century. Significant early features, which would throw light on the problem of origins, may have disappeared, in fact almost certainly must have. EGmc., on the other hand, is the earliest recorded Germanic, but there is a continuous text in one language only, i.e. in Gothic. The Gothic text arose in Moesia (Northern Bulgaria), far to the south of the main Germanic area. It is impossible to say exactly how typical this language was of EGmc. in general. It is to be emphasised that the rate of linguistic change in these largely non-literate communities could be very rapid, especially under the unsettled conditions of the Age of Migrations.

The chief source for the history of the Ancient Germans is Tacitus' *Germania*, written shortly after A.D. 98. Tacitus distinguishes three main groups, the Ingvaeonians of the North Sea coast, the Istvaeonians of the Rhine, and the Herminonians of the interior. This tripartite division has formed the basis for much linguistic speculation. Scholars have tried to find traces of it in the languages and dialects of the areas, labelling some features Ingvaeonian, other Istvaeonian, etc. New facts of detail are constantly being revealed, but their interpretation is often problematic and the main question still not satisfactorily answered.

But modern researches have at least led to important changes in general notions of classification. We have already referred to the division of PGmc. into three sub-groups, East, West and North Germanic, and to the older, erroneous view which regarded this grouping as the reflex of an ancient tripartite cleavage intermediary between PGmc. and the actually recorded derivative languages. It was also formerly supposed that Proto-WGmc. split into two halves, Anglo-Frisian and Proto-German. From the former English and Frisian were considered to have descended, from the latter both forms of German, that is to say the Low German of the north and the High German of the centre and south. But it has now been shown that Low German, especially at its earliest stage, has certain features in common with English and Frisian which appear to be basic, whereas the similarities with other German can be explained as relatively recent developments, possibly not older than the Merovingian period (481–751). The concept of Proto-German unity thus appears too schematic. The concept of one-time Anglo-Frisian unity has likewise been found inadequate; see further in the chapter on Frisian, p. 214.

We sum up by saying that whereas comparative philology is able, on the basis of the known Germanic languages, to postulate the former existence of a Primitive Germanic language and to reconstruct, in some sort, its basic vocabulary and the essentials of its phonetics and accidence, the linguistic evidence is not such that we can confidently outline the prehistory of any one of the attested languages. We have referred to the problems posed by the early records. Material known only from modern times, i.e. the evidence of the present-day dialects, is even more difficult to interpret with certainty owing to the great changes which have inevitably taken place in the course of two millennia.

BIBLIOGRAPHY

Basic grammatical statements are to be found in E. Prokosch, *A Comparative Germanic Grammar*, Philadelphia, 1939, or in a more condensed form in H. Krahe-W. Meid, *Germanische Sprachwissenschaft*[7], Berlin, 3 vols, 1967–69.

An idea of the character of research on the more general problems may be obtained from T. Frings, *Grundlegung einer Geschichte der deutschen Sprache*[3], Halle, 1957.

GERMANIC AND INDO-EUROPEAN

How long Primitive Germanic had been in existence before appearing dimly in the light of history towards the beginning of the Christian era, or where it first took shape, cannot be established. But the Germanic group of languages is ultimately related to a wider family. It is one of a number of groups which together comprise the great Indo-European family of languages which even in antiquity stretched from India to the Atlantic. Among the better known groups in this family are the Celtic (Gaelic, Welsh), Italic (Latin), Hellenic (Greek), Slavonic (Russian, Czech), Indo-Iranian (Sanskrit, Persian). Germanic speech has a marked individuality with important features not paralleled in the other groups. The sweeping character of the changes is usually attributed to substratum influence. That is to say, Germanic is an Indo-European language drastically modified by contact with an unknown non-Indo-European language. This very plausible explanation has led to the assumption that Indo-European invaders conquered and subsequently fused with an indigenous people. As the changes are as regular as they are sweeping, the process of fusion must have been a very thorough one and may be supposed to have taken place at a time when there was no contact with other Indo-European groups to disturb the process. Many scholars have suggested Scandinavia as the most likely birth place of Germanic speech. But known historical facts give no help since the changes in question are prehistoric; at the time of the earliest records the Germanic peoples already form a distinct entity. Their neighbours to the west and south were Celts. At an earlier stage their south-eastern neighbours were Illyrians, also a people of Indo-European stock.

BIBLIOGRAPHY

W. B. Lockwood, *Indo-European Philology*², London, 1971, further by the same author *A Panorama of Indo-European Languages*, London, 1972.

THE EARLIEST RECORDS IN GERMAN

When German, as distinct from Germanic, first came into being cannot be stated exactly. In fact there was no exact date and even an approximate answer would depend on a definition of the terms language and dialect, as may be inferred from what has been said about the development of the various Germanic languages in the first part of this chapter. But this much is certain. By the time sufficient written records appear, that is in the eighth century, the vernacular of Germany had passed through a number of changes which mark it off from the other Germanic languages. Furthermore, the dialects which constitute this vernacular themselves fall into two distinct groups, the first covering the north of the country, the second the centre and south. There are some differences between them in grammatical structure and in vocabulary, but what distinguishes them most sharply are the phonetic innovations of the second group. It is therefore appropriate to think of German at this period not as a single language, but as two separate languages: in the north, Low German, in the centre and south, High German. In their earliest stages—from the first beginnings to the close of the 11th century—these languages are termed Old Low German and Old High German respectively. It will be seen that these are semi-geographic terms, 'Low' referring to the low-lying plains of the north, 'High' to the higher land of the centre and south.

OLD HIGH GERMAN

The earliest continuous texts in OHG date from about 750, but not until well on in the next century do the records become at all extensive. The mid-8th century pieces, the Lay of Hildebrand and the Merseburg Charms, amount to less than eighty lines in all. A fair amount of literary activity took place during the reign of Charlemagne and a few short texts datable to about 800 have managed to survive. These are translations made from Latin religious texts, of which the longest are a portion of an apologetic treatise and a 16-page fragment of Matthew's Gospel. Charlemagne is said to have ordered the heroic songs of the Germans to be written down in a book, but no trace of such a work has ever been found. For the next 300 years writing in German is mainly theological.

The number of texts from before 1100, the end of the OHG period, would fill a dozen fair-sized volumes. Translations from Latin are very prominent, for example Tatian's Gospel Harmony and a paraphrase of the Song of Solomon. The Psalter was often translated, though some translations are today only represented by fragments of a page or two. There are translations of prayers, hymns, confessions and baptismal vows. More independent are Otfrid's so-called Gospel Harmony, a poem of 7,416 lines describing the life and teachings of Christ, and various shorter poems on biblical subjects. Secular material is much more limited. There is a German version of the Bestiary and sections from Aristotle, Martianus Capella and Boethius prepared for use in schools. A few other short texts are known. For instance, a couple of medical prescriptions and some minor legal documents. One of these is the oath of allegiance sworn by the German army at Strasbourg in 842. Although at this time Latin was the only language normally used in legal writing, as in other official work, it was occasionally necessary to draw up a German text when an oath was required of persons unable to understand Latin. Finally, mutilated fragments of what appears to have been a Latin-German phrase book have come down to us. Judging by a sentence like *Quare non fuisti ad matutinas? Quandi næ guarin ger ze metina?* 'Why weren't you at matins?', the book may have been composed to assist foreign clergy working among the Germans.

In speaking of this, the earliest period, it is customary to widen the meaning of the term 'literary remains' to embrace not only secondary productions like translations but all records of the language including word lists or even single words. The latter in fact constitute no mean part of the oldest literary remains in German. The reason is as follows. The need for a knowledge of Latin led to the vernacular glossing of Latin texts, that is to say, a German translation, or gloss, was written against each word of the Latin text or against selected, perhaps difficult, words. A large number of Latin manuscripts bearing such glosses are known and it is not improbable that a few have yet to be noticed. This is because instead of writing the German words in ink, the scribes sometimes merely impressed them on the parchment with a dry point. This makes them very difficult to see, especially now. Another favourite device was to write the glosses in cipher. Beside Lat. *amplius* we may find *mfrb* standing for *mêra* (modern Ger. *mehr*) or *bxphstbbb* glossing Lat. *elementum*, i.e. *buohstaba* (now *Buchstabe*). Sometimes lists of Latin words with their German equivalents were extracted from the glossed manuscripts and so regular glossaries arose. These were often copied and circulated as primitive dictionaries. One of these, called *Abrogans* from its opening Latin word, was made between 764 and 769 and may thus be called the first German book. Glosses are among the most ancient records of German and some occur before the earliest continuous texts. A number are known from the first half of the 8th century, technical terms in German are found in a Lombard edict dated 643, while a few words, the Malberg Glosses, seem to go as far back as the 6th century. In this last case, however, the German words have been so much corrupted by copyists

who no longer understood them that their value for linguistic
history is limited. It goes without saying that all these glosses
constitute a most important source of knowledge of the ancient
German vocabulary as they naturally include a great number
of words which are not met with in the continuous texts.
There is no doubt that it was as glosses that German first came
to be written at all.

OLD LOW GERMAN

What texts exist in OLG? Here the records are only meagre.
Everything that is known, including glosses, would not fill more
than a couple of volumes, but the main document is an epic
poem on the life of Christ called the Saviour (*Hêliand*) which
runs to 5,983 lines. The texts show that Low German literature
of this period was in all probability of the same character as
High German and perhaps to a considerable extent dependent
on it. At all events OLG literature was never so extensive as
OHG. The north was the poorer part of the country, the prosperous monasteries where most of the writing was done lay
outside the Low German area.

Such then are the records in Low and High German up to
the end of the 11th century. They do not represent, we may
suppose, more than a fraction of what was actually produced.
To those texts which are known to have existed but which are
now lost must be added an indeterminable number which have
perished without trace. All the same enough has survived to
supply the essentials of phonetics and accidence. It is possible
to write a basic account of the syntax and, in OHG at least, a
fairly extensive vocabulary has been preserved.

2

OLD HIGH GERMAN

What kind of language is revealed in the oldest documents in German? First of all, there is no indication of any overall standard form either for Low German or for High German. Indeed any such standard was not then possible. It may be stressed that a uniform standard language, like modern English for instance, implies not only widespread literacy but also a very long period of careful cultivation in writing. There was certainly not much written in German before the 9th century and even then and during succeeding centuries output remained relatively low. The overwhelming majority of the population remained entirely illiterate. German lived almost exclusively as a spoken medium and, like all languages in this situation, it existed solely in the form of its dialects. Thus all writing in German at this early period was of necessity dialect writing. The monastic scriptoria adopted for their German work forms of the language based on the speech of their own area, so that no two scriptoria wrote alike. But the documents not only bear witness to dialectal variations, they also vary chronologically, reflecting the evolution of the living language. A document written in St Gall in 800 is somewhat different in language from a document written in same place in 900. At the same time there is evidence that approximate local standards were established, though only temporarily, since the natural evolution of the spoken language eventually outmoded them. They could play no part in the grammatical evolution of the language as they were unable to affect the spoken word.

Since no two documents are exactly alike in point of orthography and language, a certain degree of normalisation is necessary in presenting the grammar of Old High German. For this purpose the East Franconian dialect is taken as the basis for the norm. It has the advantage that its consonants are essentially those used in modern standard German. These same consonants are also used in the normalised writing of Middle High German, the language of the intermediary period 1100–1350.

There are four main dialect divisions in OHG. These are Franconian in Central Germany, Bavarian and Alemannic in the south, and Langobardic. The term Franconian requires some clarification. The original home of the people known since the 3rd century as Franks was in N.W. Germany and the Low Countries, where the language is Low German (see Maps 1 and 2). In the 6th century the Franks conquered the Central German tribes (Hessians, Thuringians) and the term Franconian came to be applied to the speech of this area too. From the linguistic point of view this is a misnomer, and an inconvenient one, since the Central German dialects are High German. We must be careful to distinguish between Low Franconian, i.e. Franconian proper, which is a form of Low German, and the other Franconian, which is a form of High German. It may be called Upper Franconian. For the Old High German period Upper Franconian may be divided into the following sub-dialects: Middle, Rhenish (and South Rhenish), East. The Bavarian and Alemannic dialects, together called Upper German, were more homogeneous. Little is known about Langobardic, which became extinct about the year 1000. No continuous texts have been preserved and Langobardic is known solely from some 200 words, mostly personal names. The boundaries and sub-divisions of the OHG dialects are shown on Map 1. On Langobardic, see also pp. 176 f.

It will soon be noticed that OHG is a language which, on the whole, conforms to the overall pattern familiar from the modern language. It is chiefly in details that differences occur. They have been changes in vocabulary; many words once current have now passed out of use entirely or linger on only as local dialect words. There were more inflexions in the older language than in its present-day descendent. Its phonetic system differs in some important respects. Characteristic of OHG is the retention of full vowels, both long and short, in unstressed syllables: contrast OHG *er betalôta* with New High German *er bettelte*. We are led to suppose that German was then a more melodious language than it is today.

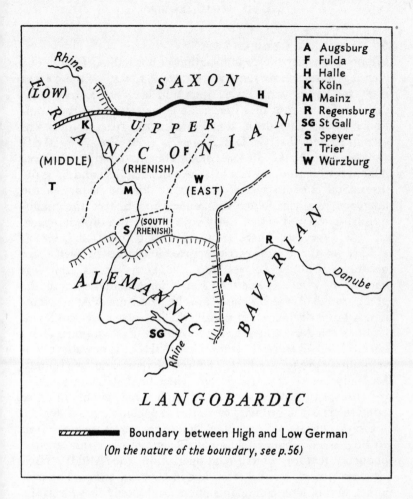

THE SOUNDS AND ORTHOGRAPHY
OF OLD HIGH GERMAN

We now consider the pronunciation of normalised OHG. The language possesses six short vowels *a, e, ë, i, o, u*. Of these *e* was close and tense, while *ë* was open and lax. The former arose through the umlaut of *a* (see below), the latter was the traditional vowel. The distinction between the two *e*-sounds was continued into MHG: OHG *mennisco* from *man, ërda*, MHG *mensche, ërde*, NHG *Mensch, Erde*. The manuscripts however seldom distinguish between these two qualities of *e* and since the distinction is of no special importance for the history of the language, we here follow the general practice of the manuscripts. Combinations of short vowels give the diphthongs *ei, ia, ie, io, iu, ou, uo*. There are the five long vowels *â, ê, î, ô, û*.

Most of the consonants are pronounced as in NHG, for instance *j* is like 'y' in 'yes' and *z* is like 'ts' in 'its', but *w* is like 'w' in 'wine'. The letter *ʒ* stands for a dental spirant, the precise value of which cannot now be determined. At all events it was quite distinct from *s* with which it was never confused. Only in modern times has it taken on the *s*-sound: OHG *lâʒan*, MHG *lâʒan*, NHG *lassen*, hence OHG *ʒ* is nowadays conventionally pronounced [s]. The letter *h* represents two sounds. Medially before consonants and when final it is the fricative [χ] (like *ch* in Scottish *loch*): *naht* 'night', *peh* 'pitch'; in other positions it is the ordinary aspirate: *hûs* 'house', *zehan* 'ten'.

OHG consonants are often long; length is expressed in writing by doubling. Consonant lengthening is an ancient phonetic feature which continued into the Middle High German period, but has been lost in German today. The pronunciation of long consonants offers no difficulties as far as the continuants go: to pronounce *ll* we simply double the length of the single *l*. But the occlusives present a problem. It may be stressed that the pronunciation, for example, of *kk* in such a word as *flekko* 'spot, mark' (NHG *Fleck*), is not to be likened to the slow pronunciation of 'k-k' in 'book-keeping', as is often stated. This is merely a forced, unnatural pronunciation of two k's side by side. The older Germanic pronunciation was a genuine lengthening of a single consonant, which in the case of the occlusives was achieved by suspending the moment of aperture. This feature also occurs in Italian; the pronunciation of OHG *kk* is to be compared with the pronunciation of Ital. *cc* in *ecco!* 'look!'

The normalised orthography does not use the letters c, v, x, y, though they often occur in the mss., e.g. 'c' may stand for *k* or *z*, 'v' for *u*. Vowel length is not usually marked, but a few early texts double the vowel to indicate length; a few others use the circumflex. The orthography of each OHG manuscript needs to be critically examined before the text can be evaluated linguistically. We must also reckon with scribal errors which have led to many corruptions, not all of which can be removed by textual criticism. The sentence quoted above, p. 9: *Quandi næ guarin ger ze metina* 'Why weren't you at matins?' reproduces the spelling of the ms. A study of this text has revealed that it was composed in the Lorraine area. It is thus written in a Franconian dialect close to our normalised OHG, but transcribed into this orthography it looks very different: *Hwanta ni wârun ir zi mettînu?* Furthermore, to be grammatically correct for normalised OHG, the form *wârun* would have to be amended to *wârut*.

A note on umlaut

Umlaut in OHG plays but a minor role. It occurs solely as a phonetic feature without any semantic function. It came about as follows. An original short *a* was modified (umlauted) to *e* under the influence of *i* in the following syllable: *kalb* calf, pl. *kelbir* from an earlier (not actually recorded) **kalbir*. When pronouncing the vowel *a*, the speakers began to anticipate unconsciously the following *i*. In other words, at the very moment of uttering the vowel *a*, they modified their tongue position in order to be ready to say *i*. As a consequence, *a* was drawn towards *i*. The vowel *i* has a high front articulation and it attracted the low vowel *a* as far forward as *e*. Though normal in OHG, the *i*-umlaut is not universal. In some dialects a consonant cluster coming between the *a* and the *i* hindered the process of modification.

There are traces of umlaut in modern English, e.g. *man*, *men* or *France, French*. This and similar forms of umlaut occur in many languages.

Outline of Old High German Accidence

NOUNS

OHG nouns fall into several classes traditionally designated *a*-stems, *ô*-stems, etc. For the most part these terms have no immediately obvious relation to the actual forms of the OHG words; the justification for these terms is theoretical. Thus it is known on comparative grounds that OHG *tag* m. 'day' is descended from a Primitive Germanic form **dagaz* (*g* = voiced *χ*), the ancestral form of the word 'day' in all the Germanic languages. This form of the word is believed to have been in use until about the beginning of the Christian era. In this form -*z* is the nominative case termination, the preceding -*a*- is the stem vowel, hence the term '*a*-stem'. The PGmc. form of OHG *wort* n. 'word' was **wordan* with -*n* as case termination and -*a*- as stem vowel. These PGmc. terminations -*az* and -*an* are cognate with the Latin endings -*us* and -*um*. Since these PGmc. words are not actually attested in writing, they are conventionally preceded by asterisks.

OHG nouns have the same four cases as NHG, but some masculines and neuters preserve, in the singular, traces of a fifth case, the instrumental: *swert* n. 'sword', *swertu* 'with the sword'. The main declensional classes are the following:

a-stems, masc. and neut.

Sg.nom.acc. *tag* m. day, gen. *tages*, dat. *tage*, inst. *tagu*; pl.nom. acc. *taga*, gen. *tago*, dat. *tagum*   PGmc. **dagaz*

Similarly *wort* n. word, except that pl.nom.acc. are uninflected.

Half-a-dozen neut. animal names regularly decline as follows: Sg.nom.acc. *kalb* calf, gen. *kalbes*, dat. *kalbe*; pl.nom. acc. *kelbir*, gen. *kelbiro*, dat. *kelbirum*. In addition a gen.sg. is attested in the place name *Kelbirisbach* 'Calf-Stream', normalised *Kelbiresbah*, and a dat.sg. occurs in a glossary as *chalbire*, normalised *kelbire*. Thus the *r*-element once belonged to the inflected cases of the singular as well. We have the confirmation of comparative evidence, for this declensional type has a parallel in Lat. *genus* n. 'race', gen. *generis*. The PGmc. equivalent of Lat. -*us* disappeared from German in the prehistoric

period, leaving only the bare root; on the other hand the
r-element remained. Subsequently it fell into disuse in the
singular, but lived on in the plural as a prominent distinguishing mark. It became productive, passing to other neuters
like *hûs* 'house', pl. originally *hûs*, but later *hûsir* as well. The
a-stems correspond otherwise to the Latin *o*-stems (*annus* m.,
bellum n.).

ô-stems, fem.

Sg.nom.acc.gen. *geba* gift, dat. *gebu;* pl.nom.acc. *gebâ*, gen.
gebôno, dat. *gebôm*   PGmc. **gebô* (*b* indicates bilabial v)
(This word is extinct in the modern language having been
replaced by a related word *Gabe*.)

The nom.sg. *geba* is not however a direct descendant of
PGmc. **gebô*. The form *geba* is historically correct only for the
acc.sg. PGmc. **gebôn*. In this declension then the accusative
has replaced the original nominative. The correct nom.sg.
ending would be -*u* in a word with a short stem syllable, i.e.
*gebu, but in other cases this ending would disappear
altogether. In fact a few examples of these survive, particularly
of the latter, e.g. *hwîl* besides *hwîla* 'time, while'. These details
will be important when we reach the strong declension of
adjectives. (As for the gen.sg. *geba* this is believed to be a recent
shortening of **gebâ* from PGmc. **gebôz*.) The *ô*-stems correspond
to the Latin *ā*-stems (*mēnsa* f.).

i-stems, masc. and fem.

Sg.nom.acc. *gast* m. guest, gen. *gastes*, dat. *gaste*, inst. *gastu;*
pl.nom.acc. *gesti*, gen. *gestio*, dat. *gestim*   PGmc. **gastiz*
Only the plural shows forms which properly belong to this
class. The singular has been reshaped to conform to the *a*-stems,
numerically a very important class which exercised an attraction
upon other classes.

Sg.nom.acc. *fart* f. journey, gen.dat. *ferti;* pl.nom.acc.
ferti, gen. *fertio*, dat. *fertim* PGmc. **farđiz* (*đ* pronounced like
th in 'this')

These stems correspond to the Latin *i*-stems (*hostis* m., *avis* f.)

The consonantal or weak declension contrasts with the above vocal or strong declension. It includes all three genders, its main types being as follows:

Sg.nom. *boto* m. messenger, acc. *boton*, gen.dat. *boten;* pl. nom.acc. *boton*, gen. *botôno*, dat. *botôm*   PGmc. **bodô*

Sg.nom.acc. *herza* n. heart, gen.dat. *herzen;* pl.nom.acc. *herzun*, gen. *herzôno*, dat. *herzôm*   PGmc. **hertôn*

Sg.nom. *zunga* f. tongue, acc.gen.dat. *zungûn;* pl.nom.acc. *zungûn*, gen. *zungôno*, dat. *zungôm*   PGmc. **tungôn*

These stems correspond to the Latin *n*-stems (*homō* m., *virgō* f., *carmen* n.).

ADJECTIVES

It is likely that in the Primitive Germanic period, i.e. before the Christian era, the declension of adjectives ran parallel to the declension of nouns. This is still the case in Old High German with the weak declension which corresponds exactly to the endings of the weak nouns declined in the previous section:

	masc.	fem.	neut.
Sg.nom.	*starko* strong	*starka*	*starka*
acc.	–*on*	–*ûn*	–*a*
gen.dat.	–*en*	–*ûn*	–*en*
Pl.nom.acc.	–*on*	–*ûn*	–*un*
gen.	–*ôno*	–*ôno*	–*ôno*
dat.	–*ôm*	–*ôm*	–*ôm*

In the strong declension, on the other hand, the original endings corresponding to noun classes have been almost obliterated by a series of newer endings which spread to the strong adjective from the pronouns. Only in certain cases of the singular do we find endings which correspond to those of noun classes. But they are sufficient to show that Germanic strong adjectives once followed the *a*-stems for the masculine and neuter, and the *ô*-stems for the feminine. This is the same arrangement as with Latin adjectives like *bonus, -a, -um*. In the following paradigm of the strong adjective an asterisk has been placed after original forms.

	masc.	fem.	neut.
Sg.nom.	stark*, –êr	stark*, –iu	stark*, –aʒ
acc.	–an	–a*	,,
gen.	–es*	–era	–es*
dat.	–emu	–eru	–emu
inst.	–u*		–u*
Pl.nom.acc.	–e	–o	–iu
gen.	–ero	–ero	–ero
dat.	–êm	–êm	–êm

Where double forms are shown, the uninflected form is usual in the predicative position. The uninflected form also spread from the sing. to the nom.pl., but is used only predicatively.

The adverb is usually formed by adding –o to the uninflected adjective: *starko* 'strongly'.

The comparative and superlative are formed by adding –iro, –isto, or –ôro, –ôsto to the uninflected positive. They follow the weak declension. Some adjectives take one set of endings and some take the other, while some may take either: *hôh* high— *hôhiro, hôhôro—hôhisto, hôhôsto.*

Adverbs chiefly have ô-forms: *hôho* highly—*hôhor*—*hôhôst.*

Four adjectives have irregular comparison: *guot* good, *beʒʒiro, beʒʒisto; ubil* bad, *wirsiro, wirsisto; mihhil* big, *mêro, meisto; luʒʒil* little, *minniro, minnisto.*

The development of a weak declension of adjectives as opposed to a strong declension is a Germanic innovation. The original function of the weak form was to denote a known or definite object. In the pre-literary period, before the full development of the article (see below under 'Articles'), the form *starko man* will have meant '*the* strong man' as distinct from *starkêr man* '*a (any)* strong man'. Later the semantic difference between such phrases was further emphasised by the addition of articles: *der starko man, ein starkêr man,* whence regularly the modern phrases *der starke Mann, ein starker Mann.* In OHG the use of articles is common, but there are traces of the older state of affairs, e.g. in the names of persons: *Brúno* 'the brown (one)', *Tumbo* 'the dumb (one)'; these are the weak forms of the adjectives *brún, tumb.* The weak adjective is usual when referring to the deity, e.g. *got almahtîgo* 'God Almighty'; here we find the weak form of *almahtîg* because the reference is to a well-known personage. But feeling for such usage weakened during OHG times and it did not survive the OHG period.

We can now see why the comparative and superlative follow the weak declension. It is commonest to compare definite things and in this way the weak form became established as a regular grammatical category, to which there are in OHG very few exceptions.

NUMERALS

The first three numerals are declinable and distinguish the three genders, a feature inherited from Indo-European times. But the corresponding treatment of the numeral four has been lost in German. The forms most commonly found in OHG are: 1 *ein* (inflects like an adj., strong and weak), 2 nom.acc.m. *zwêne*, f. *zwâ, zwô*, n. *zwei*, gen. *zweio*, dat. *zweim*, 3 nom.acc.m. *drî*, f. *drîo*, n. *driu*, gen. *drîo*, dat. *drim*, 4 *fior*, 5 *finf*, 6 *sehs*, 7 *sibun*, 8 *ahto*, 9 *niun*, 10 *zehan*, 11 *einlif*, 12 *zwelif*, 13 *drîzehan*, 14 *fiorzehan*, 15 *finfzehan*, 16 *sehszehan*, 17 **sibunzehan*, 18 *ahtozehan*, 19 *niunzehan*, 20 *zweinzug*, 21 **zweinzug inti ein* or **ein inti zweinzug*, 30 *drîzzug*, 40 *fiorzug*, 50 *finfzug*, 60 *sehszug*, 70 *sibunzug*, 80 *ahtozug*, 90 *niunzug*, 100 *zehanzug*, 1000 *dûsunt*.

For 5 an older form *fimf* is known. The forms 11 *einlif* and *zwelif* contrasting with 13 *drîzehan* etc. are explained as meaning literally 'one left' and 'two left'. Evidently the Germanic peoples here adapted the inherited Indo-European decimal system to meet the needs of an acquired duodecimal system. In the earliest OHG the decades 70 to 100 were as follows: *sibunzo, ahtozo, *niunzo, zehanzo*. The origin of the suffix, which has a correspondence in OLG *-ta*, is uncertain. During the early part of the 9th century it was replaced by *-zug* 'decade'. The cleavage between the different formations *sehszug* but *sibunzo* recalls a similar division in another language: French *soixante* but *soixante-dix* rather than *septante*, a reminder of the so-called sexagesimal system. The word for 100 *zehanzo* appears to be an analogical formation replacing the original term *hunt* which survived in the compound numerals *zwei hunt* etc.

PERSONAL PRONOUNS

These decline as follows:

Sg.nom.	*ih* I	*dû* you	*er* he	*siu* she	*iʒ* it
acc.	*mih*	*dih*	*inan*	*sia*	„
gen.	*mîn*	*dîn*	*sîn*	*ira*	*es*
dat.	*mir*	*dir*	*imu*	*iru*	*imu*

Pl.nom.	*wir* we	*ir* you	*sie* m.	*sio* f.	*siu* n. they
acc.	*unsih*	*iuwih*	„	„	„
gen.	*unsêr*	*iuwêr*	*iro*	*iro*	*iro*
dat.	*uns*	*iu*	*im*	*im*	*im*

Dual pronouns are not attested in OHG, but they were certainly in use, at least in some regions, since in the MHG period a plural *eʒ*, acc. dat. *enc*, appears in Bavarian records. Comparison with other Germanic languages, e.g. Old Saxon and Frisian, shows that in origin this was a pronoun with the meaning 'you two'.

Like the modern language, OHG has a special reflexive pronoun: acc. *sih*, gen. *sîn*, the latter being the same word as is used for the gen.sg. of *er*. Contrary to modern usage, *sih*—its form shows that it is an accusative—is not normally found in the dat., an ordinary pronoun being used instead.

The possessive pronouns are: sg. *mîn* mine, *dîn* your, *sîn* his, its, *ira* her; pl. *unsêr* our, *iuwêr* your, *iro* their. The forms *ira*, *iro* are invariable, being still felt as simply genitives, the rest inflect like strong adjectives.

ARTICLES

In origin the definite article is identical with the demonstrative pronoun, of which it is the weakest, i.e. the unstressed form. The endings are related to those of the 3rd person pronoun.

	masc.	fem.	neut.		masc.	fem.	neut.
Sg.nom.	*der*	*diu*	*daʒ*	Pl.	*die*	*dio*	*diu*
acc.	*den*	*dia*	„		„	„	„
gen.	*des*	*dera*	*des*		*dero*	*dero*	*dero*
dat.	*demu*	*deru*	*demu*		*dêm*	*dêm*	*dêm*
inst.	**diu*		*diu*				

The indefinite article has the same forms as the numeral *ein* 'one'.

The use of articles is common in OHG, but it is not so common as in later times. The development of the demonstrative (*der*) and the numeral (*ein*) as articles took place after the Common Germanic age; it belongs to the pre-historical phase of German as a separate group of dialects. There are, however, many traces in OHG of older practice from the time when the articles had not yet come into use:

> *Man giang aftar wege,*
> *zôh sîn hros in handum*

These lines are the beginning of an incantation and the modern German translation is

> '*Ein* Mann ging *den* Weg entlang,
> führte sein Pferd an *der* Hand.'

A literal transposition of the words of the second line into modern (but idiomatically impossible!) German runs '*zog sein Ross in Händen*'.

Many phrases constructed without the article became petrified and some have remained in the language to this day. Thus the phrase *in handum* of the text above is still heard in such a sentence as *er hatte die Macht fest in Händen* 'he had the power firmly in his hands'. Other examples are *mit Mann und Maus, über Berg und Tal, Tag für Tag, zu Bett* contrasting with the synonymous *ins Bett* or *im Bett*, where the use of the definite article shows them to be more recent formations. Similar developments took place in all the West Germanic languages. We have in English, too, relics of the pre-article stage, e.g. Ger. *zu Bett gehen* and *zu Bett liegen* correspond to Engl. 'go to bed' and 'lie in bed'.

VERBS

As in the modern language, the verbs in OHG fall into two main categories, strong and weak. The latter are by far the more numerous and are productive, but the former are among the commonest. The weak verbs are to a large extent derivative, that is to say derived from some other part of speech, usually a noun, whereas the strong verbs are essentially primary.

STRONG VERBS

The formation of strong verbs is one of the most characteristic and persistent features of the Germanic languages. The tenses are differentiated by internal vowel change, technically called ablaut, as in Engl. *spring, sprang, sprung* or Ger. *springen, sprang, gesprungen*. It is known that the Germanic languages have inherited this system from pre-Germanic times since considerable traces of the same system are found in other Indo-European languages, especially in Ancient Greek.

The conjugation of strong verbs in OHG is as follows:

Infin. *skríban* write

INDICATIVE

Pres.sg.1	*skríbu*	Pret.sg.1	*skreib*
2	*skríbis*	2	*skribi*
3	*skríbit*	3	*skreib*
pl.1	*skríbemês*	pl.1	*skribum*
2	*skríbet*	2	*skribut*
3	*skríbant*	3	*skribun*

Imper.sg. *skríb*, pl. *skríbet*
Past part. *giskriban*
Pres. part. *skríbanti*

SUBJUNCTIVE

Pres.sg.1	*skríbe*	Pret.sg.1	*skribi*
2	*skríbês*	2	*skribîs*
3	*skríbe*	3	*skribi*
pl.1	*skríbêm*	pl.1	*skribîm*
2	*skríbêt*	2	*skribît*
3	*skríbên*	3	*skribîn*

It may be that, having read through the pres.indic., the reader is struck by the fact that the endings are so remarkably like Latin. But we must not jump to the conclusion that Latin has 'affected' German in this respect. We have to remember that German, like Latin, is an Indo-European language. These endings are part of the common IE inheritance. In fact all the IE languages in their earlier stages have endings very much like these. Only in the course of subsequent evolution have some languages, like present-day German, lost to a great extent the distinctive endings, while others, like Russian, have preserved them better. But returning to the question of the similarity between the OHG and Latin verbal endings, it must be said that one apparent correspondence is somewhat misleading. One spontaneously thinks, no doubt, that the OHG 1st pl. ending -*emês* will be closely related to the Latin endings -*amus*, -*emus* etc. But in actual fact -*emês* appears where theoretically -*em* would be expected, and it is this shorter ending which would correspond to the Latin since, as we have seen above (under *a*-stems), German does not preserve a final syllable corresponding to Latin -*us*. No other Germanic language offers anything comparable to -*emês*. None of the theories advanced to explain the origin of the ending has won general acceptance, but at all events it is a secondary development. It did not survive the OHG period.

The vowel changes in the strong verbs follow definite patterns, as will be explained below. Here we shall only note that OHG makes a change no longer known in the language today. In NHG the pret.sg. *schrieb* has the same root vowel as the pl. *schrieben*, but in the OHG paradigm there is variation. The 1st and 3rd sg. go together with the same root vowel *ei* as against the 2nd sg. and all the plural which have *i*. This rather surprising distribution has a historical explanation. The German preterite is a conflation of two Indo-European tenses: the vowel *ei* properly belonged to the perfect, *i* to the aorist. Therefore when learning OHG strong verbs we need to note not one, but —at any rate in the majority of cases—two principal parts for the past tense.

The participles naturally decline like adjectives, the final -*i* of the present part. mostly disappearing before the inflexional endings. Most past participles take the prefix *gi*-. It may be defined as a perfective prefix, used to modify the aspect of imperfective verbs. We take an example. The OHG verb *sehan* means 'to see', *gisehan* also means 'to see' but only in the sense of 'to catch sight of'; *sehan* is an imperfective verb, *gisehan* is its perfective form. The function of *gi*- is to make the action complete. In the modern language feeling for such distinctions has been lost, though a number of verbs with the suffix still survive. Here is an instructive example. OHG *beran* means 'to carry, bear', its perfective form *giberan* therefore means 'to finish carrying'. The OHG verb *beran* is extinct, but its perfective form lives on in *gebären* with the basic sense of 'to finish carrying (a child in the womb)', i.e. 'to give birth'. It is easy to see why *gi-* regularly became attached to past participles for they naturally denote a completed action. Now, some verbs are, by their very nature, perfective, e.g. the verb 'to come'. In OHG such verbs did not take the *gi-* prefix: they did not need it, thus *queman* 'come', past part. *koman*. But later, when feeling for distinctions of aspect was waning, *gi-* spread by analogy to such participles as well, hence NHG *gekommen*, but with a relic of the form without the prefix in *willkommen* 'welcome'.

The infinitive, being a verbal noun (neuter), may also decline: gen. *skríbannes*, dat. *skríbanne*. The dative commonly occurs after the preposition *zi*, e.g. *zi skríbanne* > *zu schreiben*. The inflected forms of the infinitive are called the gerund. The regular infinitive of a small number of strong verbs ends in *-en*: three occur in the texts below: *heffen* 'raise', *liggen* 'lie', *sizzen* 'sit'.

Classes of Strong Verbs

Six main patterns of ablaut occur in the formation of strong verbs in OHG, hence one speaks of six classes of strong verbs, and most strong verbs belong to one or other of these classes. Within each class there are, however, variations. For instance, *skríban* conjugated above, belonging to Class 1, has pret.sg.1, 3 *skreib*, i.e. with the root vowel *ei*. So have most members of this group. But there are exceptions. The verb *zíhan* 'accuse' has pret.sg.1, 3 *zêh*. The irregularity is due to a special phonetic change. The diphthong *ei* nevers occurs in OHG before *h* but is altered to *ê*. Changes often affect the root vowel of the singular of the present indicative. Thus *firliosan* 'lose' has 1 *firliusu*, 2 *firliusis*, 3 *firliusit*, so that in quoting the principal parts of OHG verbs it is often important to mention one of these persons also.

Typical forms for the remaining five classes of strong verbs may be seen in the following principal parts (infin., 3rd pres.sg., 1st pret.sg. and pret.pl., past part.): 2 *firliosan* lose, *firliusit, firlôs, firlurum, firloran;* 3 *trinkan* drink, *trinkit, trank, trunkum, gitrunkan;* 4 *neman* take, *nimit, nam, nâmum, ginoman;* 5 *lesan* read, *lisit, las, lâsum, gilesan;* 6 *graban* dig, *grebit, gruob, gruobum, gigraban.*

The change of *s* to *r*, seen in the pret.pl. and past part. of *firliosan*, was a regular development of the Primitive Germanic period, and technically known as grammatical change. It likewise affected *lesan* and in the earliest OHG the forms *lârum, gileran* are found, though as early as the 9th century *lâsum, gilesan*, by analogy with the regular *s*-forms, are commoner. But *firliosan* remained much more conservative. It was not before modern times that levelling out took place and, in this case, it was the secondary *r* which replaced the original *s*: NHG *verlieren, verlor.*

A number of common strong verbs remain outside the above classification. These verbs form a seventh class. In this class the root vowel of the infinitive may be any of the following: *a, â, ei, ô, ou, uo.* The same vowels recur in the past participle. The preterite sing. and plur. always have the same root vowel (*ia* where the infin. has *a, â* or *ei*, but *io* where the infin. has *ô, ou* or *uo*): *fallan* 'fall', *fellit, fial, fialum, gifallan; stôʒan* 'push', *stôʒit, stioʒ, stioʒum, gistôʒan.* In most cases the vowel change between the preterite and the other parts has nothing to do with ablaut proper. Most of the verbs concerned originally formed their preterites by reduplication: PGmc. **fallan-* 'to fall', pret.sg. **fefall-.* The reduplicating syllable bore the stress and the second *f* was eventually lost by dissimilation; the word appears in OHG as *fial*, as above.

WEAK VERBS

Weak verbs are distinct from strong verbs in that they form the preterite and past participle not by ablaut but by means of a dental suffix. In OHG this suffix is *-t.* It is likely that the suffix is a relic of the word 'did' (OHG *teta*). Thus OHG *teilta* 'divided' is literally 'divide did'.

The weak verbs are classified according to the final vowel of the infinitive ending: *-en, -ôn, -ên,* e.g. 1 *teilen* divide, 2 *mahhôn* make, 3 *habên* have. They conjugate as follows:

INDICATIVE

Pres.sg.	1	*teilu*	*mahhôm*	*habêm*
	2	*teilis*	*mahhôs*	*habês*
	3	*teilit*	*mahhôt*	*habêt*
pl.	1	*teilemês*	*mahhômês*	*habêmês*
	2	*teilet*	*mahhôt*	*habêt*
	3	*teilent*	*mahhônt*	*habênt*
Pret.sg.	1	*teilta*	*mahhôta*	*habêta*
	2	*teiltôs*	etc.	etc.
	3	*teilta*		
pl.	1	*teiltum*		
	2	*teiltut*		
	3	*teiltun*		

Imper.sg. *teili, mahho, habe,* pl. *teilet, mahhôt, habêt*
Pres. part. *teilenti, mahhônti, habênti*
Past. part. *giteilit, gimahhôt, gihabêt*

SUBJUNCTIVE

Pres.sg.	1, 3	*teile*	*mahho*	*habe*
	2	*teilês*	*mahhôs*	*habês*
pl.	1	*teilêm*	*mahhôm*	*habêm*
	2	*teilêt*	*mahhôt*	*habêt*
	3	*teilên*	*mahhôn*	*habên*
Pret.sg.	1, 3	*teilti*	*mahhôti*	*habêti*
	2	*teiltîs*	etc.	etc.
pl.	1	*teiltîm*		
	2	*teiltît*		
	3	*teiltîn*		

A few verbs in Class 1 have the preterite in *-ita* etc., e.g. *neren* save, pret.sg.1, 3 *nerita.*

The auxiliary 'TO BE' is built up of three separate roots. The forms are as follows:

Infin. *wesan*

INDICATIVE				SUBJUNCTIVE			
Pres.sg.1	*bim*	Pret.sg.1	*was*	Pres.sg.1	*sî*	Pret.sg.1	*wâri*
2	*bist*	2	*wâri*	2	*sîs*	etc.	
3	*ist*	3	*was*	3	*sî*		

Pres.pl.1 *birum* Pret.pl.1 *wârum* Pres.pl.1 *sîm*
    2 *birut*   2 *wârut*   2 *sît*
    3 *sind*   3 *wârun*   3 *sîn*

Imper.sg. *wis*, pl. *weset*, *sît*
Pres. part. *wesanti*, past. part. *giwesan*

The infin. *sîn* is secondary, similarly the imper.pl. *sît* which is really the 2nd pl. pres.subj. 'Grammatical change' is seen in the variation *s/r* in *was/wâri* etc., but the expected corresponding past part. *giweran is never found. It had apparently been levelled out to conform with *wesan* before the literary period began.

A small group, the so-called preterite-present verbs, form their paradigms with both strong and weak forms. Here the present (strong) is in origin a preterite, the past (weak) a new formation, e.g. infin. *wiȝȝan* 'to know', originally 'to have seen', pres.sg.1, 3 *weiȝ*, 2 *weist* (exceptional ending!), pl.1 *wiȝȝum* etc.; pret.sg.1 *wista* etc., past part. *giwiȝȝan*. OHG *wiȝȝan*, *weiȝ*, *wista* may be compared with old-fashioned Engl. *to wit, wot, wist*.

COMPOUND TENSES

Having only two inflected tenses, present and preterite, OHG formed the perfect and pluperfect with the auxiliaries *habên* and *wesan* (*sîn*). The future, however, was usually expressed by the present, but *skal* (NHG *soll*) 'shall' with the infinitive also occurs; the construction *werdan* (NHG *werden*) with the infinitive is first found at the close of the OHG period. The passive is expressed by *werdan* or *wesan* (*sîn*) with the past participle.

A note on endings in OHG

The paradigms quoted in the above sketch of OHG accidence are typical of the language of the earlier texts. In later OHG many changes take place due to the weakening of unstressed endings. For instance, final *-m* tends to become *-n*, unstressed *u* tends to be lowered to *o* and eventually, at the close of the period, to be reduced to the indistinct vowel [ə] as in Engl. *father*. Hence for the OHG *-um* of the earlier records we may often find *-un*, *-om*, *-on*, *-en* in later documents, for *-eru* we may find *-ero*, *-ere*.

Specimens of Old High German

(The reader is reminded of the remarks on pronunciation, pp. 14 f. It is important not to allow oneself to be misled by the modern pronunciation of German, particularly in matters of vowel length: vowels here are short unless marked long.)

Passage from the OHG translation of Tatian's *Gospel Harmony* corresponding to Luke vii, 11–16. East Franconian, *c.* 830.

The text printed below has been normalised. In the ms. itself there are no length marks, 'z' stands for both *z* and *ȝ*; further 'uu' or 'vv' of the ms. are here normalised to *w*, similarly 'ph' and 'c' have been normalised to *pf* and *k*. But 'th' of the ms. has been left as it represents the voiced spirant as in Engl. *though*, an archaic feature of early texts in this dialect.

The translation technique is of an early type, being sometimes so slavishly literal that the result is quite unidiomatic German. It is therefore an advantage to be able to refer to the Latin original, here printed beneath the German text.

11 *Inti ward thô fon thanan thaȝ her fuor in thie burg thiu ist giheiȝan Naim, inti fuorun mit imo sîne jungiron inti ginuhtsamo menigî.*

12 *Mit thiu her thô nâhita pfortu theru burgi, sênu arstorbanêr was gitragan, einag sun sînero muoter, inti thiu was wituwa, inti menigî theru burgi mihhil mit iru.*

13 *Thia mit thiu Truhtîn gisah, miltidu giruorit ubar sia quad iru: ni kuri wuofen! Inti gieng zuo inti biruorta thia bâra.*

14 *Thie thâr truogun gistuontun, inti quad: jungo, ih quidu thir, arstant!*

15 *Inti gisaȝ thie thâr tôt was inti bigonda sprehhan, inti gab in sînero muoter.*

16 *Gifieng thô alle forhta, inti mihhilosôtun Got sus quedante: bithiu mihhil wîȝago arstuont in uns, inti bithiu Got wîsôta sînes folkes.*

Latin original:

11 *Et factum est deinceps ibat in civitatem quae vocatur Naim, et ibant cum illo discipuli eius et turba copiosa.*

12 *Cum autem appropinquaret portae civitatis, ecce defunctus efferebatur, filius unicus matris suae, et haec vidua erat, et turba civitatis multa cum illa.*

13 *Quam cum vidisset Dominus, misericordia motus super eam dixit illi: noli flere! Et accessit et tetigit loculum.*

14 *Hi autem qui portabant steterunt, et ait: adolescens, tibi dico, surge!*

15 *Et resedit qui erat mortuus et coepit loqui, et dedit illum matri suae.*

16 *Accepit autem omnes timor, et magnificabant Deum dicentes: quia propheta magnus surrexit in nobis, et quia Deus visitavit plebem suam.*

11 *inti* 'and' is the usual Franconian form, otherwise *anti*, generally umlauted to *enti;* a further variety *unti* becomes common in Late OHG and eventually replaces the others, hence MHG *und(e)*, NHG *und.* Judging from comparative evidence *anti* is the original form, the other forms being explained as vowel shadings arising in a word which is normally unstressed, cf. *arstorbanêr* 12.

ward pret.sg.3 of *werdan* 'become', NHG *werden; ward . . . thaʒ* (lit. 'happened . . . that').

thô fon thanan lit. 'then from thence' or 'da von dannen' translating *deinceps.*

her, a compromise form with *h–* from Low German *hê;* usual OHG *er.*

fuor pret.sg.3 of *faran,* NHG *fahren.*

thie fem.acc.sg., occurs in this text as well as *thia* = usual OHG *dia.*

burg f. translating *civitas.* The word originally denoted a fortified habitation. Later the sense widened to include the buildings and homes which grew up under the walls of the *burg* and which formed the beginnings of the towns, hence the many town names ending in *–burg.* Later on still, *burg* in this wider sense was replaced by MHG *stat* lit. 'place'.

giheiʒan past part. of *heiʒan,* NHG *heißen.*

jungiro m. 'disciple', NHG *Jünger.* This substantivised comparative of *jung* 'young' must have early taken on the meaning of 'pupil' after the analogy of Medieval Lat. *junior* 'younger; pupil'. Having acquired this sense it could easily be used to render Lat. *discipulus.*

ginuhtsam 'copious, large', MHG *genuhtsam.* See *menigî.*

menigî f., NHG *Menge.* This word belongs to a small class which remain unchanged in the nom.acc.pl. and the form of the qualifying adjective *ginuhtsamo* indicates a plural here, even though the Latin has a singular (*turba copiosa*). Slips like this are not rare in OHG translations.

12 *mit thiu* where *mit* governs the instrumental, lit. 'with that', the phrase
having acquired the sense of 'while, as', MHG *mit diu*.

nâhen 'approach', MHG *næhen*.

pforta f. 'gate', NHG *Pforte*. The word is an early borrowing from Lat.
porta.

sênu 'behold', a compound of *sê* and *nû* 'now'. It is natural to think of
the first element as meaning 'see', but the vowel *ê* is without parallel
in the forms of the verb known to us. The principal parts in OHG are
sehan, sihit, sah, sâhum, gisehan, the imper.sg. being regularly *sih*. It is
therefore quite possible that some other word, unrelated to 'see', lies
behind *sê*. There is a variant *sînu*.

arstorbanêr substantivised past part. of *arsterban* 'die', NHG *ersterben*
(though only used figuratively). The vowel of the prefix fluctuates
much as the vowel in the word for 'and', see 11. In this case *ur-* is the
primary form, *ar-* an early alternative, but *ir-* is more typical of the
OHG period as a whole; *er-* is also common from an early date.

gitragan past. part. of *tragan*, NHG *tragen*.

einag adj. 'only', MHG *einec*.

sun m., NHG *Sohn*.

muoter f., NHG *Mutter;* this word does not inflect in the singular.

wituwa f., NHG *Witwe*.

mihhil 'great', MHG *michel*. This once common word survived locally
in dialect until modern times. It occurs in geographical names, e.g.
in Hessen *Michelstadt* 'Big Town', in Württemberg *Michelbach* 'Big
Stream', into which flows the *Litzelbach* 'Little Stream' (MHG
lützel, OHG *luzzil*).

13 *truhtîn* m. 'lord', MHG *do*.

gisah pret.sg.3 of *gisehan* 'catch sight of'. See above under "Verbs".

miltida f. 'mercy' from *milti* 'mild, merciful' (> NHG *mild*). The
dative form *miltidu* is used to render a Latin ablative (*misericordia*).
Such use of the dative as the next best thing often occurs in translations of this sort, but such 'German' can hardly have been comprehensible without reference to the Latin.

quad pret.sg.3 of *quedan* 'speak', MHG *queden* (cf. Engl. *quoth, bequeath*).

ruoren, NHG *rühren*.

ubar 'over'; MHG, NHG *über* owe their umlaut to contamination with
OHG *ubiri* adv. 'over'.

ni kuri (felt to be imper.sg.) 'do not, *noli*'. Formally *kuri* is subj. pret.sg.3
of *kiosan* 'choose', Older NHG *kiesen*, the past part. of which survives
in *auserkoren* 'choice, elect'. On the change of *s* to *r* cf. *firliosan*, above
under 'Verbs'.

wuofen 'weep', MHG *wüefen.*

gieng, usual OHG *giang,* pret.sg.3 of *gangan* often contracted to *gân,* with a variant *gên,* NHG *gehen.*

zuo, NHG *zu.*

biruoren, NHG *berühren.*

bâra f., NHG *Bahre.*

14 *thie thâr,* usual OHG *die dâr* 'those who'. Originally *dâr* was only an adverb of place 'there', but later it took on the function of a relative particle as well. Subsequently the demonstrative pronoun *der, diu, daʒ* also assumed the functions of a relative and for a time was used together with the particle *dâr,* as here. A relic of this use still survives in NHG in archaising style, e.g. *Menschen, die da schwere Bürden tragen . . .*

truogun pret.pl.3 of *tragan.*

gistuontun pret.pl.3 of *gistantan* 'halt', perfective of *stantan* often contracted to *stân,* with a variant *stên,* NHG *stehen.*

jungo 'adolescens'. The weak form for the vocative is natural when we recall that the original function of the weak adjective was to denote a known person or thing. After the OHG period feeling for this distinction was lost.

quidu pres.sg.1 of *quedan.*

arstant imper.sg. of *arstantan,* cf. NHG *erstehen.*

15 *gisaʒ* pret.sg.3 of *gisizzen* 'sit up', perfective of *sizzen,* NHG *sitzen.*

thie masc.nom.sg., occurs often in this text beside regular *ther* = usual OHG *der.* The form *thie* in OHG is an East Franconian peculiarity, apparently due to Low German influence, cf. OS *thie* (earlier *thê*). See *her* 11.

bigonda weak pret.sg.3 of *biginnan,* NHG *beginnen.* A regular strong preterite *bigan* was also in use in OHG and this form has prevailed today, but a weak form *begonde* was still common in MHG.

sprehhan, NHG *sprechen.*

gab pret.sg.3 of *geban,* NHG *geben.*

16 *gifieng,* usual OHG *gifiang,* pret.sg.3 of *gifâhan* 'seize', formally a perfective of *fâhan* (Early NHG *fahen*) with which it appears to have been largely synonymous.

forhta f., NHG *Furcht.*

mihhilosôn 'praise, magnify', coined from *mihhil* 'great' (12) to render Lat. *magnificare.*

sus 'so', MHG *do.,* later (13th cent.) with excrescent *t: sust,* then with infixed *n* (14th cent.): *sunst,* whence with change of meaning NHG *sonst.*

bithiu, i.e. *bi* + *thiu* 'because', cf. *mit thiu* (12). Stress on *thiu*.

wîzago m. 'prophet', lit. 'knowledgeable one', related to *wizzan*, NHG *wissen*. Later in the OHG period this word was associated with *wîs* 'wise' and *-sago* 'speaker', hence *wîssago*, cf. NHG *Weissager*.

wîsôn+gen. 'visit'; the same root appears with a different ending in *wîsen* 'show', NHG *weisen*.

The First Merseburg Charm. Regarded as Franconian, c. 750.

This short text from the Cathedral Library at Merseburg is a charm spoken for the release of a prisoner. The spelling has not been normalised.

> *Eiris sazun idisi,   sazun hera duoder:*
> *suma hapt heptidun,   suma heri lezidun,*
> *suma clubodun   umbi cuoniouuidi:*
> *insprinc haptbandun,   invar vigandun!*

'Once upon a time valkyries came down, they came down here and over there: some fastened bonds, some held up the army, some loosened the fetters: leap from the binding bonds, escape from the enemy!'

eiris, found nowhere else, has been conjectured to represent a normalised **êres*, an adverbial genitive from *êr* 'earlier, before'. Equally plausible is the suggestion that *eiris* is a scribal error for *eines* (NHG *einst*). Oddly enough, both proposals yield the same sense 'once upon a time' which well fits the context.

sazun, norm. *sâzun*, pret.pl.3 of *sizzen*, NHG *sitzen*.

idisi, sg. *idis*, norm. *itis* f. 'woman'; here doubtless battle maidens akin to the Norse valkyries.

hera duoder; the former is presumably norm. *hêra* 'hither', but the latter is unexplained. It seems however reasonable to suppose that it somehow represents *dara* 'thither'. This appears to make good sense.

suma, norm. *sumo;* the pronoun *sum* 'some one' inflected like a strong adjective; it survived into the MHG period, but is now extinct.

hapt, norm. *haft* n. 'bond'; the spelling *pt* is taken to indicate that *f* before *t* had some quality which distinguished it from *f* in other positions. Bavarian mss. sometimes have *pht*.

heptidun, norm. *heftitun* (cf. *hapt*) pret.pl.3 of *heften*, NHG *do*.

heri n., NHG *Heer*.

lezidun, norm. *lezzitun* pret.pl.3 of *lezzen*, NHG *letzen* 'injure', now usually *verletzen*.

clubodun, norm. *klûbôtun* pret.pl.3 of *klûbôn*, NHG *klauben*.

umbi, NHG *um*.

cuoniouuidi is attested in glosses: *khunuuithi*, *chunuuidi*; it also occurs in Gothic *kunawidôm* dat.pl. 'fetters'. The meaning of the word is thus not in doubt, but the details of its formation and its etymology are uncertain. Comparison with the other forms, however, shows that *cuon–* in our text is erroneous for *cun–*. Without a doubt this whole half-line was obscure to the 10th-century copyist for he actually divided the words: *umbicuonio uuidi*.

insprinc, norm. *intspring* imper.sg. of *intspringan*, NHG *entspringen*; in this text original *int–* has lost the final *–t*.

haptbandun, norm. *haftbandum*; the word occurs only in this text, cf. *band* n., NHG *Band*.

invar, norm. *intfar* imper.sg. of *intfaran*, cf. NHG *entfahren*.

vigandun, norm. *fiantum* dat.pl. of *fiant*, NHG *Feind*. In our text a glide consonant, doubtless [*g*], has developed between the two vowels. The usual form carried on into MHG as *viant*, but the *a*-vowel was often weakened, hence *vient*, and finally lost giving *vînt*, whence with regular diphthongisation NHG *Feind*. The word is really a substantivisation of OHG *fianti* 'hating', pres. part. of *fian* 'to hate'.

From the 'Destruction of the World' (*Mûspilli*), a Bavarian text of the 9th century.

A notable feature of the Bavarian dialect was the shifting of *b* and *g*, especially when occurring in initial position, to *p* and *k*. The text below has been normalised to the extent that quantity marks have been added and *ʒ* distinguished from *z*.

> *Uuanta sâr sô sih diu sêla   in den sind arhevit,*
> *enti si den lîhhamun   likkan lâʒʒit,*
> *sô quimit ein heri   fona himilʒungalon,*
> *daʒ ander fona pehhe :   dâr pâgant siu umpi.*
> *sorgên mac diu sêla,   unzi diu suona argêt,*
> *ze uuederemo herie   si gihalôt uuerde.*
> *uuanta ipu sia daʒ Satanaʒses   kisindi kiuuinnit,*
> *daʒ leitit sia sâr   dâr iru leid uuirdit,*
> *in fuir enti in finstrî :   daʒ ist rehto virinlîh ding.*

'For at the moment when the soul sets out on its way and leaves the body lying, one army arrives from the heavenly stars and the other from hell. There they struggle for it. The soul may well be anxious until the decision is reached as to which army shall take it. For if Satan's company win it, they speedily lead it to a place where it is tormented in fire and in darkness. That is a truly terrible judgement.'

wanta, older *hwanta* 'for, because', MHG *want*.

sâr 'immediately', MHG *sâ(r)*.

sô 'when'; this temporal sense continued into MHG.

sêla f., NHG *Seele*.

sind m. 'road', MHG *sint*.

arheffen, NHG *erheben*.

si abbreviated for *siu*.

lîhhamo m. 'body', a kenning lit. 'body (*lîh*) covering (*hamo*)'. Another form of this compound *lîhhinamo* (i.e. *lîhhin-hamo*) survives in NHG *Leichnam*.

likkan, norm. *liggen*, NHG *liegen*.

lâʒ(ʒ)an, NHG *lassen*.

queman, NHG *kommen*.

himilzungal n. 'heavenly star'.

peh n., NHG *Pech*.

pâgan, norm. *bâgan* 'quarrel, struggle', MHG *bâgen*. Doubtless the NHG verb *balgen* 'do.', though of entirely different origin, owes something to the earlier word.

mac, norm. *mag* pres.sg.3 of *magan*, later *mugan* 'be able', NHG *mögen*.

unzi 'until', MHG *unz(e)*.

suona f. 'decision, judgement', NHG *Sühne*.

argên, NHG *ergehen*.

wedar, older *hwedar* 'which (of two)', MHG *weder*, with change of meaning NHG *weder*. Cf. archaic Engl. *whether of the twain*.

halôn, with a variant *holôn*, NHG *holen*.

ipu, norm. *ibu* 'if', also *ubi, oba*, NHG *ob*.

Satanazses, norm. *Satanases* gen. of *Satanas* 'Satan'.

kisindi, norm. *gisindi* n., NHG *Gesinde*, lit. 'companions of the road', formed from *sind* 'road'.

dâr here 'there where'.

finstrî f. 'darkness', MHG *vinstere*, from *finstar*, NHG *finster*.

rehto 'truly, right', adv. from *reht*, NHG *recht*.

virinlîh, norm. *firinlîh* 'terrible' from *firina* f. 'crime', MHG *virne*.

ding n. 'thing; court; judgement', NHG *Ding*.

From Notker's translation of Martianus Capella's *Nuptiae Philologiae et Mercurii*. Alemannic, c. 1000.

Alemannic shares with Bavarian the tendency to shift *b* to *p* and *g* to *k;* also to shift initial *d* to *t*. When initial or after consonants *k* is shifted to *kχ*, here '*ch*' and thus not distinguished in spelling from the (double) spirant *hh*. In Notker's orthography length is indicated by the circumflex. Stressed short vowels take the acute accent. Certain diphthongs have the circumflex, e.g. *ûo*, others the acute, e.g. *éi*. Notker's orthography is a very precise reflexion of the spoken dialect of his time. We add here only the distinction between *ʒ* and *z*.

Téro zuéio (i.e. Mars et Liber) *uuás ter fórderôro éin rôt iúngeling, uuánda sîn stérno rôt íst, únde slíndare ióh túrstesare des plûotes. Pedíu héiʒet er* Mars, *álso* mors.

Ter ánder uuás mámmende únde mínnesám. Uuáʒ íst húgelichera únde mínnesámera uuîne?

Sîn rébeméʒers án dero zéseuuún trágende únde sînen sláfmáchigen chópf án dero uuínsterûn.

Ióh spílogérnêr chád man, dáʒ er uuâre.

Sîne génge uuâren scránchelige.

Únde feruuúndene fóne déro trúncheni des stárchen uuînes.

'The first of the two was a red youth, for his star is red, and he is a devourer and a thirster after blood. Therefore he is called *Mars*, that is *mors*.

The other was gentle and lovable. What is more delightful and more lovable than wine?

Carrying in his right hand the grape knife and in his left hand his drowsy cup.

They said that he was wanton, too.

His steps were unsteady.

And affected by the intoxicating power of the strong wine.'

fórderôro, norm. *fordarôro*, also *fordaro* 'former', NHG *vordere*.

slíndare, norm. *slindâri* m. 'devourer' from *slindan* 'to devour', MHG *slinden*.

túrstesare, norm. *durstisâri* 'one who is thirsty' from *durstisôn* 'be thirsty' from *durst* 'thirst', NHG *Durst*. Doubtless a word coined to render Lat. *sititor* of the original.

plûot, norm. *bluot* n., NHG *Blut*.

Mars ... mors: we need not follow this etymology!

mámmende, norm. *mammundi* 'gentle', MHG *mammende*.

minnesám, norm. *minnasam* 'lovable', MHG *minnesam*.

húgelich, norm. *hugilíh* 'delightful', MHG *hügelích*.

rébemézers, i.e. *rébe*, norm. *reba* f., NHG *Rebe*, and *mézers*, norm. *mezzers* n. 'knife'. By the MHG period *mezzers* was felt to be a genitive form, so *-s* was dropped in the other cases, hence MHG *mezzer*, NHG *Messer*. The form *mezzers* is Late OHG, earlier *mezziras*, earlier still *mezzirahs* which arose by dissimilation of *s* to *r* from *mezzisahs*, a compound of *mezzi* 'food' and *sahs* 'knife'. All these stages are actually recorded in OHG. The second element *sahs* is ultimately identical with Lat. *saxum* 'stone'. In Germanic *sahs* must originally have had this meaning too. Subsequently specialised to mean 'stone for cutting', it eventually came to denote 'knife', its original sense being quite forgotten. But etymology reveals that we are dealing with a term which arose in the Stone Age.

zeseuuûn, norm. *zesawûn* dat.sg. pf *zesawa* f. 'right hand', MHG *zesewe*.

slâfmáchich, norm. *slâfmahhîg* lit. 'sleep-making'.

chopf, norm. *kopf* m. 'cup'; NHG *Kopf* is the same word.

uuínsterûn, norm. *winstarûn* dat.sg. of *winstara* f. 'left hand', MHG *winstere*.

ióh, norm. *joh* 'and, also'.

spílogérnêr (strong ending) 'wanton', cf. NHG *Spiel*, *gern*.

chad, norm. *quad*. In Notker, *qu-* loses the labial: the stages were *quad* > **kad* > *chad*.

genge, norm. *gengi* pl. of *gang* m. 'step, walk', NHG *Gang*.

scránchelich, norm. *skrankalîh* 'unsteady', cf. *biskrankolôn* 'stagger', allied to *skrenken* 'set at a slant', NHG *schränken*.

feruuíndene, norm. *firwundane* past part. pl. of *firwindan*, NHG *verwinden*.

trúncheni, norm. *trunkanî* f. 'intoxication', formed from the old past part. *trunkan*, NHG *trunken*.

BIBLIOGRAPHY

The standard handbook on OHG is W. Braune, *Althochdeutsche Grammatik*, a work which is continually appearing in new editions. A selection of representative texts is given in W. Braune, *Althochdeutsches Lesebuch*, likewise frequently re-edited. Shorter works edited in English are J. Ellis, *Elementary Old High German Grammar*, Oxford, 1953, and C. C. Barber, *An Old High German Reader*, Oxford, 1951.

R. Schützeichel, *Althochdeutsches Wörterbuch*, Tübingen, 1969, contains the vocabulary of the literary texts. A dictionary embracing all the sources has been appearing in fascicles since 1952; it is E. Karg-Gasterstädt and T. Frings, *Althochdeutsches Wörterbuch*, Berlin.

3

OLD LOW GERMAN

The term Old Low German designates the dialects spoken in the northern part of the German-speaking area from the time of the first record in the second half of the 8th century up to about 1100. Two main dialects are represented: Old Low Franconian spoken in the west of the area, corresponding roughly to the Netherlands and Flanders, and Old Saxon, the language of the centre and east (see Map 2). The former is only poorly represented, most of the surviving records being in Old Saxon. It is this dialect of OLG which we shall consider here. As with OHG, it will again be necessary to present the outline of accidence in a normalised orthography. The actual manuscripts themselves reveal many peculiarities, in some cases the language has been influenced by the neighbouring High German.

THE SOUNDS OF OLD LOW GERMAN (OLD SAXON)

Old Saxon has the same six short vowels as OHG: *a, e, ë, i, o, u*, and the same five long vowels *â, ê, î, ô, û*. Combinations of short vowels give the diphthongs *ei, io, iu, au, eu*. Most of the consonants are pronounced as in OHG. Doubling is frequent. The letter *h* denotes either the aspirate or the fricative according to position exactly as in OHG. The letter *ƀ* stands for bilabial v. Initially and when geminated *g* is an occlusive, but medially in voiced surroundings is generally the voiced spirant [g], becoming voiceless when final. The dental spirant, written *th* or *đ*, is voiceless when initial or final, but voiced when medial in voiced surroundings. At a later stage in the language this spirant must have become voiced in all positions, since it appears as *d* in the succeeding Middle Low German period. The most prominent phonetic feature distinguishing OLG from OHG is the so-called High German Sound Shift described in the next chapter.

MAP 2

Old Saxon in the 9th century

As in OHG, vowel length is not usually indicated in the manuscripts. The mss. also use letters not occurring in the normalised spelling, e.g. 'c' for *k*. The letters *ƀ* and *đ* are part of the ms. tradition; they are usual in the *Hêliand*.

Outline of Old Low German (Old Saxon) Accidence

NOUNS

The Old Saxon declensions are rather similar to those of Old High German.

a-stems, masc. and neut.

Sg.nom.acc. *dag* m. day, gen. *dages*, dat. *dage*, inst. *dagu;* pl. nom.acc. *dagos*, gen. *dago*, dat. *dagun*

A few traces of the older dat.pl. ending *-um* occur, but *-un* is normal here and in all classes.

Similarly *word* n. word, except that pl.nom.acc. are uninflected. A few neuters however preserve a nom.acc.pl. ending *u-*, e.g. *skip* ship, *skipu* ships, an archaism without parallel in OHG.

Owing to the restricted amount of material surviving, words belonging to the class of OHG *kalb* (OS *kalf*) are not fully attested. What remains suggests that, unlike the corresponding OHG, this was a declining group being mostly assimilated to the *word*-class.

ô-stems, fem.

Sg.nom.acc.gen. *geƀa* gift, dat. *geƀu;* pl.nom.acc. *geƀa*, gen. *geƀono*, dat. *geƀon*

Traces of the older uninflected nom.sg. remain e.g. *hwîl* beside *hwîla* 'time, while'.

i-stems, masc. and fem.

Sg.nom.acc. *gast* m. guest, gen. *gastes*, dat. *gaste*, (no inst.); pl.nom.acc. *gesti*, gen. *gestio*, dat. *gestiun*

Sg.nom.acc. *fard* f. journey, gen.dat. *ferdi;* pl.nom.acc. *ferdi*, gen. *ferdio*, dat. *ferdin*

n-stems, all genders

Sg.nom. *bodo* m. messenger, acc. *bodon*, gen.dat. *boden:* pl. nom.acc. *bodon*, gen. *bodono*, dat. *bodon*

Sg.nom.acc. *herta* n. heart, gen.dat. *herten;* pl.nom.acc. *hertun*, gen. *hertono*, dat. *herton*

Sg.nom. *tunga* f. tongue, acc.gen.dat. *tungun;* pl.nom.acc. *tungun*, gen. *tungono*, dat. *tungon*

ADJECTIVES

The adjectival declension shows the same main features as in OHG. The weak declension follows the weak declension of nouns:

	masc.	fem.	neut.
Sg.nom.	*starko* strong	*starka*	*starka*
acc.	–*on*	–*un*	–*a*
gen.dat.	–*en*	–*un*	–*en*
Pl.nom.acc.	–*on*	–*un*	–*un*
gen.	–*ono*	–*ono*	–*ono*
dat.	–*on*	–*on*	–*on*

The strong declension has been reshaped by secondary pronominal endings to almost the same extent as in OHG. In the following an asterisk has been placed after original forms:

	masc.	fem.	neut.	all genders
Sg.nom.	*stark**	*stark**	*stark*́*	Pl. *starke*
acc.	–*an*	–*a**	,,	,,
gen.	–*es**	–*era*	–*es**	–*ero*
dat.	–*emu*	–*eru*	–*emu*	–*un**
inst.	–*u**		–*u**	

The uninflected form, historically a singular only, occurs as nom.pl., but only predicatively.

The adverb is usually formed by adding –*o* to the uninflected adjective: *starko*.

The comparative and superlative of adjectives are formed by adding –*iro*, –*isto*, or –*oro*, –*osto* to the uninflected positive. But owing to the weakening of vowels in unaccented syllables, the most usual forms recorded are -*era*, -*ara*, and -*ista*, but chiefly -*osta*. Adverbs usually show -*or*, -*ost*.

The irregular comparison is in essentials as in OHG: *gôd* good, *betera*, *betsta;* *uƀil* bad, *wirsa*, *wirsista;* *mikil* big, *mêra*, *mêsta;* *luttil* little, *minnera*, *minnista.*

NUMERALS

The numerals in OS show the same general stage of evolution as the OHG numerals. The first three are declined and there is a break in the decades after 60 when the suffix alters. Indeed, the break is further emphasised in OS by a prefix as well. Since the records are rather sparse, several of the forms below are not found exactly as printed here in a normalised orthography: 1 *ên* (inflects like an adjective, strong and weak), 2 nom.acc.m. *twêne*, f. *twâ, twô,* n. *twê,* gen. *tweio,* dat. *twêm,* 3 nom.acc.m.f. *thria,* n. *thriu,* gen. **thrio,* dat. *thrim,* 4 *fiuwar,* 5 *fîf,* 6 *sehs,* 7 *siƀun,* 8 *ahto,* 9 *nigun,* 10 *tehan,* 11 *elleƀan,* 12 *twelif,* 13 *thriutein,* 14 *fiuwartein,* 15 *fîftein,* 16 *sehstein,* 17 *siƀuntein,* 18 *ahtotein,* 19 *niguntein,* 20 *twêntig,* 21 **ên endi twêntig,* 30 *thrîtig,* 40 *fiuwartig,* 50 *fîftig,* 60 *sehstig,* 70 *antsiƀunta,* 80 *antahtoda,* 90 *antnigunta,* 100 *hund,* 1000 **thûsund, thûsundig.*

The prefix *ant-* in *antsiƀunta* etc. is unstressed; it is held to be a corruption of *hund-,* a prefix which appears in Old English, e.g. *hundseofontig* 70. The suffix *-da* in *antahtoda* instead of the expected *-ta* is explained as contamination from the ordinal *ahtodo* 8th. Later analogical forms for 70–90 occur as follows: *siƀuntig, ahtotig, niguntig.* The development of intervocalic *g* in *nigun* is secondary, cf. OHG *niun,* via the intermediary stage **niwun.* In addition to *hund* a compound recorded as *hunderod* lit. 'hundred number' occurs once. The form **thûsund* doubtless existed as *dûsent* is the normal form in Middle Low German, but only *thûsundig,* with analogical *-ig,* is actually met with in the surviving texts.

PERSONAL PRONOUNS

These decline as follows:

Sg.					
nom.	*ik* I	*thû* you	*hê, hi*[2] he	*siu* she	*it* it
acc.	*mik, mî*[1]	*thik, thî*[1]	*ina*	*sia*	,,
gen.	*mîn*	*thîn*	*is*	*ira*	*is*
dat.	*mî*	*thî*	*imu*	*iru*	*imu*

---

[1] These originally dat. forms have largely replaced the older *mik, thik.*
[2] *hî* occurs in one ms. only.

Pl.	nom.	*wî* we	*gî* you	*sie, sia, siu*[1] they
	acc.	*ûs*	*iu*	,,
	gen.	*ûser*	*iuwer(o)*[2]	*iro*
	dat.	*ûs*	*iu*	*im*
Du.	nom.	*wit* we two		*git* you two
	acc.dat.	*unk*		*ink*
	gen.	*unkero*[2]		**inker(o)*[2]

[1] Feeling for ancient distinctions of gender apparently lost in OS, as all these forms occur for each of the three genders.

[2] *-o* by secondary association with other gen.pl. in *-o* as in *iro*, also in nouns and adjectives.

Unlike OHG, OS has no special reflexive pronoun.

The possessive adjectives are: sg. *mîn* my, *thîn* your, *sîn* or *is* his, its, *ira* her; pl. *ûsa* our, *iuwa* your, *iro* their; *unka* our two, *inka* your two. The forms *is, ira, iro*, being still felt as simply genitives, are invariable; the rest inflect like strong adjectives, *ûsa* and the others in *-a* dropping the final vowel in the inflected forms; e.g. sg.masc.acc. *ûsan*, gen. *ûses*.

ARTICLES

The definite article declines as follows:

		masc.	fem.	neut.	all genders
Sg.	nom.	*thê*	*thiu*	*that*	Pl. *thê (thia, thiu)*
	acc.	*thena*	*thia*	,,	,,
	gen.	*thes*	*thera*	*thes*	*thero*
	dat.	*themu*	*theru*	*themu*	*thêm*
	inst.	**thiu*		*thiu*	

The indefinite article has the same form as the numeral *ên* one.

VERBS

The OS verb may be closely compared with its OHG counterpart, but is distinguished from High German by one fundamental innovation which it shares with the other North-West Germanic languages. The separate endings of the plural have been replaced by a single ending, as follows. In the pres.indic. the ending of the 2nd person has ousted the 1st and 3rd persons, while in other tenses the endings of the 1st and 3rd person have fallen together and ousted the 2nd person. See p. 218.

STRONG VERBS

The conjugation of strong verbs in OS is as follows:

Infin. *skrîƀan* write (Class 1)

INDICATIVE

Pres.sg.		Pret.sg.			
1	*skrîƀu*	1	*skrêf*	Imper.sg. *skrîf*,pl. *skrîƀad**
2	*skrîƀis*	2	*skriƀi*	Past. part. *giskriƀan*
3	*skrîƀid**	3	*skrêf*	Pres. part. *skrîƀandi*
pl.	*skrîƀad**	pl.	*skriƀun*	

*final -*d* often devoiced to *t;* the termination *d* also occurs.

SUBJUNCTIVE

Pres.sg.1, 3	*skrîƀe*	Pret.sg.1, 3	*skriƀi*
2	*skrîƀes*	2	*skriƀis*
pl.	*skrîƀen*	pl.	*skriƀin*

Principal parts (infin., 3rd pres.sg., 1st pret.sg., pret.pl., past part.) of other ablaut classes: 2 *farliosan* lose, *farliusid, farlôs, farlurun, farloran;* 3 *drinkan* drink, *drinkid, drank, drunkun, gidrunkan;* 4 *neman* take, *nimid, nam, nâmun, ginoman;* 5 *lesan* read *lisid, las, lâsun, gilesan;* 6 *graƀan* dig *greƀid, grôf, grôƀun, gigraƀan.*

WEAK VERBS

Weak verbs in OS fall into two main classes corresponding to Classes 1 and 2 of OHG. The OS infinitive endings are 1. -*ian*, 2. -*o(ia)n*. Most forms in Class 2, however, show a development parallel to OHG, where only the shorter forms are found. Typical paradigms follow.

Infin. *dêlian* divide, *mako(ia)n* make

INDICATIVE

Pres.sg.			Pret.sg.		
1	*dêliu*	*makon*	1	*dêlda*	*makoda*
2	*dêlis*	*makos*	2	*dêldes*	etc.
3	*dêlid*	*makod*	3	*dêlda*	
pl.	*dêliad*	*mako(ia)d*	pl.	*dêldun*	

Imper.sg. *dêli, mako;* pl. *dêlid, mako(ia)d*
Pres. part. *dêliandi, mako(ia)ndi* Past part. *gidêlid, gimakod*

SUBJUNCTIVE

Pres.sg.1, 3 *dêlie*   *mako(ie)*   Pret.sg.1, 3 *dêldi*   *makodi*
   2 *dêlies*   *makos*   2 *dêldis*   etc.
  pl.   *dêlien*   *mako(ia)n*   pl.   *dêldin*

A few verbs have the preterite in *-ida* etc., e.g. *nerian* 'save', pret.sg.1, 3 *nerida*.

A 3rd class corresponding to the OHG type with infin. *-ên* no longer exists in OS, the verbs originally belonging to it having been attracted into the other classes. Only very occasionally does a verb still show a form proper to the 3rd class. Examples are pres.sg.2 *haƀes*, 3 *haƀed* in the paradigm of *hebbian* below, but analogical *haƀis*, *haƀid* (like *dêlis*, *dêlid*) occur as well.

THE AUXILIARIES 'TO BE' AND 'TO HAVE'

The following forms may be regarded as typical:

Infin. *wesan, hebbian*

INDICATIVE

Pres.sg.1 *bium*   *hebbiu*   Pret.sg.1 *was*   *habda*
   2 *bist*   *haƀes*   2 *wâri*   *habdes*
   3 *ist*   *haƀed*   3 *was*   *habda*
  pl.   *sind*   *hebbiad*   pl.   *wârun*   *habdun*

Imper.sg. *wes, haƀi;* pl. ———, *hebbiad*
Pres. part. *wesandi, hebbiandi* Past part. *giwesan, gihabd*

SUBJUNCTIVE

Pres.sg.1, 3 *sî*   *hebbie*   Pret.sg.1, 3 *wâri*   *habdi*
   2 *sîs*   *hebbies*   2 *wâris*   *habdis*
  pl.   *sîn*   *hebbien*   pl.   *wârin*   *habdin*

COMPOUND TENSES

These are formed as in OHG.

A note on the endings in OS

The paradigms above have been compiled according to the same principles as in the OHG section. It may be emphasised that owing to the weakening of unstressed endings, which began earlier in OS than in OHG, the vowels of the terminations are very variable. The dat.sg.m.n. ending of strong adjectives is quoted above as -*emu*. This is the oldest form, but in fact it occurs only rarely. The ending appears in no less than 13 other forms as well: -*emo*, -*imo*, -*amu*, -*amo*, -*omu*, -*omo*, -*umu*, -*um*, -*un*, -*an*, -*om*, -*on*, -*en*. Variations may occur within the same document. The *Héliand* is no exception, for not only do the two main mss. (M and C) vary as between each other, but each ms. varies within itself. Most of the above developments of original -*emu* occur in the *Héliand*. In its first half M has more commonly -*un*, less commonly -*um*, rarely -*on*, -*om*, but in its second half -*umu* predominates, with -*omu*, -*omo*, -*emu* as rare alternatives. C on the other hand has chiefly -*on*, rarely -*an*, -*om*, -*un*, -*en*, -*emo*, -*amo*. In reading OS we may not expect orthographical—and morphological—consistency any more than in OHG.

Specimens of Old Saxon

A charm spoken to cure a horse's lameness. From a 10th-century ms.

Visc flôt aftar themo uuatare, verbrustun sîna vetherun : thô gihêlida ina ûse druhtin. Thê selvo druhtin, thie thena visc gihêlda, thie gihêle that hers theru spurihelti.

'A fish was swimming through the water, its fins broke: then Our Lord healed it. The Lord Himself, who healed the fish, may he cure the horse of its lameness.'

The forms in the following glossary have been normalised :

fisk m. 'fish'; OHG do., NHG *Fisch*.

fliotan 'swim'; OHG *fliozan*, NHG *fließen*.

aftar 'through'; OHG do., MHG *after*.

watar n. 'water'; OHG *wazzar*, NHG *Wasser*.

firbrestan 'break'.

federa f. 'feather'; OHG *federa*, NHG *Feder*.

thô 'then'; OHG, MHG *dô*.

gihêlian 'heal, cure'; OHG *giheilen*, MHG *geheilen*. The simplex *hêlian* also occurs, similarly OHG *heilen*, NHG do.

druhtin m. 'lord', OHG, MHG *truhtîn*.

self '(him)self', OHG, MHG *selb*, cf. NHG *selber*, *selbst*.

hers apparently a regional variant of the usual form *hros* n. 'horse'; OHG *do.*, NHG *Roß*. The form *hers* shows transposition of *r* (metathesis), just as the English form, OEngl. *hors*, an older form still in the proper name *Horsa*. Metathesis of *r* is not unusual, but the origin of the vowel *e* in the OS variant is problematic.

spurihelti f. 'lameness of the foot joint', cf. OHG *spurihalz* 'lame in the foot joint', likewise used in reference to a horse. The first element of the compound *spuri-* is not found elsewhere in German, but its meaning is established by comparing related words such as OEngl. *spure* 'heel' or the verb *spurnan* 'kick' (Mod.Engl. *spurn*). The second element of the compound *-helti* is formed from the adjective *halt* 'lame'; OHG, MHG *halz*.

From 'The Saviour' (*Hêliand*), lines 2906–19. Second quarter of the 9th century.

> Thô lêtun sie suîdean strôm,
> hôh hurnidskip   hluttron ûdeon,
> skêdan skîr uuater.   Skrêd lioht dages,
> sunne uuarð an sedle;   the sêolîdandean
> 2910 naht nebulo biuuarþ;   nâdidun erlos
> forðuuardes an flôd: uuarð thiu fiorðe tîd
> thera nahtes cuman   — neriendo Crist
> uuarode thea uuâglîdand   — thô uuarð uuind mikil
> hôh uueder afhaban: hlamodun ûdeon,
> 2915 strôm an stamne;   strîdiun feridun
> thea uueros uuiðer uuinde: uuas im uurêd hugi,
> sebo sorgono ful: selbon ni uuândun
> lagulîdandea   an land cumen
> thurh thes uuederes geuuin.

'Then they caused the high prowed ship to part the strong current, the pure water with clear waves. The light of day passed, the sun went to rest; night encompassed the seafarers with darkness; the men pressed forwards on the flowing tide: the fourth hour of the night was come—redeeming Christ protected the wavefarers—then a strong wind arose, a mighty storm: the waves, the current resounded against the stem; the men sailed with difficulty against the wind: their hearts were dismayed, their minds full of anxieties: the oceanfarers themselves did not believe they would reach land because of the force of the tempest.'

The forms in the following glossary have been normalised:

lâtan 'cause, let'; OHG *lâȝ(ȝ)an*, NHG *lassen*.

swîdi 'strong'; MHG *swinde*, also with *ge-* prefix *geswinde* 'impetuous, quick', NHG *geschwind*.

strôm m. 'current, stream'; OHG, MHG *stroum*. The vocalism of this word in High German varies remarkably, cf. MHG *strâm, strûm*, further OHG, MHG *strôm*, whence the modern standard form *Strom*.

hurnidskip n. lit. 'horned ship', a term not found elsewhere. The absence of the perfective prefix *gi-* suggests an old formation. With *skip* compare OHG *skif*, NHG *Schiff*.

hluttar 'clear'; OHG *hlûttar*, NHG *lauter*.

ûdia f. 'wave'; OHG *undia*, MHG *ünde*.

skêdan 'part, cut'; OHG *skeidan*, NHG *scheiden*.

skîr 'pure'. This word regularly became *schîr* in MLG and in this form passed into High German where it is now spelt *schier*.

lioht n. 'light'; OHG do., NHG *Licht*.

sunna f. 'sun'; OHG do., NHG *Sonne*.

an sedle werdan 'go to rest', an idiom known only from this poem. The sense *sedal* n. 'rest' is secondary, the original meaning being 'seat'. This expression is doubtless a euphemism. It is paralleled in MHG *diu sunne gie* (=*gieng*) *ze gnâden* 'the sun went to rest' and in Early NHG *die sonne gieng zu röst und gnaden* 'do.'. In former times men showed a marked disinclination to refer to the setting sun in so many words. The literal term *untergehen* was felt to be too drastic and was often avoided ('linguistic taboo').

sêolîdandi m. 'seafarer', a poetic compound to be compared with *wâglîdand, lagulîdandi* below, terms only to be found in this poem. The second element *-lîdandi* is the pres. part. (declined weak) of *lîdan* sv. 'fare, travel'; OHG *lîdan*, NHG *leiden* 'suffer'. The modern sense 'suffer' is attested as early as the 9th century, the semantic change from 'travel' being achieved through an intermediary stage where the word took on the sense of 'go through', cf. Engl. *think what he went through*.

2910   *naht* f. 'night', OHG do., NHG *Nacht*.

neƀal m. 'darkness'; OHG *nebal*, NHG *Nebel*. The form in the text is the instrumental.

biwerpan 'encompass'; OHG *biwerfan*, NHG *bewerfen*.

nâdian 'press on'; OHG, MHG *nenden*.

erl m. 'man'; OHG do.

forðwardes 'forwards' (lit. 'forth-wards'), i.e. *forð* (OHG, NHG *fort*), *-wardes*, cf. OHG *-wertes*, NHG *-wärts*.

flôd m., f. 'flood, flowing tide'; OHG *fluot*, NHG *Flut*.

fiorðo 'fourth'; OHG *fiordo*, NHG *vierte*.

tîd f. 'hour', OHG *zît* 'hour; time', NHG *Zeit*.

nahtes: in OS a number of feminine words adopted this genitive ending from the masc. and neut. declensions. In OHG, too, *nahtes* was used in the sense 'by night'; it even came to be regarded as a masc. form, hence *des nahtes*. Both these forms survive today: *nachts*, *des Nachts*.

neriandi pres. part. of *nerian* 'save, redeem'; OHG *neren*, NHG *nähren*. In the form *neriendo* in the present text, *i* has been lost before the inflexional ending, as often.

waron 'protect'; OHG *-warôn*, NHG *wahren*.

wâglîdand, see *sêolîdandi*. Here the original pres. part. has been completely substantivised and the formal connection with the adjectival declension has been broken. With others like it, e.g. *hêliand* 'saviour', it formed a special declensional class in which the nom.pl. is often the same as the nom.sg. The first element in this compound is *wâg* m. 'wave'; OHG *wâg*, NHG *Woge*.

mikil 'strong, great'; OHG *mihhil*, MHG *michel* (p. 31). The OS word lives on in the name *Mecklenburg*.

wedar n. 'storm'; OHG *wetar*, NHG *Wetter*.

afhebbian sv. 'arise'; OHG *-heffen*, NHG *-heben*. OS *af* corresponds to OHG *ab(a)*, NHG *ab*.

hlamon 'resound'; OHG *hlamôn*.

2915 *stamn* m. 'stem', the same word as OHG *stamm*, NHG *Stamm*, where original *n* has been assimilated to *m*.

strîdiun 'with difficulty', an adverbial use of the dat.pl. of *strîd* m. (*i*-stem) 'strife, trouble, difficulty'; OHG *strît*, NHG *Streit*.

ferian 'travel (over water)'; OHG *feren*, MHG *vern*.

wer m. 'man'; OHG *wer*, cf. NHG *Werwolf*.

widar 'against'; OHG *widar*, NHG *wider*.

wrêð 'dismayed; angry'. This word is unknown in High German, but survives in modern Low German as *wrede* 'angry'.

hugi m. 'mind, heart'; OHG do., MHG *hüge*.

seƀo m. = *hugi*; cf. MHG *beseben* 'perceive'.

sorga f. 'anxiety'; OHG do., NHG *Sorge*.

ful 'full'; OHG *fol*, NHG *voll*.

wânian 'believe'; OHG *wânen*, NHG *wähnen*.

lagulîdandi, see *sêolîdandi*. The first element, not otherwise attested in German, must be the same word as OEngl. *lagu* 'sea, water'.

thurh 'through, because of'; OHG *durh*, NHG *durch*.

giwin n. 'force, struggle'; OHG *do*. A noun formed from the verb *winnan* 'struggle, win'.

BIBLIOGRAPHY

G. Cordes, *Altniederdeutsches Elementarbuch*, Heidelberg, 1973.
F. Holthausen, *Altsächsisches Wörterbuch*[2], Cologne, 1967.

4

THE HIGH GERMAN SOUND SHIFT

High German is distinguished from Low German and from all other Germanic languages by a striking innovation termed the High German Sound Shift. This was a development which affected particularly the occlusive consonants *p, t, k,* transforming them to a remarkable extent. Thus original *p* is variously changed to *f, ff* or *pf* according to its position in the word. To a lesser extent the voiced occlusives and the corresponding spirants were affected. The changes took place in the pre-literary period, but the forms of ancient personal and topographical names and of words borrowed at an early date from Latin afford some evidence for dating the shift approximately. It arose in the south in the alpine area, presumably as the result of contact with speakers of other languages. We may think here of the Celts, the Illyrians or the Rhaetians—the last a non-Indo-European people—who are known to have preceded the Germans in the alpine region. For three centuries or more the area was under Roman rule, secured against Germanic invasion from the north by the *Limes* on the Danube. It is likely that the natives of this wide area, at least in the more accessible parts, became romanised in speech. They would speak their own variety of Vulgar Latin, pronouncing it more or less in accordance with their native phonetic system, just as happened elsewhere in the Roman Empire. When the Bavarians and Alemanni, and perhaps other German-speaking groups from the east (Bohemia), established themselves among them, the native inhabitants will have gone over to the Germanic speech of their conquerors, but again still retaining by and large their old phonetic habits. This is, of course, the normal development in such circumstances. We have only to remember the Irish brogue or the accent of English-speaking Welshmen, who may not know a word of Welsh. The language is English, but the phonetics are Celtic. Similarly in the alpine area, early on in the period of the migrations, un-Germanic pronunciations must have become general. Then they became expansive. The reasons are not now ascertainable with certainty, but it is to be supposed that migrations from the mountainous regions helped to spread the shifted forms. There is no doubt that such movements took place. At any rate, changes were reaching the Franconians in the centre of the country by the 6th century. At the beginning of the literary period, the whole Franconian area, except the north-west, had been largely affected by the sound shift, so that the oldest German is seen to fall into two main divisions, High German and Low German.

The northward thrust of the shifted forms in the pre-literary period was abruptly halted on the Franconian-Saxon frontier. Franconian power now extended over the centre and south of the country, but it had not yet broken the independence of the Saxon confederacy, an aim not finally achieved until 804 after twenty years of warfare. The rising political tension between Saxons and Franks in the 8th century will have made the Franconian-Saxon borderland a very real frontier and it was this political frontier which determined the linguistic boundary between Low German and High German. On the other hand, the shifted forms continued to move forward in the Rhineland area; this was old Franconian territory. Certain changes definitely took place after the beginning of the literary period. For instance, Otfrid of Weissenburg writing Rhenish Franconian about 860 has unshifted *p*, e.g. *pad* 'path', where the modern dialect of the area has *pf-*. We shall say more below about the nature of the boundary between High and Low German.

The changes do not affect the dialects uniformly. They are most numerous in Upper German, but become fewer in Franconian. Since, however, the consonant system of the modern standard language is in essentials Franconian, it will be convenient to base a description of the sound shift on examples from this dialect. The changes are seen most clearly in the oldest forms of the language, so that we may begin by comparing OHG (Old East Franconian) with OLG (Old Saxon).

CHANGES AFFECTING ORIGINAL
VOICELESS OCCLUSIVES

Two groups of positions are to be distinguished:

1. When occurring medially between vowels, *p*, *t*, *k* were shifted
to the corresponding double spirants *ff*, *ʒʒ*, *hh*: OLG *opan* open
(adj.), *etan* eat, *makon* make, OHG *offan*, *eʒʒan*, *mahhôn*.

A similar change is observed when these occlusives occur
between a vowel and a consonant or when final after a vowel,
except that the spirant is not doubled. Contrast OHG *bouhhan*
signal (OLG *bôkan*) with *bouhnen* give a signal, OHG *âʒ* ate, but
eʒʒan.

Except in the earliest texts, the double spirant is usually
reduced after a long vowel or diphthong in conformity with a
general tendency to reduce double consonants of whatever
origin in this position: Early OHG *slâffan* sleep, *lâʒʒan* let, but
later *slâfan*, *lâʒan* (OLG *slâpan*, *lâtan*); likely also Early OHG
zeihhan sign (OLG *têkan*) became *zeihan*, though in this case the
written form of the later period is the ambiguous *ch*.

2. When occurring initially, after a consonant or if geminated, *p*
and *t* are shifted to the voiceless affricates *pf*, *z* [ts]: OLG *plegan*
take charge of, *helpan* help, *skeppian* make, OHG *pflegan*, *helpfan*,
skeppfen; OLG *tiohan* draw, *holt* wood, *settian* set, OHG *ziohan*,
holz, *sezzen*.

In Central Franconian and usually in Rhenish Franconian *p*
is not affected, hence *plegan* etc.

In Upper German *k* in these positions was shifted to *kh*
[kχ]: OLG *korn* corn, *werk* work, *wekkian* wake (tr.), Upper
OHG *khorn*, *werkh*, *wekkhen*, normally written *chorn*, *werch*,
wechen. Such pronunciations are still a common feature of many
Upper German dialects today.

It will be noticed that OHG *helpfan* conflicts with NHG
helfen. The same applies to OHG *werpfan* throw > NHG *werfen*
(OLG *werpan*). In such cases further shifting reduced *pf* after *l*
and *r* to *f*.

Note

The sound shift does not affect occlusives in the following combinations: *sp*, *st*, *sk*, *ft*, *ht*, *tr*, hence OLG, OHG *spil* game,
stilli quiet, *skaft* shaft, *naht* night, *triuwa* faith.

CHANGES AFFECTING ORIGINAL VOICED OCCLUSIVES AND SPIRANTS

In this case it will be convenient to treat each consonant separately.

Labial series

OLG has the occlusive in the initial position, after a consonant and when geminated, otherwise the spirant: *beran* carry, *lamb* lamb, *sibbia* clan; *sibun* seven. In the High German area, Central Franconian was not affected at this point, and preserves the distinction between occlusive and spirant exactly as in OLG. East and Rhenish Franconian, on the other hand, change the spirant into the occlusive: *sibun*. In Bavarian this occlusive, of whatever origin, is shifted to *p:* *peran, lamp, sippa, sipun;* in Alemannic it is shifted to *p* where it corresponds to OLG *b*, but is retained where it corresponds to OLG *ƀ: peran* etc., but *sibun*. At the end of the OHG period, however, *p* generally reverted to *b*, except in gemination: Late Upper OHG *beran* etc., but *sippa*.

Dental series

In this case only the occlusive survives in the West Germanic languages, the corresponding spirant having been changed into the occlusive in the pre-literary period. OLG (WGmc.) *d* is shifted in High German to *t:* OLG *dohter*, OHG *tohter*. This change does not however reach Central and Rhenish Franconian.

Velar series

Although the script is ambiguous, the evidence of the modern dialects strongly suggests that the Old Franconian values corresponded to those of OLG, i.e. occlusive in *gast* guest, *ruggi* back, spirant in *stîgan* climb. Thus at this point the sound shift did not affect Central Germany at all. Only Upper German shifted the voiced velars, both occlusive and spirant being changed to the voiceless occlusive: Upper OHG *kast, rukki, stîkan*. But the voiced occlusive is also common, especially in the medial position, and eventually becomes dominant, except in gemination: Late Upper OHG *gast, stîgan* but *rukki*.

MAP 3

High and Low German today

Note

The often observed correspondence between Engl. *th* as in *three*
and Ger. *d* as in *drei* has nothing to do with the High German
Sound Shift. It is true that High German was again the inno-
vating language, but the change of the originally unvoiced
(WGmc.) spirant *th*, subsequently voiced, to the occlusive *d*
is much later than the sound shift, and moreover it spread to
Low German and to Frisian. The development is first noticed
in Upper German about the middle of the 8th century. By
800 it was reaching the Middle Franconian area, though not
becoming general until after 900—Tatian *c.* 830 and Otfrid
c. 860 still use *th*. At a later date the change is seen to have
affected all the Low German dialects : Middle Low German
and Middle Dutch have only *d*. Frisian resisted the innovation
longest, but by 1300 or so the old spirant was lost in Frisian
as well.

THE NATURE OF THE BOUNDARY BETWEEN HIGH AND LOW GERMAN

It is apparent from the foregoing that even though the boundary
between High and Low German is a basic feature of the linguistic configuration, it is not clear-cut in the sense that all the
High German changes reach the boundary. There are further
complications. In the Rhineland, High German penetration has
staggered the changes over a wide area. Map 3 gives details of
certain shifts affecting *p, t, k*. Here we see that the shift of *k*
has advanced furthest north, followed at some distance by *p*
and then by *t*. Moreover the boundary LG *ik/* HG *ich* (Ürdin-
gen Line) lies further north than the boundary LG *maken*/HG
machen (Benrath Line) in the west, but the reverse is the case in
the east. Map 3 also shows the boundary for the shift of *pp*,
from which we see how geminated *p* has resisted High German
influence much better than single *p*. Elsewhere the boundary
has remained remarkably stable since the early Middle Ages,
though even here High German forms have made small
advances, most of all at the eastern end.

THE MIDDLE PERIOD

5

MIDDLE HIGH GERMAN

The literary remains from the last decades of the Old High German period are scanty indeed, and the position is not greatly altered after 1100 when the Middle High German period formally begins. But a change was on the way. By the middle of the 12th century Germany was hastening towards a period of literary floraison which was to raise the German language out of local obscurity and assert its European importance. This was the Golden Age of the Hohenstaufen dynasty, the age of the great courtly poets Der von Kürenberg, the two Reinmars, Wolfram von Eschenbach, Hartmann von Aue, Walther von der Vogelweide, Gottfried von Strassburg, Heinrich von Morungen, Neidhardt von Reuenthal. The years between about 1170 and 1230 are now known as the First Classical Age in German literature. The great works themselves are essentially secular, though often permeated with profound religious feeling; they are all in verse. There was no drama as yet, but the genres of epic and lyric flourished and revealed, for the first time, the full resources of the German language. The poems themselves fill dozens of volumes and are consequently too numerous to detail here. By contrast, prose was hardly written at all—this was still mainly the province of Latin—a collection of sermons being the most important text. But later, and especially during the last fifty years of the MHG period, that is between 1300 and 1350, the number of prose documents greatly increases as German replaces Latin as the language of administration, see p. 130.

The spoken language of the MHG period was, as in the previous period, characteristically dialectal. This is not to say that all speakers of any given dialect spoke in the same way. There will have been differences, for instance, between the speech of the educated and the uneducated, even though the dialect basis for both was the same. This must indeed be the case in any community except for the most primitive and socially undifferentiated. But in the chivalrous society of 12th-century Germany with its rigid concept of a man's station in life, a concept heartily sanctioned by the law of state and church alike, differences must have been very real. We can imagine the speech of the cultured circles characterised by a refined pronunciation, a careful choice of words and attention to formal grammatical accuracy, the criterion being acceptability in other cultured circles in at least the neighbouring parts of the country. Educated speech would be uniform over wider areas than the rustic language of the villagers. It would have regional validity and sometimes transcend the dialect boundaries proper.

Spoken language of this sort must have become normal at the princely courts where Germans from all over the country regularly met together. In fact a high degree of uniformity is presupposed by the diction of the poets of the classical period. Though their native dialect may be recognisable here and there, the language of their works is remarkably uniform. We must not, however, think here in terms of modern standard German, where the spelling and inflexion of every word are regulated. Such uniformity was never reached in medieval German. But it is nevertheless apparent that, in the classical MHG period, approximate regional standards in writing and speaking could be achieved and that these approximate regional standards affected each other. Thus we find the Alemannic poets avoiding certain traits peculiar to their own area. For instance, as we shall note again below, a typical feature of MHG phonetics is the general reduction of unstressed vowels to the indistinct vowel [ə], written e, regardless of whether they were short or long in the previous, OHG period. From archival materials, however, it has been established that in the MHG of the Alemannic area the change affected at first only those vowels which had been short in OHG, the originally long vowels retaining their full quality and quantity, as in OHG, until well on in the 13th century. But the Alemannic poets of the classical age do not use such forms, they habitually substitute the indistinct vowel e which had become the rule in all dialects but their own.

The classical writers established, for the first time in the history of German, something like a standard literary form. We can see its evolution in perspective. It was made possible not only by greater intercommunication, but above all by the rise and influence of the Imperial court in the 12th century. But this literary language grew and matured only within the ruling feudal circles. It exercised no tangible effect on the illiterate peasantry and when, in the next century, feudal institutions fell into decay, the standard language of the Hohenstaufen Age was lost. Henceforward, and for some time to come, the German language had a regional, rather than a national character.

The form of language employed by the classical MHG poets is technically called *die mittelhochdeutsche Dichtersprache*. Since the poets wrote in an approximately uniform language, it is permissible, when editing their works, to normalise the orthography following the system elaborated by Karl Lachmann (1793–1851) in his scholarly editions of the Middle High German poets. For the minute study of a textual tradition, exact diplomatic reproduction is naturally essential, but for general historical and comparative purposes the normalised orthography is perfectly reliable, in fact indispensable.

THE SOUNDS AND ORTHOGRAPHY OF MIDDLE HIGH GERMAN

Middle High German retained the six short vowels of Old High German: *a, e, ë, i, o, u*, where *e* is close and *ë* open. (In the following we write *e* for both sounds, as explained in the section on OHG.) But the spread of i-umlaut to all back vowels without exception gave rise to three new short vowels. Umlaut of *o* and *u* gave *ö* and *ü*. Furthermore *a* was now affected in cases where in OHG the mutation had been checked by a following consonant cluster, e.g. OHG *naht* night, pl. *nahti*, but MHG *naht*, pl. *nähte*. This new vowel *ä* was very open and distinct from *ë* and more so from *e*, though it subsequently merged with them. In Central German mss. *ä, ë* and *e* are usually all written "e", but Upper German documents often distinguish the first by writing 'å', i.e. in the actual handwriting *å*. Later the superscript 'e' was reduced to ", whence the umlaut sign ·· current today.

The five traditional long vowels remained in MHG: *â, ê, î, ô, û*. These were joined by three new ones arising from *â, ô, û* by i-umlaut: *æ, œ, iu*. These are, of course, the long forms of *ä, ö, ü*. (Notice that in MHG the digraph *iu* does not represent a diphthong, but is an orthographical device to represent long *ü*.) Of the OHG diphthongs *ei* remains, likewise *ie* which, though not prominent in OHG, now becomes very common as the frequently occurring OHG *io* is weakened to *ie;* the rarer OHG *ia* also weakens to *ie*. OHG *iu* becomes the monophthong long *ü*—hence the 'orthographical device' mentioned above. The OHG diphthongs *ou* and *uo* continue into MHG. As they contained back vowels, they were liable to i-umlaut, hence two new diphthongs arose: *öu* and *üe*, the latter with weakening of *o* to *e* parallel to the development of OHG *io* above.

The consonant system of MHG continues that of OHG with but few changes. The lengthening of consonants remains a feature of the language. MHG *w* is still like Engl. 'w' in 'wine' and the dental spirant *ʒ* remains distinct from *s*. On the other hand *s* itself took on new values approximating to [ʃ] and [ʒ]. The actual phonetic distinction between *s* and *ʒ* was maintained throughout the classical MHG period, but by the close of the 13th century voiceless *s* and *ʒ* had coalesced as [s], so that, for instance, *las* could now rhyme with *laʒ*. The spellings of these words today: *las* and *laß*, i.e. *lasz*, are reminders of the old phonetic distinction. When reading MHG today the differences between *s* and *ʒ* are usually disregarded, the letters being pronounced as NHG *s* and *ß* respectively.

A number of observations confirm the values of classical MHG *s*. One indication is seen in the spelling conventions of the Hungarian language, where *s* stands for [ʃ], while [s] is written *sz:* the Hungarian pronunciation of *Budapest* is [budɔpɛʃt], of *Liszt* [list]. Hungarian orthography was taking shape at the time and the Hungarians looked to contemporary German spelling for guidance. There is further evidence for MHG pronunciation from other foreign languages. During the period in question several German words containing *s* passed into the neighbouring Slavonic languages; in such words the original MHG *s* appears either as [ʃ]: Czech *šlechta*, Polish *szlachta* < MHG *slahte* race, origin (cf. NHG

Geschlecht) or as [ʒ]: Czech *růže*, Polish *róża* < MHG *rôse* rose. Such facts enable us to understand the evolution of the sounds represented by MHG *s*. It has been as follows. In the oldest period of the German language *s* stood for [s]. It is quite possible that voicing occurred in those positions where *s* is voiced today, thus OHG *rôsa* may have been pronounced [ro:za]. Later, *s* shifted to sounds approximating to [ʃ] and [ʒ], subsequently reverting to [s] and [z], but not in all positions. When initial before a consonant, MHG *s* developed into [ʃ], the sound now written *sch*: MHG *slâf*, *smal*, *snel*, *swinden*, NHG *Schlaf*, *schmal*, *schnell*, *schwinden*. We can now see why words like NHG *Spiel* and *Stein* are pronounced as though spelt **Schp-*, **Scht-*. The pronunciation has changed according to rule, but the spelling has remained at the MHG stage. If the modern orthography were consistent one would write **Schpiel*, **Schtein*, or else **Slaf* etc. A further change associated with *s* is as follows. In MHG the *k* of the OHG combination *sk* became the fricative [χ], written *ch*, thus OHG *sk* appears in MHG as *sch*, i.e. *s* + [χ], but by the second half of the 13th century *sch* had probably acquired its present value [ʃ]. It is most likely that MHG *ch* was velar in all positions, thus *ich* may be pronounced [iχ], not [iç] as is usual today. The velar pronunciation may still be heard in southern dialects.

There were a few other changes in the pronunciation of certain consonants. Originally voiced occlusives were regularly devoiced when final: *tac* day, gen. *tages*. This tendency, which survives today though not indicated in the orthography (*Tag*, *Tages*), began to show itself during the OHG period as may be inferred from manuscript spellings. Finally, we notice that original *f* becomes (weakly) voiced *v* in MHG when initial or medial between vowels: OHG *findan* find, MHG *vinden;* MHG *hof* court, gen. *hoves*. This was the position in the classical period, but later in the 13th century *v* ceased to be voiced, reverting to *f* as in the modern language: MHG *vinden*, *hoves*, NHG *finden*, *Hofes*.

Apart from the phonetic changes outlined above, we also note the following purely orthographic changes. MHG *h* has the same phonetic values as OHG *h*, but when final after vowels the MHG spelling is *ch*: OHG *peh* pitch, MHG *pech*.

Similarly OHG *hh* is now written *ch*: OHG *mahhôn* make, MHG *machen*. Further, *c* not *k* is written when final in a syllable: *senken* (cause to) sink, pret. *sancte*.

DIFFERENCES BETWEEN OHG AND MHG

The basic linguistic differences between OHG and MHG are of phonetic origin. Two developments are most significant. The first is the spread of i-umlaut, the second the reduction of vowels in unstressed syllables. Whereas in OHG i-umlaut was confined to short *a*, it spread in MHG to all back vowels, as explained in the preceding section. In OHG all simple vowels, both long and short, could stand in unstressed syllables, but in MHG the vowels of most unstressed syllables were uniformly reduced to the indistinct vowel [ə], written *e*, e.g. OHG *firstôzan*, MHG *verstôzen* (NHG *verstoßen*), OHG *betalôta*, MHG *betel(e)te* (NHG *bettelte*). This process was well under way in Late OHG. Thus the language of the Middle Period lost in sonority through the wholesale reduction of vowels in unstressed syllables, but on the other hand it gained a large number of new sounds through the extension of i-umlaut.

Both these developments, though purely phonetic in origin, were to lead to great changes in the grammatical structure of German. The weakening of unstressed endings was particularly fateful. Compare, for instance, the declension of nouns in OHG and MHG and see how many of the once distinct endings became conflated in the Middle Period. It is clear that the traditional classification of nouns valid for OHG is only to a limited extent applicable to MHG. Inflexional variety ceases to be a prominent feature. The masc. *a*-stems and masc. *i*-stems have now identical endings throughout. The same applies to the fem. *ô*-stems and the fem. *i*-stems. But a new feature is now coming to the fore as a classifying element. This is the umlaut. Thus *gast* 'guest' is distinguished from *tac* 'day' solely by umlaut in the plural: *geste* contrasting with *tage*. At this stage speakers of the language would inevitably come to feel that umlaut could be a sign of the plural. They would have no recollection of its phonetic origin, in fact it would only enter their consciousness at all as it took on a meaningful function as an indicator of the plural. Notice how in *vart* 'journey' the older, regular sg.gen.dat. *verte* (from OHG *ferti*) was replaced by *vart*. The tendency was to reserve the umlauted form for the plural. It wasn't long before this tendency became productive and so we find, about this time, that *mantel* 'cloak' is suddenly provided with a pl. *mentel*.

Outline of Middle High German Accidence

NOUNS

a-stems, masc. and neut.

Sg.nom.acc. *tac* m. day, gen. *tages*, dat. *tage;* pl.nom.acc.gen. *tage*, dat. *tagen*. Similarly *wort* n. word, except that pl.nom.acc. are uninflected.

Sg.nom.acc. *kalp* n. calf, gen. *kalbes*, dat. *kalbe;* pl.nom.acc. *kelber*, gen. *kelber(e)*, dat. *kelber(e)n*. This sub-class continues to be productive in MHG.

ō-stems, fem.

Sg. *gebe* gift; pl.nom.acc. *gebe*, gen.dat. *geben*

i-stems, masc. and neut.

Sg.nom.acc. *gast* m. guest, gen. *gastes*, dat. *gaste;* pl.nom.acc. gen. *geste*, dat. *gesten*

Sg.nom.acc. *vart* f. journey, gen.dat. *vart*, older *verte;* pl. nom.acc.gen. *verte*, dat. *verten*

Consonantal declension, all genders.

Sg.nom. *bote* m. messenger, obl. and pl. *boten*
Sg.nom. *zunge* f. tongue, obl. and pl. *zungen*
Sg.nom.acc. *herze* n. heart, gen.dat. and pl. *herzen*

ADJECTIVES

The evolution of the MHG adjectival endings from the OHG period is precisely the same as for the comparable noun classes, the sole change being the weakening of the terminations. Hence the weak adjective declines as follows:

Sg.masc.fem.nom. *starke* strong, obl. and pl. *starken*
Sg.neut.nom.acc. *starke*, gen.dat. and pl. *starken*

The strong declension :

		masc.	fem.	neut.
Sg.	nom.	*stark(er)*	*stark(iu)*	*stark(eʒ)*
	acc.	*–en*	*–e*	,,
	gen.	*–es*	*–er(e)*	*–es*
	dat.	*–em(e)*	*–er(e)*	*–em(e)*
Pl.	nom.acc.	*–e*	*–e*	*–iu*
	gen.	*–er(e)*	*–er(e)*	*–er(e)*
	dat.	*–en*	*–en*	*–en*

In the predicative position the uninflected form *starc* is usual.

The adverb in MHG is generally formed by adding *-e* to the uninflected adjective: *starke* strongly.

Comparative and superlative adjectives are formed by adding *-er* (for older *-ere*, OHG *-iro*, *-ôro*) and *-este* (OHG *-isto*, *-ôsto*) to the uninflected positive. In the superlative degree the endings *-iste* and *-ôste* are not unknown in MHG, but as a rule these full vowels have been regularly reduced. The frequently occurring umlaut in the root vowel of the comparative and superlative adjective is due to the former presence of *-iro*, *-isto;* absence of umlaut, on the other hand, indicates that the earlier endings were *-ôro*, *-ôsto*. As in OHG, some words in MHG occur in both forms, e.g. *lang* long, comp. *lenger, langer,* superl. *lengeste, langeste*. The adverbial endings are regularly *-er*, *-est*.

Irregular comparison continues: *guot* good, *beʒʒer, beste; übel* bad, *wirser, wirste; michel* big, *mêrer, meiste; lützel* little, *minner, minste.*

Whereas in OHG the comparative and superlative inflect according to the weak declension, in MHG they inflect strong or weak. In other words, they are now made to conform to the ordinary rules governing the inflexion of the positive.

NUMERALS

Commonly occurring forms are : 1 *ein* (inflects like an adj., strong and weak), 2 nom.acc.m. *zwêne,* f. *zwâ, zwô,* n. *zwei,* gen. *zweier,* dat. *zweien,* 3 nom.acc.m.f. *drî,* n. *driu,* gen. *drîer,* dat. *drîen,* 4 *vier,* 5 *vünf,* 6 *sehs,* 7 *siben,* 8 *ahte,* 9 *niun,* 10 *zehen,* 11 *einlif, eilf,* 12 *zwelf,* 13 *drîzehen,* 14 *vierzehen,* 15 *vünfzehen,*

16 *sehzehen*, 17 *sibenzehen*, 18 *ahzehen*, 19 *niunzehen*, 20 *zweinzic*, 21 *ein unde zweinzic*, 30 *drîzic*, 40 *vierzic*, 50 *vünfzic*, 60 *sehzic*, 70 *sibenzic*, 80 *ahzic*, 90 *niunzic*, 100 *zehenzic*, later *hundert*, 1000 *tûsent*.

It will be noticed that the first three numerals inflect as in OHG, but that 2 and 3 have acquired new analogical endings in the gen. and dat. The word *zehenzic* continued into the 12th century when *hundert* becomes common. This form is of northern origin, occurring first in OSax. as *hunderod*. The word is a compound, lit. 'hundred-number'. The simple *hunt* 'hundred', known in OHG, occurs sporadically in MHG too.

PERSONAL PRONOUNS

These decline as follows:

Sg.	nom.	*ich* I	*dû* you	*er* he	*siu* she	*eʒ* it
	acc.	*mich*	*dich*	*in*	*sie*	,,
	gen.	*mîn*	*dîn*	*sîn*	*ir(e)*	*es, sîn*
	dat.	*mir*	*dir*	*im(e)*	*ir(e)*	*im(e)*

Pl.	nom.	*wir* we	*ir* you	*sie* m.f.	*siu* n. they
	acc.	*unsich*	*iuch*	,,	,,
	gen.	*unser*	*iuwer*	*ir(e)*	*ir(e)*
	dat.	*uns*	*iu*	*in*	*in*

These forms are substantially those of the earlier period. The form *eʒ* is a weakened variety of *iʒ*; this still occurs occasionally. The acc. *uns*, properly the dat., has generally replaced *unsich*. The forms *siu*, *sie* are the oldest. However, *sie* may replace *siu*, and both may be replaced by *sî* or *si*.

A plural pronoun nom. *eʒ* you, acc.dat. *enc*, is recorded in Bavarian documents since the 14th century. Comparison with other Germanic languages shows that this was originally the dual pronoun 'you two' (see pp. 43, 231). The pronoun survives widely in modern Bavarian dialects (see p. 101).

The special reflexive pronoun *sich*, *sîn* functions as in OHG, i.e. it is not yet found in the dat., an ordinary pronoun being used instead.

The possessive pronouns are: sg. *mîn* mine, *dîn* your, *sîn* his, its, *ir(e)* her; pl. *unser* our, *iuwer*, Bavarian also *enker* your, *ir(e)* their. The forms *ir(e)* are generally invariable like the corresponding words in OHG, but occasionally they take the strong inflexions like the others. They had hitherto been felt simply as genitives, but when the inflexional -*e* disappeared, *ir* was by analogy treated like an adjective.

ARTICLES

The MHG definite article is regularly descended from the OHG forms: Sg.nom.m. *der*, f. *diu*, n. *daȝ*, acc.m. *den*, f. *die*, n. *daȝ*, gen.m.n. *des*, f. *der(e)*, dat.m.n. *dem(e)*, f. *der(e)* ; pl.nom.acc.m.f. *die*, n. *diu*, gen. *der(e)*, dat. *den*.

The indefinite article has the same forms as the numeral *ein* one.

VERBS

The MHG weakening of endings caused changes in the classification of verbs comparable to the changes noted for the nouns. The three OHG classes of weak verbs are now merged into one main type. The pret.indic. and subj. are now indistinguishable, while in the pres.indic. and subj. only the 3rd persons are different. In the case of the strong verbs formal simplification has not gone so far since here the tenses and in part the moods, too, are distinguished by ablaut. But all the same the changes were considerable enough to lead to important modifications in the syntax. Where the subjunctive became formally identical with the indicative, it could no longer play a part in the language. Perforce other devices had to be created to express what the subjunctive could no longer do. We take an example. Otfrid wrote in OHG *bimîde ih thaȝ wîȝi* 'may I escape the punishment'. The infinitive is *bimîdan*, cf. NHG *meiden, vermeiden*. The form *bimîde* is the 1st sg.pres.subj., the 1st sg.pres.indic. being *bimîdu*. If Otfrid had written *bimîdu ih thaȝ wîȝi*, he would have meant 'if I escape the punishment'. Subsequently OHG *bimîde* and *bimîdu* coalesced in MHG as *bemîde*. When this happened, the two OHG constructions became formally identical. But the force of the latter, the more frequently used indicative construction inevitably prevailed. The old subjunctive construction had to be replaced by a paraphrase, as in modern German, where Otfrid's sentence would run *möge ich der Strafe entgehen.*

The paradigm of a STRONG VERB in MHG:

Infin. *schrîben* write

INDICATIVE

Pres.sg.1	*schrîbe*	Pret.sg.1	*schreip*
2	*schrîbest*	2	*schribe(st)**
3	*schrîbet*	3	*schreip*
pl.1	*schrîben*	pl.1	*schriben*
2	*schrîbet*	2	*schribet*
3	*schrîbent*	3	*schriben*

* As early as the 12th century, especially in Central German, i.e. in the Franconian of Central Germany, *schribest* is found after the analogy of the other tenses. Later in the MHG period this form becomes the rule everywhere.

Imper.sg. *schrîp*, pl. *schrîbet* Pres. part. *schrîbende*, past part. *geschriben*

SUBJUNCTIVE

Pres.sg.1	*schrîbe*	Pret.sg.1	*schribe*
2	*schrîbest*	2	*schribest*
3	*schrîbe*	3	*schribe*
pl.1	*schrîben*	pl.1	*schriben*
2	*schrîbet*	2	*schribet*
3	*schrîben*	3	*schriben*

Principal parts of verbs from other ablaut classes (infin., 3rd pres.sg., 1st pret.sg. and pl., past part.): 2 *verliesen* lose, *verliuset, verlôs, verlurn, verlorn;* 3 *trinken* drink, *trinket, tranc, trunken, getrunken;* 4 *nemen* take, *nimet, nam, nâmen, genomen;* 5 *lesen* read, *liset, las, lâsen, gelesen;* 6 *graben* dig, *grebet, gruop, gruoben, gegraben.*

As in OHG, the vowel of the 3rd pres.sg. occurs throughout the singular, e.g. 1 *verliuse*, 2 *verliusest.*

Notice that the pret.indic.sg.2 of these verbs takes umlaut: *verlüre(st), trünke(st), næme(st), læse(st), grüebe(st)* from OHG *firluri, trunki, nâmi, lâsi, gruobi.* Likewise the pret.subj.: 1 *verlüre,* 2 *verlürest,* etc. from OHG *firluri, firluris,* etc.

The paradigm of a WEAK VERB in MHG

Infin. *machen* make

INDICATIVE

Pres.sg.1 *mache*	Pret.sg.1 *machete*
2 *machest*	2 *machetest*
3 *machet*	3 *machete*
pl.1 *machen*	pl.1 *macheten*
2 *machet*	2 *machetet*
3 *machent*	3 *macheten*

Imper.sg. *mache*, pl. *machet* Pres. part. *machende*, past part. *gemachet*

SUBJUNCTIVE

Pres.sg.1,3 *mache*, 2 *machest;* pl.1,3 *machen*, 2 *machet*
Pret. (as Indicative)

The auxiliary 'TO BE':

Infin. *wesen, sîn*

INDICATIVE

Pres.sg.1 *bin*	Pret.sg.1 *was*
2 *bist*	2 *wære*
3 *ist*	3 *was*
pl.1 *birn, sîn*	pl.1 *wâren*
2 *birt, sît*	2 *wâret*
3 *sint*	3 *wâren*

SUBJUNCTIVE

Pres.sg. 1 *sî*	Pret.sg.1 *wære*
2 *sîst*	etc.
3 *sî*	
pl.1 *sîn*	
2 *sît*	
3 *sîn*	

Imper.sg. *wîs*, pl. *weset, sît*
Pres. part. *wesende*, past part. *gewesen, gewest*

The forms *birn, birt* disappear in the course of the 13th century, the other alternative forms are found throughout the period.

The verb 'TO HAVE' in MHG may keep its regular full form *haben* (OHG *habên*), but contracted forms occur in the infin., indic., and pret. subj., and these are usual when the verb is used as an auxiliary. The contracted forms are:

Infin. *hân*
Indic.pres.sg.1 *hân*, 2 *hâst*, 3 *hât;* pl.1 *hân*, 2 *hât*, 3 *hânt*
Indic.pret.sg.1 *hâte* etc. Subj.pret.sg.1 *hæte* etc.

Specimens of Middle High German

(The reader is reminded of the remarks on pronunciation, pp. 59 ff. We beg indulgence for repeating what has already been said in connection with the reading of OHG. It is important not to be misled by the modern pronunciation of German, particularly in matters of vowel length; vowels here are short unless marked long.)

From a sermon by the Franciscan preacher Berthold von Regensburg (about 1220–1272).

Eȝ stênt siben sternen an dem himel, dar an sult ir lesen unde tugende lernen, wan unser herre hât uns alliu dinc ze nutze und ouch ze guote geschaffen, einhalp zuo dem lîbe und anderhalp zuo der sêle, als ich ê sprach. Und alsô hât unser herre die sternen ouch geschaffen, die habent gar grôȝe kraft über alliu dinc diu ûf erden sint under dem himel. Als er den steinen unde den wurzen unde den worten kraft hât gegeben, alsô hât er ouch den sternen kraft gegeben, daȝ sie über alliu dinc kraft hânt, ân über ein dinc ... Daȝ ist des menschen frîiu willekür; dâ hât nieman gewalt über danne dû selber.

'There are seven stars in the sky, these you are to read and learn virtues, for Our Lord has created all things for our benefit and good, on the one hand for our bodies and on the other hand for our souls. And so the Lord has created the stars too, they have great power over all things which are on earth beneath the sky. Just as he has given power to the stones and the plants and the words, so has he also given the stars power, that they have power over all things, except over one thing ... That is man's free will; over that no one has authority except yourself.'

stênt, pres.pl.3 of *stên* 'stand', NHG *stehen*, which together with its variant *stân* replaced OHG *stantan* in the Middle Period.

sternen 'stars', pl. of *sterne* weak m., OHG *sterno* beside *stern*, from which comes the modern word. Forms without *n* also exist, e.g. MHG *ster*, *sterre* and these are more original, like Engl. *star*, Dutch *ster*. It is thought that the *n*-forms arose through the influence of such words as sun and moon, e.g. OHG *sunna*, *mâno*.

sult, NHG *sollt*.

tugende, sg. *tugent* f., NHG *Tugend* with new pl. *Tugenden*.

wan, OHG *hwant*, in NHG replaced by *denn*, but still in Du. *want*.

und, not the full form *unde* as the following word begins with a vowel.

einhalp, adv. lit. 'one half, one side'.

erde, weak f., hence dat.sg. *erden*. Notice that the words *ûf erden* survive in NHG in the set phrase *auf Erden* 'on earth', even though *Erde* no longer normally inflects in the singular.

sint: according to modern standard syntax it would stand at the end of its clause. But in natural German this rule may be frequently disregarded, as other considerations such as emphasis or sentence rhythm can lead to a different order. This is very noticeable in Luther's Bible and in writing today there is an increasing tendency to disregard the standard rules of word order, where necessary, to reproduce naturally spoken German.

wurz f. 'plant'; the word is best known today in compounds, e.g. *Brechwurz* 'ipecacuanha', the ordinary word for plant now being *Pflanze*.

ân, for usual *âne* 'without', *-e* being elided as in the case of *und* (above). NHG *ohne* is from a Central Ger. dialect variant **ône*.

willekür, lit. 'choice of will', *-kür* being connected with the verb *kiesen* 'choose', now obsolete, though its petrified past participle survives in *auserkoren* 'elect'. NHG *Willkür* now means 'arbitrariness'.

dâ hât . . . über: the normal construction in NHG is *darüber hat . . .*, but the MHG construction is still common locally in spoken German.

nieman, OHG *nioman* < *ni* + *ioman* 'nobody', lit. 'not any-man (person)', i.e. the negative of *ioman* 'anybody'. The final *d* in NHG *niemand* is a post-MHG development; it effects a number of words, thus MHG *ieman*, *mâne*, NHG *jemand*, *Mond*.

danne 'then', a variant of *denne*, which still occurs in NHG in certain applications: *stärker denn je*, *besser als Herr denn als Knecht*.

A poem by Walther von der Vogelweide. The poet expresses his thanks for the grant of a fief. About 1220.

Ich hân mîn lêhen, al die werlt, ich hân mîn lêhen!
nû enfürhte ich niht den hornunc an die zêhen
und wil alle bœse hêrren deste minre vlêhen.

der edel künec, der milte künec hât mich berâten,
daʒ ich den sumer luft und in dem winter hitʒe hân.
mîn' nâhgebûren dunke ich verre baʒ getân:
sie sehent mich niht mêr an in butʒen wîs, als sî wîlent tâten.
ich bin ʒe lange arm gewesen ân' mînen danc.
ich was sô volle scheltens, daʒ mîn âtem stanc.
daʒ hât der künec gemachet reine und dar ʒuo mînen sanc.

The following prose translation by H. Böhm, *Die Gedichte Walthers von der Vogelweide*, Berlin, 1944, will enable the reader to compare the language of 700 years ago with the idiom of today:

'Ich habe mein Lehen, ihr alle, ich habe mein Lehen! Nun fürchte ich nicht, den Hornung an die Zehen zu bekommen, und nehme mir vor, alle geizigen Herren umso weniger anzugehen. Der großmütige König, der gütige König hat mich versorgt, so daß ich es den Sommer über luftig und im Winter warm habe. Meinen Nachbarn komme ich jetzt weit hübscher vor: sie sehen mich nicht mehr wie früher an, als sei ich ein Schreckgespenst. Ich bin zu lange, leider, arm gewesen. Ich war so voller Schmähsucht, daß mein Atem stank. Das alles hat der König rein gemacht und obendrein mein Singen.'

al die werlt, lit. 'all the world'. The form *die* sometimes occurs besides the usual *diu*. NHG *Welt* has lost the original *r*. By contrast Du. *wereld* is much more archaic, cf. OLG *werold*, OHG *weralt*. Engl. *world*, too, preserves *r*, at least in the spelling. Only in Scotland is *r* still heard in the pronunciation.

nû: the modern standard form *nun* is attested since the 13th century, clearly secondary. Descendents of MHG *nû* survive in the modern dialects.

enfürhte ich niht 'I fear not': *en-* . . . *niht* is a double negative, its oldest form being OHG *ni* . . . *niowiht*. Here *ni* is the original negative particle which in the oldest German sufficed of itself to indicate negation. It preceded the verb, the second word *niowiht* lit. 'nothing' < *ni* + *io* + *wiht*, i.e. 'not-any-thing', being added after the verb to strengthen the original particle. It had thus the function of an adverb. Later it must have taken the stress as it came to be regarded as the main carrier of the negative idea. As a consequence the original particle *ni* weakens to *ne* and becomes a mere proclitic, appearing in MHG either as *ne-* or usually *en-*. As the proclitic particle now fulfilled no essential purpose it gradually fell into disuse and was obsolete by the end of the MHG period. The evolution of the negative in French (*ne* . . . *pas*, etc.) offers many parallels. Doubtless the two languages have influenced each other in this respect.

hornung m., an old name for February, surviving in South-West Germany. A derivative of *horn* 'corner', its literal meaning is something like 'bastard' in opprobrious allusion to February's having fewer days than the other months. For the ancient Germans a month was a lunar month and therefore the present term cannot have come into existence before the use of the Roman calendar in Germany. It first occurs in a list of the German names of months written during Charlemagne's reign.

bœse, NHG *böse*, though this does not preserve the sense of 'greedy' found in MHG, where it can be used (as here) as the opposite of *milte*, see below. Notice that in NHG the adjective would be weak: *alle bösen* . . .

hêrren 'lords', pl. of *hêrre*. This form with the long root vowel is more archaic than that with the short—i.e. shortened—vowel, an example of which occurs in the previous passage. In origin the word is a substantivised comparative adjective, hence its weak inflections. Its oldest form is OHG *hêriro* from *hêr* 'distinguished, lofty, sublime' (>NHG *hehr*). It is a calque on the Latin comparative *senior* used as a term of address for a feudal lord. In modern times, of course, the term has become general. Ger. *der Herr* is thus exactly parallel to Ital. *il signore* or Span. *el señor*, while Du. *mijnheer* reflects French *monsieur*.

deste minre, NHG lit. *desto minder*, which is not, however, an everyday combination in the modern language—as is *umso weniger* of the translation. MHG *deste* < Late OHG *desde*, a contraction of earlier *des diu*, where *des* is the gen.n.sg. of the article and *diu* its instrumental. Besides *deste* Low German has a variant *desto*. The latter arose though confusion of *-te* in *deste* with the word *te* 'to' which had an alternative form *to*. This Low German form has now become standard German. As for *minre*, this is an alternative form of *minner* 'less', which continues in NHG as *minder* with excrescent *d*, the same phenomenon as was noted in the previous passage under *nieman*.

vlêhen, NHG *flehen*.

edel for usual *edele*.

künec 'king'. In some districts the vowel of the suffix had an *i*-quality in this and similar words, hence the alternative spelling *künic*, continued in NHG *König*. In the modern form, original *ü* has been replaced by secondary *ö* from Central German dialect. The MHG forms go back to OHG *kuning*, the second *n* being lost by dissimilation. The modern Dutch form *koning* is thus more archaic in this respect than even MHG.

milte 'generous', a sense common in MHG, NHG *mild(e)* 'mild'. The modern language preserves a trace of the old sense 'generous' in the expression *eine milde Gabe* 'a charity, charitable gift', but normally MHG *milte* in the present sense must be rendered in NHG by *freigebig* (or a synonym).

berâten: MHG *rât* means both *Rat* and *Vorrat*, i.e. 'advice' and 'provisions', consequently *berâten* can mean both 'advise' and (as here) 'provide for'. NHG *beraten* now only means 'advise'.

den sumer, temporal accusative. The construction survives in NHG to some extent, e.g. *er blieb den Sommer dort*, but is now often supplemented by an adverb, cf. the translation *den Sommer über*.

mîn for *mîne*.

nâhgebûren 'neighbours', pl. of *nâhgebûre*, i.e. *nâh* 'near' (NHG *nah*) and *-gebûre* 'dweller'. NHG *Nachbar* is a contraction of this word, but the full form survives in the surname *Nachgebauer*, also *Nachbauer*.

dunken 'appear' (with acc.) a southern, non-umlauted form beside *dünken*, now the standard modern form. In reading, *-e* in *dunke* will be elided before *ich*.

verre 'far'. NHG *fern* is from MHG *verne*, earlier *verrene*, OHG *ferrana* 'from afar'.

baz, adv. 'better'. This old adverbial form survives locally in NHG with various meanings, e.g. *ich war baß erstaunt* 'I was much surprised'.

in butzen wîs 'like a scarecrow', lit. 'in scarecrow wise'; *butze* m. survives locally in the modern language, also the compound *Butzemann* with the same meaning.

wîlent 'formerly', NHG *weiland*. The MHG form *wîlent* arose in the 12th century from *wîlen*, OHG *hwîlôm*, in origin dat.pl. of *hwîla* 'period of time, while', but used as an adverb. Archaic Engl. *whilom* is the same form.

ân' mînen danc, an idiomatic phrase, lit. 'without my thanks', but used to mean 'against my wishes', here rendered by *leider* 'unfortunately'.

volle: the weak ending is unusual in the predicative position.

The opening stanzas of the Lay of the Nibelungs. Author unknown. About 1200.

1 *Uns ist in alten mæren   wunders vil geseit*
   von heleden lobebæren,   von grôzer arebeit,
   von vröuden hôchgezîten,   von weinen und von klagen,
   von küener recken strîten   muget ir nu wunder hæren sagen.

2 *Ez wuohs in Burgonden   ein vil edel magedîn,*
   daz in allen landen   niht schæners mohte sîn,
   Kriemhilt geheizen: si wart ein schæne wîp.
   dar umbe muosen degene   vil verliesen den lîp.

3 *Der minneclîchen meide   triuten wol gezam.*
   ir muotten küene recken: niemen was ir gram.
   âne mâzen schæne   sô was ir edel lîp:
   der juncvrouwen tugende   zierten anderiu wîp.

(This passage is more difficult to translate adequately than the previous one. It is not that the style is more involved, it is the highly idiomatic language in these stanzas which makes a closely literal translation well-nigh impossible. About fifty modern German versions of this famous poem have appeared during the last hundred years, but the translators have usually been content with renderings which merely transpose the MHG words into their NHG forms as far as possible. Needless to say, this is not translation.)

1 'In ancient poems are we told many wondrous things of heroes famed, of great travail, of joys ineffable, of weeping and lament, of the strife of daring soldiers, you may now hear marvels told.

2 There came to age in Burgundy a high-born maid, none in any land could be more comely, Kriemhild her name: she grew into a handsome woman. On her account many a fighting man was doomed to lose his life.

3 This desirable maid was meant to be loved. Daring soldiers yearned for her: none was ill-disposed towards her. Fair beyond words was her high-born self: this maiden's qualities would have been a boon to other women.'

1 *mære* n.f. 'tale, report, poem'. This once common word survives now only in literary style as NHG *Mär(e)*, from which however is derived the well-known diminutive *Märchen* 'fairy story'.

wunders vil lit. 'of wonder much'.

geseit, a widespread southern form for *gesaget*, past. part. of *sagen* 'say'. Such forms have today been mostly replaced, but there are a few traces of them in the modern standard language. For example: beside MHG *maget* 'maid' there occurs the common variant *meit*; the former gives NHG *Magd*, the latter NHG (poetic) *Maid*.

heleden, usually in the contracted form *helden* 'heroes', pl. of *helt*—older forms *helde, helede*—NHG *Held*. The word is not found in OHG and seems to be a northern word which penetrated to the south in the 12th century. It is attested in OS *helith;* see also below under *degen*.

lobebære 'praiseworthy', but NHG *lobenswert*.

arebeit, the sense 'travail' is found everywhere in the older records of the language and appears to be the primary one.

vröude, NHG *Freude—hôchgezît* 'festival; joy; wedding'; a variant *hôchzît* occurs, whence NHG *Hochzeit.*

Many editors put a comma after *vröuden* and translators generally render the line very literally, only *hôchgezîten* having to be changed since the meaning of NHG *Hochzeiten* 'weddings' is too specialised to be possible here. So we read in the well-known rendering by K. Simrock: 'Von Freud' und Festlichkeiten, von Weinen und von Klagen.' But even the alliteration gained in the modern version doesn't remove the impression that we seem to have a line made up of rather incongruous elements. But perhaps the original is not to blame. In the Lachmann edition, *vröuden* is not followed by a comma, for Lachmann realised that *vröuden* could be used idiomatically to qualify a following noun in order to impart to it a superlative quality. The word *hôchgezîten* is common in the meaning *'Festlichkeiten'*, i.e. 'festivities', but it is also amply attested in the abstract sense 'joys'. If we assume this meaning here and qualify it with *vröuden,* we can translate the first half line 'of joys ineffable', i.e. as one abstract concept. In the second half of the line, the often occurring phrase *weinen und klagen* likewise constitutes a single abstract concept. Thus we have a perfect balance. There are no festivities in this line at all, just supreme joy on the one side, bitter sorrow on the other. Now, at last, we have poetry.

This example may serve to draw attention to a very delicate aspect of the interpretation of the older literature. There is no native feeling now for these ancient words and no way of recapturing the nuances contained in them except by such a procedure as has just been illustrated. For the German of today, MHG is effectively a dead language. Many problems of translation are scarcely solvable at all for want of evidence, doubtless others are not even recognised, for inevitably a language changes considerably in the course of seven centuries, to say nothing of the revolutions in thought and ideals which remove us still further from the intellectual life of the Middle Ages.

küene, NHG *kühn;* the OHG prototype was *kuoni.*

recke, from OHG *wrekkio.* After the Middle Ages the word virtually disappeared from the language, but was revived at the end of the 18th century as a result of an awakened interest in medieval poetry. See below under *degen.*

mugen (also *mügen*) 'be able', NHG *mögen* with *ö* from Central German dialect.

2 *wuohs,* NHG *wuchs.*

magedîn: diminutive form of *maget* 'maid' (NHG *Magd*). Whether the word had any diminutive sense proper at this stage seems doubtful, for it was already ancient and the suffix *-în* no longer productive. The use of *-în* as a diminutive suffix is found in all West Germanic languages. A weakened relic occurs in NHG *Küken* 'chick' (in origin a Low German form contrasting with High German *Küchlein,* still common in the spoken language of the south as *Küchel*), cf. Engl. *chicken* beside *chick*, and, of course, in Engl. *maiden* which is in origin identical with *magedîn*.

daʒ . . . niht schœners mohte sîn lit. 'which . . . nothing more comely could be'. It will be noticed that *niht* is here used in its original sense of 'nothing', see commentary on the phrase *enfürhte ich niht* in the previous passage.

ein schœne wîp 'a handsome woman'. The final -*e* in MHG *schœne* (< OHG *skôni*) is not an inflexion, but belongs to the absolute form as in the case of *küene* above. Final -*e* in such cases is nearly always lost in NHG, hence *schön*, but for an exception cf. *milde* in the previous passage. MHG *wîp* (> NHG *Weib*) had meanings today associated with *Frau*. MHG *vrouwe*, on the other hand, meant essentially 'lady'. Since the Middle Ages, the status of both these terms has declined. Except in certain phrases with a restricted use, such as *Weib und Kind*, or in consciously archaic or historical style, the word *Weib* today has a derogatory ring. To fill the vacuum at the top, *Dame* has come into the language from French.

dar umbe 'on her account', in modern German '*um derentwillen*', since NHG *darum* cannot refer to a person.

muosen, an often used form beside *muosten*, NHG *mußten* 'had to'.

degene, gen.pl. of *degen*, from OHG *degan*. Like *recke*, mentioned above, this term became very rare by the end of the Middle Ages, but was revived in the closing years of the 18th century. The chief reason for the virtual demise of these words was the disappearance from the social scene and from literature of the persons designated by the words. This is at the same time the reason why *recke* and *degen* are so difficult to translate into a modern idiom; the Germans, as we have seen, simply restored the old words. We may regard *recke* and *degen* as close synonyms. They denoted brave fighting men of high rank. Furthermore, the term *helt* was at least a near-synonym. For want of anything better, we translate the word as 'hero', but the paraphrase 'courageous armed man' would doubtless be nearer the mark. Unlike the other two terms, *helt* remained in common use and has in modern times become the conventional equivalent of 'hero' in all senses.

lîp 'life', NHG *Leib*, which however normally means 'body'. The older meaning survives in *Leibrente* 'life-pension'. The sense 'body' first develops in MHG; an example occurs in the next stanza.

3   *minneclîch*, restored in NHG as *minniglich*. The basic noun is *minne* 'love, esp. courtly love'. By the close of the Middle Ages the meaning of the word had become so degraded that it could not be used in literature. Later it must have disappeared from colloquial use too, or nearly so, for it could be revived at the same time as *degen* and *recke* as the technical term for '(medieval) courtly love'.

meide dat.sg. of *meit* 'maid,' governed by *gezam;* see above under *geseit*.

triuten 'to love,' a derivative of *trût* 'beloved,' NHG *traut* 'familiar'.

gezam pret. of *gezemen* (+ dat.) 'suit, be appropriate'.

muotten for *muoteten*, pret. of *muoten* (+ gen.) 'yearn for'. The verb is a derivative of *muot* 'thought, mind, etc.', NHG *Mut*.

niemen 'nobody', a weakened form beside *nieman*, see first passage.

gram 'ill-disposed', surviving in NHG in the phrase *jemandem gram sein* 'to bear someone a grudge'. The noun (*der*) *Gram* 'grudge' arose in MHG; it is based on the adjective.

âne mâ3en lit. 'without measure' (*mâ3e* f.), a common cliché.

ir edel lîp lit. 'her high-born body', but the reference is not to her figure only, but to her person in its entirety. MHG *lîp* is regularly used periphrastically in this way, cf. a similar development of Engl. *body* in *anybody, nobody, somebody*, 'Gin a body meet a body ...' For the original meaning of *lîp* i.e. 'life', see above.

juncvrouwe: the term denoted a maiden; it was more widely used than NHG *Jungfrau*.

BIBLIOGRAPHY

There are several publications available for the elementary study of Middle High German, one of which particularly recommends itself to English-speaking beginners. This is M. F. Richey, *Middle High German*, Edinburgh, 1952. It contains, in Part I, a few short texts carefully annotated, and in Parts II and III, a survey of the phonology and accidence followed by more short texts to which a select glossary is appended. This handy little introduction assumes no previous philological training and is ideal for self-instruction. Another volume designed for self-instruction is J. Zupitza, *Einführung in das Studium des Mittelhochdeutschen*, a book which has appeared in many editions, the latest being by F. Tschirch, Jena, 1953.

Well-known books of reference are H. Paul, *Mittelhochdeutsche Grammatik*, and M. Lexer, *Mittelhochdeutsches Taschenwörterbuch*. Both works frequently appear in reprints or new editions.

6

MIDDLE LOW GERMAN

Middle Low German follows Old Low German (essentially Old Saxon) in the north of Germany just as Middle High German follows Old High German in the centre and south. It would be convenient if the term MLG could cover the same period as MHG, i.e. from 1100 to 1350. But the problems of periodisation in the north are different from those in the High German area. To begin with, there is a long gap between the texts of the OLG period (mainly 9th century) and those of the MLG period, the earliest of which date from the 13th century. To be sure, these MLG texts show the weakening of endings and the spread of i-umlaut, the two most characteristic features of the Middle Period, already noted in connection with MHG. But as we see from the OLG documents, the weakening of endings developed more rapidly in the north which would presumably reach the middle stage before the centre and south. Then, at the other end of the period, it is usual to apply the term MLG to the language of the north for as long as it was used as an official written medium, i.e. until it was supplanted in this respect by High German. High German had been gaining ground at certain points on the southern fringe for some time. For instance, official documents in Merseburg ceased to appear in Low German about the middle of the 14th century. After that, High German was used. In Halle the last official document in Low German is dated 1417. But the main change-over took place in the 16th century. Berlin abandoned Low German in 1504. Magdeburg began to use High German about the middle of the century; the last official ordinance to be issued there in Low German is dated 1570. Hamburg retained Low German, at least for local administration, until the very end of the century. The demise of MLG as an official language was a direct reflexion of the general supremacy of the High German area at this time. Literary MLG had been a product of Hanseatic enterprise and prestige. When the Hansa declined, there were no other local forces strong enough to continue the economic and political independence of the north or to maintain a degree of cultural autonomy.

We note, *en passant*, that MLG exerted an enormous influence upon the Scandinavian languages. The Low German loans, particularly in Danish and Swedish, are legion. In fact, Low German influence on Scandinavian may be compared to the influence of Norman French upon English. Low German was the commercial language of the whole Baltic area during the Middle Ages and North Germans played a most significant part in the rising Scandinavian towns. The merchants were often Germans and so were the craftsmen; their guilds were organised on German lines. The City Law of Stockholm stipulated that not more than half of its aldermen could be Germans.

The surviving texts in MLG are very extensive, but consist predominantly of prose documents of an administrative and legal character. There are many translations or adaptations from High German and from Dutch. Poetry is poorly represented. A fair degree of standardisation in the written form was attained by the 15th century, the classical period of MLG.

SOUNDS AND ORTHOGRAPHY OF MIDDLE LOW GERMAN

MLG continued the six short and the five long vowels of OLG, though not all were preserved in all positions. As in MHG, the spread of i-umlaut to all back vowels created new, modified vowels. In MLG these were short *ö* and *ü*, long *ô* and *û*. Umlaut of *a* and *â* is written *e* and *ê*, any original difference between these and the corresponding inherited vowels not being apparent from the script. The OLG diphthong *ei* remains (written *ei*, *ey*), *eu* and *iu* fall together as the monophthong *û*, *io* becomes *ê*, *au* appears as *ou* and may be modified to *öu*.

Two general features of the phonology of the MLG vowels may now be mentioned. Firstly, there was a marked tendency to reduce originally long vowels before two consonants. On the other hand, originally short vowels in stressed open syllables were lengthened. In the case of original short *i* and *u*, lengthening was accompanied by qualitative changes: OLG *stiki* prick, stab (noun), *mugan* be able, MLG *steke, mogen*. Here the stressed *e* and *o* are long. A diacritic mark is not really necessary, since their length is apparent from their position in a stressed open syllable, though it may be marked thus: *stēke, mōgen*. These vowels had an open quality and were therefore distinct from old *ê* and *ô*, which were closed vowels continuing unchanged from OLG times.

It will be noticed that the two features, shortening and lengthening, are complementary. The language was building up a phonological system in which a stressed vowel was characteristically short in a closed syllable, but long in an open one. Purely phonetic reasons are ultimately responsible for this development. The same strong dynamic stress which, falling on the root syllable, led to the weakening of unstressed syllables, led also to the lengthening of the stressed vowel where possible, i.e. in open syllables. Thus OLG *stiki*, i.e. *sti-ki*—syllables begin with consonants—becomes MLG *steke* with long root vowel. But in closed syllables, that is to say syllables which are closed by a consonant, lengthening did not take place, e.g. OLG *bindan* bind, i.e. *bin-dan*, MLG *binden*. This development was not confined to Low German, but is common to the whole of German in the widest sense, including the Low Countries. Only a few particularly conservative Swiss dialects have not been involved in this movement. The changes, however, did not take place everywhere at the same time. In High German, lengthening does not become noticeable until after the Classical MHG period (see p. 90), whereas in the Low Countries the phenomenon is at least as old as in the North of Germany. Quite possibly it is even older as Middle Dutch shows no trace of the distinction between *ē/ō* and *ê/ô* found in MLG. In MDu. only the closed varieties occur, whatever their origin.

The consonant system of MLG continues that of OLG with but little change. The spirant *th* (*đ*) becomes *d*, *sk* changes to *sch* as in MHG, but the change was not general; *sk* has persisted in some areas down to the present day. The final voiceless velar spirant is written *ch*. Miscellaneous other changes will be apparent from the examples; they are all paralleled in MHG.

Outline of Middle Low German Accidence

NOUNS

a-stems, masc. and neut.

Sg.nom.acc. *dach* m. day, gen. *dages*, dat. *dage;* pl.nom.acc. gen. *dage*, dat. *dagen*. Similarly *word* n. word, except that pl. nom.acc. are uninflected, and *kalf* n. calf, but with pl.nom.acc. gen. *kelver*, dat. *kelvern* beside *kalver*, *kalvern*, where the umlauted vowel has been replaced by analogy with the singular.

ô-stems, fem.

Sg. *sêle* soul, gen.dat. also *sêlen*; pl.nom.acc. *sêle(n)*, gen.dat. *sêlen*. The alternative forms are due to the influence of the weak declension (*tunge*, below).—OLG *geƀa* does not survive in MLG.

i-stems, masc. and fem.

Sg.nom.acc. *gast* m. guest, gen. *gastes*, dat. *gaste;* pl.nom.acc. gen. *geste*, dat. *gesten*

Sg. *vart* f. journey; pl.nom.acc.gen. *verde*, dat. *verden*

Consonantal declension, all genders.

Sg.nom. *bode* m. messenger, obl. and pl. *boden*

Sg.nom. *tunge* f. tongue, obl. *tungen* (acc. also commonly *tunge*); pl. *tungen*

Sg.nom.acc. *herte* n. heart, gen.dat. and pl. *herten*

ADJECTIVES

The weak declension :

Sg.masc.fem.nom. *starke* strong, obl. and pl. *starken*
Sg.neut.nom.acc. *starke*, obl. and pl. *starken*

The strong declension:

	masc.	fem.	neut.		all genders
Sg. nom.	*stark*	*stark*	*stark*	Pl.	*starke*
acc.	*−en*	*−e*	,,		,,
gen.	*−es*	*−er*	*−es*		*−er*
dat.	*−em*	*−er*	*−em*		*−en*

The adverb is usually formed by adding *−e* to the uninflected adjective: *starke* strongly.

The comparative and superlative of adjectives and adverbs are formed by adding *-er* and *-est* to the positive, with or without umlaut, as in other German. Irregular comparison continues, but some of the traditional words have been lost: *gôt* good, *beter, best; övel* bad (*wers, werst*); *vele* big, *mêr, mêst; lüttel* little, *minner, minst*. Here *vele* has replaced *mekel* (< OLG *mikil*), which is occasionally attested, e.g. in (*to der*) *Mecklenburg* lit. '(at the) Big Town'. The forms *wers, werst* are only used adverbially.

NUMERALS

Commonly occurring forms are: 1 *ên* (inflecting like an adj., strong and weak), 2 nom.acc.m. *twêne,* f. *twô,* n. *twey,* gen. *twîger,* dat. *twên,* 3 nom.acc.m.f. *drê,* n. *drû,* gen. *drîger,* dat. *drin,* 4 *vêr,* 5 *vîf,* 6 *ses,* 7 *seven,* 8 *achte,* 9 *negen,* 10 *tein,* 11 *elven,* 12 *twelf,* 13 *drüttein,* 14 *vertein,* 15 *veftein,* 16 *sestein,* 17 *seventein,* 18 *achtein,* 19 *negentein,* 20 *twintich,* 21 *ên und twintich,* 30 *drüttich,* 40 *vertich,* 50 *viftich,* 60 (*t*)*sestich,* 70 (*t*)*seventich,* 80 (*t*)*achtentich, achtich,* 90 (*t*)*negentich,* 100 *hundert,* 1000 *dûsent*(*ich*).

The forms of the decades with initial *t-*, a relic of OLG *ant-*, occur only in the areas adjoining the Netherlands. In *tsestich,* the initial *t-* is secondary after the analogy of *tseventich* etc.

PERSONAL PRONOUNS

Typical forms are:

Sg.					
nom.	*ik* I	*dû* you	*hê* he	*sie* she	*it* it
acc.	*mî*	*dî*	*en*	,,	,,
gen.	*mîn*	*dîn*	*is*	*er*	*is*
dat.	*mî*	*dî*	*em*	,,	*em*
Pl.					
nom.	*wî* we	*gî* you		*sie* they	
acc.	*ûs*	*jû*		,,	
gen.	*ûser*	*jûwer*		*er*	
dat.	*ûs*	*jû*		*em*	

There is no trace of the dual in MLG texts, but it survived at least locally throughout the period, as is made certain by its occurrence in the modern dialects of the Hamm-Dortmund-Iserlohn region.

MLG acquired a reflexive pronoun: acc.dat. *sik*, gen. *sîn*. These are no more than an adaptation of MHG *sich*, *sîn*.

The possessive adjectives are: sg. *mîn* my, *dîn* your, *sîn* his, its, *er* her; pl. *ûse* our, *jûwe* your, *er* their.

ARTICLES

Typical forms of the definite article are:

	masc.	fem.	neut.	all genders
Sg. nom.	*dê*	*dû*	*dat*	Pl. *dê*
acc.	*den*	*die*	„	„
gen.	*des*	*der*	*des*	*der*
dat.	*dem*	„	*dem*	*den*

The indefinite article has the same form as the numeral *ên* one.

VERBS

As in MHG, the inflexions of the MLG verb show many formal simplifications by comparison with the old period, particularly in the case of the weak verb, of which there is now only one class. At this stage, both strong and weak verbs have most of the endings in common.

STRONG VERBS

The conjugation of strong verbs is as follows:

Infin. *schrîven* write

INDICATIVE

Pres.sg.1	*schrîve*	Pret.sg.1	*schrêf*	Imper.sg.	*schrîf*
2	*schrifst*	2	*schrevest*	pl.	*schrîvet*
3	*schrift*	3	*schrêf*		
pl.	*schrîvet, schrîven*	pl.	*schreven*		

SUBJUNCTIVE

Pres.sg.1, 3	*schrîve*	Pret.sg.1, 3	*schreve*
2	*schrîvest*	2	*schrevest*
pl.	*schrîven*	pl.	*schreven*

Pres. part. *schrîvende*   Past part. *geschreven*

The indic.pres.pl. ending *-et* occurs to the west, *-en* to the east of the Elbe. In many areas *ge-* of the past part. is either reduced to *e-* or lost altogether.

Principal parts (infin., 3rd pres.sg., 1st pret.sg., pret.pl., past part.) of the other ablaut classes: 2 *vorlêsen* lose, *vorlüst, vorlôs, vorloren, vorloren;* 3 *drinken* drink, *drinkt, dranc, drunken, gedrunken;* 4 *nemen* take, *nimt, nam, nêmen, genomen;* 5 *lesen* read, *list, las, lêsen, gelesen;* 6 *graven* dig, *greft, grôf, grôven, gegraven.* The forms *nêmen, lêsen* have widely replaced the regular *nåmen, låsen;* the new root vowel *ê* has been taken over from the pret. subj.

WEAK VERBS

The conjugation is as follows:

Infin. *maken* make

INDICATIVE

Pres.sg.1	*make*	Pret.sg.1	*makede*	Imper.sg.	*make*
2	*makest*	2	*makedest*	pl.	*maket*
3	*maket*	3	*makede*		
pl.	*maket, maken*	pl.	*makeden*		

SUBJUNCTIVE

Pres.sg.1, 3 *make*, 2 *makest;* pl. *maken.* Preterite (as Indicative)
Pres. part. *makende*   Past part. *gemaket*

The auxiliaries 'TO BE' and 'TO HAVE'. Typical forms are:
Infin. *wesen* or *sîn, hebben*

INDICATIVE

Pres.sg.1	*bin, hebbe*	Pret.sg.1	*was, hadde*
2	*bist, he(f)st*	2	*wêre, haddest*
3	*is, he(f)t*	3	*was, hadde*
pl.	*sîn, hebbet, sint, hebben*	pl.	*wêren, hadden (wêren* for older *wåren* with vowel from subj.)

Imper.sg. *wes* or *sî,* — ; pl. *weset* or *sît, hebbet*

SUBJUNCTIVE

Pres.sg.1, 3 *sî, hebbe,* 2 *sîst, hebbest;* pl. *sîn, hebben*
Pret.sg.1, 3 *wêre, hedde* etc.

Pres. part. *wesende* or *sînde, hebbende* Past part. *gewesen* or *gewest, gehat*

Specimen of Middle Low German

From the *Weltchronik* of Hermann Korner (†1438). Normalised.

Dô it quam vor middernacht, dô sach dê jungelinc, dat sik des vogedes graf up dede unde dê dôde lîcham richtede sik up unde nam dat laken, dar hê inne gewunden was, unde want dat to hôpe unde leide dat in ênen horne des graves. Dê wîle dê dôde aldus dorch dê stat lêp, dô stêch dê jungelinc den torne dale unde ginc up den kerkhof bi dat graf unde stêch dar in unde nam dat laken unde drôch dat mit sik up den torn unde slôt vaste tô unde wolde sên, wô sik dê dôde teren wolde, wan hê des lakens missede. Dô dat spôk dê stat ummelôpen hadde unde sîn tît quam der rouwe, dô quam it weder up den kerkhof unde ginc to deme grave. Alsô it dô des dôkes nicht envant, dô ginc it rûkende bi der erden alsô en hunt unde sochte dat laken. To deme lesten lêp dê dôde dê mûren des tornes bûten up alsô en katte.

'As midnight approached, the lad saw the bailiff's grave open and the dead body got up and took the shroud it was wrapped in and folded it up and laid it in a corner of the grave. While the dead man was thus walking through the town, the lad climbed down the tower and went up the churchyard to the grave and climbed in and took the shroud and carried it with him up the tower and locked (the door) firmly and wanted to see how the dead man would behave when he missed the shroud. When the ghost had walked round the town and its time came for rest, it came back to the churchyard and went to the grave. When it did not find its shroud, it went sniffing along the ground like a dog and searched for the shroud. Finally the dead man climbed up the walls of the tower on the outside like a cat.'

dô ... dô lit. 'then ... then', i.e. 'when', cf. MHG *dô*, a variety of *dâ*, older *dâr*.

sach infin. *sên* 'sehen', cf. Du. *zag* (infin. *zien*).

jungelinc 'Jüngling', cf. Du. *jongeling*.

voget, gen. *vogedes* 'Vogt', cf. Du. *voogd*.

up dede infin. *up dôn* 'auftun', cf. Du. *opdoen*.

licham m., older *lichame*—as in Middle Dutch (ModDu. *lichaam*)—OLG *likhamo* 'body', lit. 'body (*lik*) covering (*hamo*)'. The word occurs in High German too: OHG *lihhamo*, MHG *lichame*. The form seen in NHG *Leichnam* with the specialised sense 'corpse' is closely related to the foregoing (see p. 35).

laken n. lit. 'sheet', OLG *lakan*, also OHG *lahhan*, MHG *lachen;* the High German form survives sporadically in NHG dialect *Leilach(en)* 'bed-sheet', properly *Leinlachen* lit. 'linen sheet'. Through the North German (Westphalian) linen trade the term *Laken* found its way into Early NHG with the specialised sense 'bed-sheet'. Today it competes with *Bettuch* and *Leintuch*.

dar . . . inne 'wherein'. Here *dar* is a relative particle, as also in older High German; it is ultimately identical with *dô*, see above.

to hôpe 'zuhauf'; MLG *hôp* 'heap', MHG *houf(e)* beside the ablaut variant *hûfe* which fell together giving NHG *Haufen*.

leide occurring beside *legede*, infin. *leggen* 'legen'. MHG showed an analogous development: *leite* beside *legete*, but the modern standard has, of course, only the descendent of the latter form *legte*. In Modern Dutch, however, both forms are acceptable: *leide* (also *lei*) or *legde*, infin. *leggen*.

horne m. 'corner' shows a semantic development of the basic meaning 'horn' via such senses as 'prominent part, (protruding) corner', cf. also Engl. *corner* ultimately from Latin *cornu* 'horn'.

aldus 'thus', lit. *al* ' all' + *dus* ' thus'. The words *aldus* and the simplex *dus* are unknown in High German, but are usual in Dutch.

lêp infin. *lôpen* 'laufen', cf. Du. *lopen*.

stêch infin. *stîgen* 'steigen', cf. Du. *stijgen*.

torn(e) m. 'Turm', cf. Du. *toren*. These words go back to Old French *torn from Latin *turrem* (acc.) 'tower'; the NHG form is secondary.

dale 'down', formally dat. of *dal* 'valley', beside more usual *dal* (adverbial acc.). Cf. MHG *ze tal* 'down', lit. 'to valley', NHG *zu Tal*.

ginc infin. *gân* 'gehen', cf. Du. *gaan*.

drôch infin. *dragen* 'tragen', cf. Du. *dragen*.

slôt 'schloß' corresponds exactly to MHG *slôz* (> NHG *schloß*), but the MLG infin. is *slûten*, as in Middle Dutch (>ModDu. *sluiten*), whereas MHG has *sliezen* (> NHG *schließen*).

wô 'wie' < OLG *hwô*; an ablaut variant is OHG *hwio*, MHG, NHG *wie* (see p. 202).

sik teren, with a variant *tieren*, 'to behave'. Possibly the same as NHG *sich zieren* 'adorn oneself'.

missen governs the genitive. This verb is attested in MHG, but in NHG *vermissen* is more usual.

spôk n. 'Spuk m.', cf. Du. *spook* n. This word is typically Low German (incl. Dutch) contrasting with High Ger. *Gespenst.* NHG *Spuk* does not appear before 1691, clearly taken up from Low German dialect.

ummelôpen infin. *do.*, see *lôpen* above; *umme* < OLG *umbi.*

quam 'kam', infin. *komen*, cf. Du. *kwam* (infin. *komen*).

rouwe 'Ruhe' presupposes OLG *rôwa, parallel to OHG *ruowa*, MHG *ruowe*, NHG *Ruhe* (where *h* is purely orthographical).

alsô, cf. MHG *do*. (> NHG *als*); the word is also Dutch (ModDu. *alzo*). Here it strengthens *dô . . .dô.*

. . .des dôkes nicht envant '. . . das Tuch nicht fand'. The genitive construction with the negative is paralleled in MHG *. . . des tuoches niht envant.* For the negative *nicht en-*, see p. 71.

rûken 'riechen'; for the different stem vowel in Low and High German, cf. *slûten* above (under *slôt*).

bûten 'außen', cf. Du. *buiten* (see p. 201).

BIBLIOGRAPHY

Since but little creative literature was originally written in MLG, it is much less studied than MHG and the means to its study are consequently more restricted. There is no handy dictionary comparable to Lexer's *Mittelhochdeutsches Taschenwörterbuch.* The student must consult A. Lübben and C. Walther, *Mittelniederdeutsches Handwörterbuch*, 1888, now being replaced by a second edition prepared by A. Lasch and C. Borchling, Neumünster, 1956–.

The standard grammar is by A. Lasch, *Mittelniederdeutsche Grammatik*[2], 1974. A wide selection of texts, both prose and verse, but without a glossary, is given in W. Stammler, *Mittelniederdeutsches Lesebuch*, Hamburg, 1921.

THE MODERN PERIOD

7

FROM MEDIEVAL TO MODERN GERMAN

PERIODISATION

There was no problem in dating the end of the Old High German period and the beginning of Middle High German. This is because there are very few texts from the second half of the 11th century. When, in the next century, texts became plentiful, we see that the weakening of unstressed full vowels, sporadically observed in Late OHG, has become the general rule and has led to various grammatical changes. This language we properly call MHG.

But it is far less easy to find a convenient dividing line between Middle High German and New High German. There is no lack of texts and they amply illustrate the fundamental rule that change in living language is continuous and mostly gradual, though there are periods at which the rate of change appears to be quicker than at others. Changes arise locally. They may spread and involve the whole language, but may take centuries to do so.

A striking phonetic difference between medieval and modern German is the lengthening of originally short vowels in open syllables (see below). The change was already taking place in the north as early as the 12th century, i.e. at the beginning of the MHG period, and by about the middle of the 14th century it had affected practically all High German. This is why, following a number of authorities, we have regarded 1350 as marking the end of the MHG period (p. 57). Others would postpone the beginning of NHG until 1500, so that to all intents and purposes NHG begins with Luther. That a new epoch in the history of German opened with the Reformation is indisputable (see Chap. 8), but it is concerned primarily with the creation of a standard language and not with the

organic evolution of the sounds and forms of German. These
are made the criteria in fixing the change from OHG to MHG;
we are consistent if we apply the same principles in dating the
transition from MHG to NHG.

New High German may be said to have begun, therefore,
over 600 years ago. Inevitably, great changes occur during
six centuries and language historians have felt the need to
subdivide so long a period. The language of the first half, i.e.
from 1350 to 1650, is qualified as Early New High German.
The closing date 1650 is also taken by those who prefer to date
Early NHG from 1500.

The most striking feature of the MHG period was the rise of
the classical *Dichtersprache* (pp. 58 f.). But this achievement was
lost with the disintegration of courtly society, and writing in
German became regional once more. In the early Middle Ages
the regional centres had been the monastic scriptoria. Now, in
accordance with the changed mode of life, the towns were the
influential centres.

The Early NHG period witnessed the gradual development
of the modern literary idiom, a development which received a
significant impetus and took on a new aspect with the discovery
of printing. Then came the Reformation and Luther's Bible
with its unprecedented circulation. Towards the end of the
period the activity of the Language Societies and the gram-
marians brings us within sight of a uniform written language in
the modern sense. Further details of these developments are
to be found in Chapter 8.

In the following section on sounds and inflexions we take as
contrasting poles the classical MHG and the modern standard
forms (NHG). Naturally intermediary stages are found in many
cases, as will be indicated in the comments.

The Main Phonetic Differences between
MHG and NHG

VOWELS

VOWEL LENGTHENING

An important feature distinguishing modern German from
classical MHG is the lengthening of short stressed vowels in

open syllables. The change began in the north (see pp. 79 f.), spreading over the whole High German area—except for part of Switzerland—during the 13th and 14th centuries.

According to the rules of German prosody, a consonant begins a syllable. MHG *tages* 'day's' is therefore divided *ta-ges*. A syllable ending in a vowel is said to be 'open', a syllable ending in a consonant 'closed'. Following the law of lengthening, MHG *tages* (where *a* is pronounced short) becomes NHG *Tages* (where *a* is pronounced long)—the use of capitals for nouns in modern German is purely an orthographic convention. Similarly MHG *bote* 'messenger' (*o* short), NHG *Bote* (*o* long), MHG *gewesen* 'been' [gəwesən], NHG *do.* [gəve:zən]. Further examples: MHG *nemen* 'take', NHG *nehmen* (where *h* is introduced—as often—in the modern spelling as a sign of vowel length, see below on the development of MHG *h* in NHG), MHG *siben* 'seven', NHG *sieben* (where *ie* is a modern spelling convention to represent long *i*, see below on the development of MHG *ie* in NHG), MHG *treget* 'carries' (from *tragen*), NHG *trägt*. Today *ä* is generally used instead of *e* in order to show the relationship between umlauted and unumlauted forms. Thus *ä* does not necessarily continue MHG *ä* since the historical distinction between MHG *ä* and *e* has been lost in the modern standard language. In NHG the spellings *ä* and *e* therefore denote the same sound, whether short or long. Some, however, pronounce long *ä* (as here in *trägt*) as open [ɛ:] to distinguish it from long *e* (as in *nehmen*) i.e. the close [e:]; this pronunciation is most commonly heard when people read aloud. But a distinction in pronunciation between *ä* and *e* today is purely arbitrary and due entirely to the spelling.

By contrast with these examples of lengthening in open syllables, we have the regular retention of the short vowels in closed syllables. MHG *helfen* is divided *hel-fen*, hence NHG *do.* also with short vowel. Similarly the vowels of MHG *ist* 'is', *von* 'of, from' are unchanged in the modern language.

There are, however, a considerable number of exceptions to the main rule of lengthening. They may be considered under two main headings:

1. Analogical lengthening. If we study the paradigm of MHG *tac* (p. 63), we see that regular lengthening of *a* would take place in NHG in all the inflected forms. Only in the uninflected nom.acc. *tac*, a word consisting of one closed syllable, would *a* remain short. In practice, however, this short vowel is lengthened after the analogy of the other declensional cases, hence NHG *Tag* [ta:k] with long *a*. We must now mention that in the Low German dialects analogical lengthening is not the rule and this feature has influenced the pronunciation of High German in this area, hence *Tag* is normally [taχ] in the north to this day, cf. Low Ger. *dach* 'day'.

As a further example we may take MHG *wec* 'way', gen. *weges* which become NHG *Weg*, *Weges* where *e* is long in both cases. On the other hand, the modern adverb *weg* 'away', though formally identical with MHG *wec* and therefore with NHG *Weg* also, regularly keeps the short vowel. This is because the adverb was no longer consciously associated with the noun and was accordingly not influenced by the analogical lengthening.

There are many instances of analogical lengthening in the past tense of strong verbs: MHG *las* 'read', *nam* 'took', but NHG *las*, *nahm* following the plural forms *lasen*, *laset*, *nahmen*, *nahmet* < MHG *lâsen*, *lâset*, *nâmen*, *nâmet*—it will be noticed again that the modern spelling is inconsistent: in the one verb *h* is used as length-indicator, in the other it is omitted.

2. Lengthening did not take place before *m* and especially before *t* in a number of words: MHG *komen* 'come', *gate* 'companion, husband', NHG *kommen*, *Gatte*. Lengthening never occurs before *m* and *t* if these are followed by -*el* or -*er*: MHG *himel* 'heaven', *hamer* 'hammer', *satel* 'saddle', *bleter* 'leaves', NHG *Himmel*, *Hammer*, *Sattel*, *Blätter*, and occasionally before other consonants: MHG *doner* 'thunder', NHG *Donner*.

In these cases gemination of the consonant had already occurred in Late MHG before the law of lengthening could take effect. In other words, early and classical MHG *komen*, *gate* etc. changed in later MHG to *kommen*, *gatte* etc., i.e. with consonants lengthened according to Old German practice. Such words were now prosodically divided *kom-men*, *gat-te* and the

short stressed vowels were consequently not involved in
the lengthening. At a still later stage, at the beginning of the
modern period, *mm, tt* etc. were reduced in pronunciation to
give single consonants [m, t], but the gemination was retained
in the spelling where it serves to indicate that the preceding
vowel is short.

VOWEL SHORTENING

Vowel shortening in stressed syllables is much less common than
lengthening. It chiefly affects originally long vowels when these
occur before two or more consonants, more rarely before a
single consonant: MHG *dâhte* 'thought', *hôrchen* 'hearken',
hôchzît 'festival, wedding', *nâchgebûre* 'neighbour', *jâmer* 'misery',
slôȝ 'lock', NHG *dachte, horchen, Hochzeit, Nachbar, Jammer,
Schloß*. The forms with shortened vowel first appear in the
north and occur in the Central German area during the MHG
period itself.

MONOPHTHONGISATION

The MHG diphthongs *ie, uo, üe* became the long monophthongs *ie, u, ü:* MHG *nie* 'never', *guot* 'good', *küene* 'bold',
NHG *nie, gut, kühn*. It will be noticed that MHG *ie* is retained
in the modern spelling, though the sound is now that of the
simple vowel [i:]. This monophthongisation took place in
Central German about the beginning of the MHG period,
but it did not spread to the south; the dialects there have
largely preserved diphthongal sounds down to the present day.
On the other hand, the Central German monophthongs
became usual in the colonial territories east of the Elbe; from
here they entered into the formation of the Standard German
vowel system.

DIPHTHONGISATION

The MHG long vowels *î, û, iu* (pronounced [y:]) have become
diphthongs: NHG *ei, au, eu*. Hence MHG *mîn* 'my', *hûs* 'house',
liute 'people', NHG *mein, Haus, Leute*. The spelling *äu* instead of
eu is used to show the affinity of obviously related forms: MHG
hiuser 'houses', NHG *Häuser* because of *Haus*, cf. MHG *treget*,
but NHG *trägt* above. Unlike other features so far mentioned

the present change began in eastern Bavaria. It has been traced back to the 12th century. This 'Bavarian diphthongisation' spread northwards into Central German.

OTHER VOWEL CHANGES

MHG *ou, öu* change to NHG *au, eu*, most commonly written *äu* (cf. *ä* for *e* above): MHG *vröuwen* 'be pleased', NHG *freuen;* MHG *boum* 'tree', pl. *böume*, NHG *Baum, Bäume.*

MHG *ei* remains in the spelling: MHG *ei* 'egg', NHG *Ei* now pronounced [a:e, a:i].

MHG *u, ü* correspond to NHG *o, ö* in a number of words, especially before a nasal: MHG *sun* 'son', pl. *süne*, NHG *Sohn, Söhne.*

In many cases unstressed *e* of a MHG form has been lost: MHG *küene* 'bold', NHG *kühn.* On the other hand, unstressed *e* lost in MHG has sometimes been analogically restored in the modern standard language: OHG *ih faru*, Late OHG *ih fare* 'I go', MHG *ich var*, NHG *ich fahre.* All the same this final *e* is not usually heard in ordinary, everyday speech.

CONSONANTS

The consonant changes between MHG and NHG are less striking than the vowel changes. We give below the more signnificant.

Some differences between MHG and NHG are purely orthographical, e.g. MHG *tac* 'day', gen. *tages*, but NHG *Tag, Tages* where *g* has been generalised though the pronunciation is unaffected [ta:k, ta:ges].

At the beginning of the modern period the long (double) consonants of MHG were reduced to short (single) consonants; they continued, however, to be written double, see above (2): MHG *alle* [al:ə] 'all', pl., NHG *do.* [alə]; similarly *ch* < OHG *hh*: MHG *machen* [maχ:ən], NHG *do.* [maχən].

MHG *mb* (when final: *mp*) was assimilated to *mm;* likewise MHG *ng* [ŋg] was assimilated to [ŋ:]. These double consonants were then simplified to [m, ŋ] in the general reduction of long consonants: MHG *lamp* 'lamb', gen. *lambes*, NHG *Lamm,*

Lammes, MHG *lanc* 'long', pl. *lange* [laŋgə], NHG *lang, lange* [laŋ, laŋə]—but in some areas the pronunciation [laŋk] survives as a relic of older conditions.

Intervocalic *h* ceased to be pronounced at the end of the MHG period, though it continued to be written: MHG *sehen* [sehən] 'see', NHG *do.* [ze:ən]; loss of *h* was sometimes followed by contraction: MHG *stahel* 'steel', NHG *Stahl*. From such examples arose the practice of using *h* as an indicator of vowel length, thus MHG *stuol*, NHG *Stuhl*.

The development of MHG *s* and *ʒ* has already been discussed (pp. 60 f.); the modern standard pronunciation of *s* as [z], e.g. in *so* [zo:], is a feature which came into being in the north and subsequently moved southwards into the High German area, but many of the southern dialects still use [s]. MHG *v* became *f* during the 13th century (see p. 61); the MHG spelling is sometimes retained: MHG *vogel* 'bird', NHG *Vogel*. MHG *w* became [v] in the modern language and *w* is still written: MHG *wîn* [wi:n], NHG *Wein* [va:en].

MHG *w* is lost in NHG after *u*: MHG *bûwen* 'till, build', *vrouwe* 'lady', *vröuwen* 'be pleased', NHG *bauen, Frau, freuen*.

The MHG combinations *lw, rw* appear as NHG *lb, rb*: MHG *swalwe* 'swallow', *varwe* 'colour', NHG *Schwalbe, Farbe*.

MHG final *m* becomes *n*: MHG *buosem* 'bosom', NHG *Busen*, but *Busem* is still common in the Early NHG period.

A singular development, the beginnings of which go back to Late MHG times, is the so-called excrescent *t*: MHG *anderhalp* 'other side', *wesen(t)lîch* 'real, essential', NHG *anderthalb* 'one and a half', *wesentlich;* compare also NHG *eben*, colloquially often *ebent*.

Accidence

At the beginning of modern times German accidence was more radically changed than at any other time in the history of the language. By and large, MHG continued the declension and conjugation patterns of OHG in spite of considerable phonetic attrition. But in the modern period developments went much further. Since the endings were no longer so distinct, sweeping analogical changes literally reshaped the accidence of the German language. The point was reached when the old system, which had been wearing out in MHG, finally broke down and let in a flood of changes. In the declensions analytical tendencies come strongly to the fore and the position of the genitive is much weakened, with correspondingly important syntactical changes. These changes, however, are not always apparent from the texts because of the inherent conservatism of literary language. But there is enough evidence to show that, in point of syntax, the average position of the modern dialects was reached by the 15th century.

NOUNS

We saw that the MHG declension system regularly continued the OHG system, but the weakening of the old full vowels in the terminations in MHG led to a simplification of inflexional types. For instance, in OHG the words *tag* and *gast* had different endings in the plural (pp. 16 f.), but the differences were lost in MHG (p. 63). In fact, by the MHG stage, the only difference between the declension of *tag* and *gast* was the contrast between the root vowels in the plural: *tage, geste*. In the consciousness of speakers of MHG the word *gast* formed its plural by means of vowel change, *tag* did not. It is clear that the umlauted plurals are more distinctive than the un-umlauted ones and so, naturally, umlaut came to be associated with the formation of the plural (see pp. 62 f.). As a consequence, many nouns which originally belonged to the *tag*-class were attracted into the *gast*-class, in other words they began to take umlaut analogically. This process started in the MHG period. For example, MHG *stap* 'rod' belonged originally to the *tag*-class, hence pl. *stabe*, but *stebe* occurs in MHG many times as well. MHG *boum* 'tree' normally makes its plural regularly, i.e. *boume*, but in later MHG *böume* begins to appear. This tendency to introduce umlaut analogically in the plural increased greatly in NHG times: Classical MHG *hof* 'court', *koch* 'cook', pl. *hove, koche*, NHG *Hof, Koch*, pl. *Höfe* (but *-hofen* the old dat.pl. in place names, e.g. *Waidhofen*), *Köche;* similarly in two-syllable words: MHG *vadem* 'thread', *vogel* 'bird', pl. *vademe, vogele*, NHG *Faden, Vogel*, pl. (with loss of unstressed final *e* in words of more than one syllable) *Fäden, Vögel*. We may fairly say that umlaut has quite reshaped the original pattern of declension. In OHG most masculine nouns in the language belonged to the *tag*-class, but today their number is greatly reduced. Since the types represented by *tag* (*a*-stem) and *gast* (*i*-stem) fell together in MHG in all cases where the vowel is not modifiable, e.g. *visch* (*a*-stem), *tisch* (*i*-stem), pl. *vische*, *tische*, the classes as such are partly confused, but we can say that only about a dozen masculine monosyllables go like *Tag* now, i.e. without umlaut in the plural, e.g. *Arm, Hund, Schuh*, pl. *Arme* etc.

In one sub-class of nouns in MHG the modification of the plural was associated with a very distinctive ending, namely *-er*. This sub-class was composed of neuters only, e.g. *kalp* 'calf', pl. *kelber* (p. 63). It was not a numerous class, but had been slowly gaining ground since OHG times. For instance, *tal* 'valley' now usually formed its plural *teler*, whence NHG *Tal*, *Täler*, whereas in OHG the ordinary plural was *tal*, like *wort* (p. 16). But the great expansion of this ending took place towards the end of the medieval period and at the beginning of modern times: Classical MHG *kint* 'child', *kleit* 'garment', *wort* 'word' form their plural without change, but NHG sg. *Kind, Kleid, Wort*, pl. *Kinder, Kleider, Wörter*. (This last word, however, seems to be losing ground to an alternative form *Worte*. Many speakers are unfamiliar with *Wörter*, except in *Wörterbuch* 'dictionary', while even educated people often confuse the two both in speaking and writing, so that the usual dictionary distinction between *Wörter* 'separate words' and *Worte* 'expressions' is not always typical in practice.) In NHG the *-er*-class has also attracted a number of common masculine nouns: MHG *geist* 'spirit', *lîp* 'life, body', *wurm* 'worm', pl. *geiste*, *lîbe*, *würme*, but NHG *Geist, Leib, Wurm*, pl. *Geister, Leiber, Würmer*.

Uninflected monosyllabic neuter plurals, though once the commonest neuter pattern, are obsolete in the modern language—apart from a few stereotype phrases like *zwei Glas Bier* 'two glasses of beer', *drei Pfund Butter* 'three pounds of butter', otherwise *Gläser, Pfunde*. Most monosyllabic neuters now take the distinctive ending *-er* with umlaut where possible, but a few add *-e* without umlaut following masculines of the type *Tag, Tage*, e.g. *Worte, Pfunde, Haare, Jahre*. Nowadays only neuters of more than one syllable retain the old uninflected plural: MHG sg.pl. *meʒʒer* 'knife', *waʒʒer* 'water', NHG sg.pl. *Messer, Wasser.*

The *vart*-class of feminine nouns continues in modern German, but as a less numerous category. The only words which have remained in this class are a number of those capable of umlaut: MHG *kraft* 'strength', *sû* 'sow', pl. *krefte, siuwe*, NHG *Kraft, Sau*, pl. *Kräfte, Säue.* Our paradigm example *vart* 'journey', pl. *verte* (p. 63) has undergone a two-fold development. MHG *vart* is now *Fahrt* which forms its plural *Fahrten*, but MHG *verte* survives in *Fährte* 'spoor'. In modern German this form was felt to be a singular and a new plural *Fährten* was created for it. Most of the nouns originally belonging to the *vart*-class now form their plural by adding *-en* (without umlaut) as *Fahrt, Fahrten*, see below. All those nouns incapable of umlaut now take *-en :* MHG *arebeit* 'work, trouble, *zît* 'time', pl. *arebeite, zîte*, NHG *Arbeit, Zeit*, pl. *Arbeiten, Zeiten.*

Turning now to the *gebe*-class (p. 63), we see that this class has now generalised *-en* throughout the plural. This was due to contamination with the consonant (weak) declension of the *zunge*-type. As a result the plural ending *-en* became particularly strong and this led to the assimilation of many nouns originally belonging to the *vart*-class, cf. the examples in the previous paragraph. The word *gebe* itself is obsolete in the standard language; it retreated in face of the advance of *gâbe*, a related formation of the same declension. Examples of *-en* plurals: MHG sg.pl. *gâbe* 'gift', *varwe* 'colour', *vrâge* 'question', NHG sg. *Gabe, Farbe, Frage*, pl. *Gaben* etc.

Whereas the *gebe*-declension altered its plural to agree with the *zunge*-declension, in the singular the opposite happened. In the standard language, *zunge* gave up its inflexional *-n* in the oblique cases of the singular. In practice, then, the two declensions fell together and the ancient difference between the vocalic and consonantal (between the strong and weak) declensions, which went back to early Germanic times at least, was finally obliterated.

The masculine consonant stems, on the other hand, have to a limited extent preserved the inherited declensional type. Thus the inflexions of MHG *bote* 'messenger' remain unchanged in present-day German. But many words have now left this class.

The inflexional *n* of the singular has been very commonly generalised and the words have passed into the strong class: MHG *boge* 'bow', gen. *bogen*, NHG *Bogen*, gen. *Bogens;* in a few words the plural is distinguished by analogical umlaut: MHG *garte* 'garden', pl. *garten*, NHG *Garten*, pl. *Gärten*. Occasionally a noun keeps the *-e* of the MHG nom.sg., e.g. *Name*, *Glaube*, though until recent times the forms *Namen*, *Glauben* were commonly used as well. The termination is lost in the formation of diminutives: MHG *hûfe* 'heap; troop', NHG *Haufe* 'do.', diminutives *Häufchen* 'little heap', *Häuflein* 'small troop', similarly *Gärtchen* 'little garden' etc. In some other cases forms without a termination occur beside forms with the usual *-en* desinence: MHG *schrecke* 'fright', NHG *Schreck* or *Schrecken;* both words are common, though the latter is the usual literary form. Sometimes differences of meaning are involved: NHG *Tropf* 'worthless, silly person, drip', *Tropfen* 'drop', both from MHG *tropfe* 'do., do.'

The few neuter consonant stems remain weak in the plural in NHG, but have variously modified the singular: MHG *herze* 'heart', NHG sg.nom.acc. *Herz*, gen. *Herzens*, dat. and pl. *Herzen;* MHG *ôre* 'ear', *ouge* 'eye', NHG sg. *Ohr*, *Auge*, pl. *Ohren*, *Augen*.

In addition to the main developments within the declensional system as outlined above, there are numerous examples of gender change between MHG and NHG. Sometimes different genders have been present in the different dialects for some time. Thus MHG *sanc* 'song' and *tranc* 'potion, drink' are neuter in southern texts, but masculine in Central German texts. In the modern language, the masculine gender has established itself as the indisputable standard. On the other hand, there are cases where the gender has actually changed as between MHG and NHG. Such genuine changes are usually associated with other changes. A good example is NHG *Wange* f. 'cheek' which in MHG was a neuter going like *herze*. When this small sub-group broke down, *wange* was attracted into the important feminine class represented by *Gabe* and *Zunge* (see above) and its gender was accordingly changed. MHG *locke* 'curls', the plural of *loc* m., came to be regarded first as a collective singular—cf. the use of *Haar* 'hair' in German or

English—then as a singular pure and simple, hence NHG sg. *Locke* 'curl'. At this stage the word took on the feminine gender by analogy with the many feminine endings in *-e* and the new plural *Locken* followed automatically. MHG *wolken* n. 'cloud(s)' —the same word as poetic Engl. *welkin*—came to be felt as a plural, from which a singular *wolke* was extracted. In some dialects the newly formed singular was used as a masculine, in others it was feminine and this latter gender has become the present standard: *die Wolke*, pl. *Wolken*. Changes of this sort can easily occur. In English we have made *pea* the singular of *peas*, though in reality this is itself a singular, in fact we still use it as such if we talk about *pease-pudding*.

ADJECTIVES

In general, the modern declensions continue the medieval pattern with the appropriate phonetic changes. Notice that the ending *-iu* of the nom.sg.fem. and neut.nom.acc.pl. is reduced to *-e* in NHG. The weak ending *-en* has, however, gained ground, penetrating into the strong declension where it has replaced the old masc.neut.gen.sg. *-es*. Today we may say only *guten Mutes* 'of good courage', but Goethe wrote in Götz von Berlichingen *gutes Mutes*. Traces of the use of the *-en* form first appear in the 15th century, but the old form is normal with Luther. Schottel in his *Haubtsprache* of 1663 recommends *-es*— though he unconsciously uses *-en* himself! The schoolmasters campaigned in vain against the weak form. By 1800, present usage was firmly established; the mature Goethe has *-en*.

The NHG use of strong and weak adjectives corresponds basically to MHG practice. But there have been a number of shifts which have given rise to the 'Mixed Declension' in modern German, that is to say a declension composed of both originally strong and weak endings. Thus one says today *mein alter Hut* (strong), but *meine alten Hüte* (weak)—MHG usually *mîne alte hüete*.

NUMERALS

In the evolution of the numerals into NHG we note that of the inflected forms for 'two' only the MHG neuter *zwei* survives. A descendent of the MHG masc. *zwêne* is still met with in biblical language: *ihr könnt nicht zween Herren dienen*. On the other hand the often heard *zwo* is not ancient; it is a creation of the telephone age. OHG masc. *drî* eventually absorbed the old fem. *drîo*, hence MHG *drî* m.f., which then pushed out the special neut. *driu*, so that NHG *drei* (from *drî* with regular diphthongisation) is the sole form in use today.

PRONOUNS

The medieval pronouns have survived in modern German, but there have been a number of changes. The MHG acc. *unsich* 'us' has been replaced by *uns*, originally a dative only, while the MHG dat. *iu* 'you' has been replaced by *euch* (< MHG *iuch*). The usual MHG dat. *in* 'them' appears in Alemannic texts as early as the 13th century with the ending *-en*, obviously after the analogy of the declension of nouns. This distinctive form tended to spread and from it we have the modern *ihnen*. A new development in the use of the reflexive *sich* is noteworthy. In MHG, *sich* was accusative only, a special reflexive pronoun was not used in the dative. But today *sich* has taken over the functions of the dative, too. Here the southern dialects have remained more conservative than the literary language. Corresponding to standard Ger. *Haben Sie Geld bei sich?* we may often hear Bavarian *Haben Sie Geld bei Ihnen?*

MHG neut.gen.sg. *es* has been lost as a syntactical case. Doubtless its demise was rapid from the moment when it fell together phonetically with the neut.nom.acc.sg. *ez*. It remains, however, in such phrases as *ich bin's zufrieden*, though the ordinary speaker is not aware of it; in his linguistic consciousness '*s* is an accusative. The genitive today is usually *dessen*, e.g. *ich bin mir dessen bewußt*. In medieval German a considerable number of verbs governed the genitive, but very few of them do so today. Examples are *bedürfen*, e.g. *sie bedarf keiner Hilfe*, and *walten*, especially in stereotype phrases like *er waltet seines Amtes*. The great majority of such verbs now take the accusative: MHG *vergiz mîn niht* 'don't forget me' survives in the flower name *Vergißmeinnicht*, but today one otherwise says *vergiß mich nicht*. Consequently, the genitive of the pronoun is not common today. By the analogy of *unser*, *euer* (< MHG *iuwer*), they all now take the *-er* ending: *meiner* etc.

The MHG Bavarian plural (originally dual) pronoun nom. *eȝ*, acc.dat. *enc*, survives in modern Bavarian *es*, *enk*, used instead of *ihr*, *euch*, e.g. *tummelt's enk* 'beeilt (ihr) euch'. These are purely dialect words, but are very widespread. Their use in Vienna is regarded as vulgar, but curiously enough even educated Viennese use the nom. *es* unconsciously every time they form the 2nd plural of the verb: *ihr habt* in the Viennese *Umgangssprache* becomes *ihr habt's*. Similarly the imperative *seid* is in Vienna *seid's*, cf. *tummelt's enk* above.

The possessive pronouns in NHG inflect like strong adjectives except for the uninflected masc.nom.sg. and neut.nom.acc.sg. *mein:* fem.nom.acc.sg. *meine*, etc.

A full history of the development of the pronouns of address in German would be a chapter to itself. We summarise the essentials.

In the Middle Ages, *ir* was used instead of *dû* by the upper classes amongst themselves and by the lower orders to their betters. In the early 17th century, *Er* 'he' and *Sie* 'she' appear as the most polite forms of address. This use of the 3rd singular (with the 3rd sg. of the verb naturally) is comparable to the use of such phrases as *Euer Gnade* 'Your Grace' (cf. Dutch usage, p. 195). Then towards the end of the same century, *Er* and *Sie* were faced with competition from the still more select *Sie* 'they', which may be compared to the hyper-polite title *Euer Gnaden* 'Your Graces' in reference to a single person. By the second half of the 18th century, the plural *Sie* had established itself, but had not yet replaced its competitors. Apparently one tried to distinguish degrees of formality. This is illustrated in 'Faust'. Mephisto and the Scholar address each other with *Ihr*. Wagner likewise uses *Ihr* when talking to Faust, but his master also uses *Er* and *du* in his replies. When speaking to Faust, Mephisto rings the changes on all three pronouns. When speaking to Marthe, he uses *Ihr* and *Sie* (sg.); Marthe replies only with *Ihr*. Today the situation is more stabilised: *du* with its plural *ihr* are the pronouns of familiarity, *Sie* the polite pronoun, single and plural. The only problem is to decide where politeness ends and familiarity begins. Children are, of course, addressed with *du*, but it is often a tricky matter to know whether a young girl is old enough to be addressed as *Sie*.

It should be noticed, by the way, that in the south *Sie* is commonly used only as the polite singular; the plural is then always *Ihr*. In other words, there is no polite pronoun in the plural.

We should like to observe, in conclusion, that the solitary English *you* seems socially far more desirable than the German system.

ARTICLES

When we consider the use of the articles in medieval and modern German a number of differences become apparent. Contrast, for example, the following MHG sentence with its NHG translation. The peasant's son praises his ox and says *nie rint sô genæme wart geweten under joch* (Meier Helmbrecht, 824/5) 'nie (zuvor) wurde *ein* so brauchbares Rind ins Joch gespannt'. On the other hand certain uses of the article in MHG are no longer permissible in standard NHG: *der hêrre mîn* 'mein Herr' or *wîz als ein snê* 'weiß wie Schnee'. But the older diction is occasionally preserved, for instance in folksong: *Es fiel ein Reif in der Frühlingsnacht.* Generally speaking, however, NHG makes freer use of the articles than MHG.

It remains to be said that in southern German, both in pure dialect and in forms of speech which otherwise closely follow the standard, the use of the articles is well-nigh universal. In other words, an article is normally found before every noun. The sentence 'one must have patience with children' runs in Standard German: *mit Kindern muß man Geduld haben*, but in familiar Bavarian or Austrian colloquial: *mit den Kindern* (*mit die Kinder* would be more familiar still) *muß man eine Geduld haben.*

VERBS

Apart from regular phonetic changes, notably the loss of unstressed *e* in certain endings, the NHG weak verb continues the MHG pattern with only one small change. This is the levelling out of the ending of the 3rd pl. pres. indic.—MHG *machent*—to agree with the 3rd pl. of the other tenses, hence NHG *machen*.

On the other hand, the modern strong verb shows further innovations of great consequence. MHG maintains the ancient distinction, found in the majority of strong verbs (Classes 1 to 5), between (a) the 1st and 3rd singular of the preterite and (b) the 2nd singular and the plural. The distinction concerns the root vowel. Thus MHG sg.1,3 *schreip* 'wrote' contrasts with sg.2 *schribe(st)*, pl.1,3 *schriben*, 2 *schribet*. In NHG this distinction is no longer made, the root vowel being in all cases levelled out. In some verbs it has been the vowel of the 2nd singular and the plural which has replaced the vowel of the 1st and 3rd singular. In this way MHG *schreip* has given way to MHG *schrieb*, after the analogy of *schribe(st)*, *schriben*, *schribet*, where MHG *i* in open syllable was regularly lengthened in NHG (and in this case, as often, written *ie*): *schriebst*, *schrieben*, *schriebet*.

It will be remembered that in MHG the preterite of strong verbs in Classes 2–6, whose root was capable of modification, showed three different root vowels (p. 67): sg.1,3 *nam* 'took', 2 *næme(st)*, pl.1,3 *nâmen*, 2 *nâmet;* here *næme(st)* had arisen by umlaut about the beginning of the MHG period (< OHG *nâmi*). In cases like this, the exceptional 2nd sing. was usually levelled out first: *næmest* became *nâmest*. In other verbs it was the vowel of the 1st and 3rd sing. which superseded the vowel of the other persons, e.g. MHG *tranc* 'drank', pl. *trunken*, NHG sg. *trank*, pl. *tranken*. Similarly MHG sg. *verlôs* 'lost', pl. *verlurn*, NHG sg. *verlor*, pl. *verloren*. And then this generalised vowel spread to the preterite subjunctive; MHG *verlüre* became NHG *verlöre*. With this word, however, the pret.subj. is perhaps more theoretical than real, for in the present-day language only a limited number of verbs can employ this tense in ordinary contexts; the others use a periphrastic construction instead. One could say, for instance, either *er sagte, dass er käme* or *er sagte, dass er kommen würde*, but only *er sagte, dass er es verlieren würde*.

The above changes developed over a considerable period of time, beginning in Bavaria in the 15th century. Luther still observes without exception the ablaut distinctions, and some of these are retained in his Bible as printed today, e.g. *Was hülfe es dem Menschen, so er die ganze Welt gewönne, und nähme doch Schaden an der eigenen Seele?* The present stage was not generally reached until the end of the 17th century.

In MHG the whole of the pres.sg.indic. has the same root

as the 3rd sing., e.g. 1 *lise* 'read', 2 *lisest*, 3 *liset*, contrasting with pl. *lesen* etc., so that in such verbs the vowel contrast corresponds to the difference between singular and plural. This contrast is still living in the dialects and familiar *Umgangssprache* of the south: 1 *lies*, 2,3 *liest;* pl. *lesen* etc. But in other places there was a tendency to generalise the vowel of the plural throughout; this was common in northern, i.e. Low German, dialects. Central German usage made an awkward compromise between these two practices: here the 1st sing. follows the plural, while the 2nd and 3rd sing. retain their traditional vowel. This arrangement was adopted by the standard language, hence NHG 1 *lese*, 2,3 *liest*. In verbs of Class 2 the vowel of the plural has been generalised: MHG sg.1 *verliuse*, 2 *verliusest*, 3 *verliuset;* pl. *verliesen* etc., NHG sg.1 *verliere*, 2 *verlierst*, 3 *verliert;* pl. *verlieren* etc.

We saw (p. 66) that the transition from OHG to MHG did not bring great changes to the system of strong verbs since the ablaut distinctions were not affected by the phonetic changes taking place at the time. But in the modern period, levelling out in the preterite led to the breaking down of many old distinctions. The old patterns were irrevocably lost and the way was then open to all manner of analogical changes impossible before, so that the traditional system of ablaut patterns has but limited relevance for a synchronic classification of the strong verbs in present-day German.

Specimens of Early New High German
with translations into modern style

From 'The Yeoman from Bohemia' by John of Saaz (Johannes von Saaz), written in Saaz/Žatec, 1400. The Yeoman (really John himself) has indicted Death for the loss of his beloved wife. The defendant attempts to justify himself, but the Yeoman reveals contradictions in his arguments:

Nach ewer wechselrede kan sich niemant gerichten. Solten alle irdische dinge so bose, snode vnd vntuchtig sein beschaffen vnd gewurket? Des ist der ewig schepfer von anegenge der werlte nie gezigen. Tugent lieb gehabet, bosheit gehasset, sunde vbersehen vnd gerochen hat got vnz

her. Ich gelaube, hin nach tue er auch das selbe. Ich han von jugent
auf gehoret lesen vnd gelernet, wie got alle dinge beschaffen habe. Ir
sprechet, wie alle irdisch wesen vnd leben sullen ende nemen : so sprichet
Plato vnd ander weissagen, das in allen sachen eines zeruttunge des
andern geberunge sei vnd wie alle sache auf vrkunfte sint gebawet vnd
des himels lauf vnd der erden alle von einem in das ander verwandelt
wurkunge ewig sei.   (A. Bernt, *Der Ackermann aus Böhmen*,
                                      Heidelberg, 1929, p. 49)

A modern German version of the above:

'Nach Eurer widerspruchsvollen Rede kann sich niemand
richten. Sollten alle irdischen Dinge so böse, kläglich und
unnütz geschaffen und gestaltet sein? Dessen ist der ewige
Schöpfer vom Anbeginn der Welt niemals geziehen worden.
Tugend lieb gehabt, bösen Sinn gehaßt, die Sünde verziehen
und gestraft hat Gott bis zum heutigen Tage. Ich meine,
weiterhin tut er das gleiche. Ich habe von Jugend auf in
Büchern gelesen und gelernt, wie Gott alle Dinge geschaffen
habe. Ihr sagt, wie alles Wesen und Leben der Erde ein Ende
nehmen soll. Dem entgegen aber spricht Plato und andere
Philosophen, daß in allen Dingen des einen Zerstörung des
anderen Gebärung sei und daß alle Dinge auf Wiedergeburt
aufgebaut sind und daß das Geschehen im Himmel und auf
Erde nur eine von einem ins andere verwandelte ewige
Wirkung sei.'   (A. Bernt, *Der Ackermann und der*
                                      Tod, Insel-Verlag, Leipzig, p. 62)

ewer, uninflected form, i.e. gen. of *ir*.

alle irdische dinge, now *alle irdischen Dinge*: the strong ending after *alle* was
usual until modern times.

bose, snode etc., read *böse, snöde* etc.; such vowel modification is not shown in
the spelling of this text.

sein beschaffen und gewurket, NHG (mechanically) '*beschaffen und gewirkt sein*':
the strict rule which prescribes that *sein* must come last has only arisen in
the modern period, cf. also *sint gebawet* (below), NHG '*gebaut sind*'; *gewurket*
(= *gewürket*) pp. of *würken*, a variant of *wirken* the now standard form.

des still found in *deshalb, deswegen*, but otherwise replaced by *dessen*.

ewig, see under *irdisch* (below).

schepfer: now with rounding *Schöpfer*, a development first noticed in Late
MHG but which did not reach all dialects.

anegenge n. 'beginning', MHG *do.*, OHG *anagengi.*

gezigen pp. of *zeihen* (+ gen.) 'accuse', now replaced by analogical *geziehen.* This verb occurs most commonly today in the compound *verzeihen* 'excuse'.

gerochen pp. of strong verb *rechen* 'avenge', now written *rächen* to show its etymological affinity with *Rache* 'revenge'. NHG *rächen* is conjugated weak (avoiding homonymity with *riechen* 'smell'), though *(un)gerochen* '(un)-avenged' still survives, in spite of its now jocular associations.

unz 'until', MHG, OHG *do.*, cf. Engl. *un til*, *un to;* replaced in NHG by the neologism *bis.*

han '(I) have' (MHG, OHG *hân*), a contracted form surviving in dialect but replaced in the standard language by *habe.*

alle irdisch leben und wesen: down to the modern period uninflected forms of the attributive adjective, when in the nom.sing., are commonly found, cf. further *verwandelt wurkunge* (below), also *der ewig schepfer* (above), though an uninflected form after the def. art. is less usual. Uninflected adjectives occur today only in a few set phrases, e.g. *etwas auf gut Glück tun* 'take a chance with something'.

sullen, an often attested variant of *sollen.*

ander: the inflected form *andere* has been more normal in all periods.

weissage m. 'prophet' (MHG *wissage*, OHG *wissago*), but NHG *Weissager* with analogical *-er* ending.

geberunge f. 'birth', MHG *do.*

sache f. 'thing', in origin an ô-stem, does not change in the nom.acc.pl., but in more recent NHG it has become weak: pl. *Sachen.*

urkunft f. 'rebirth, resurrection', MHG *do.*, from *ur-* 'out of' and *-kunft* 'coming', verbal noun from *kommen*, cf. NHG *An-*, *Zukunft.*

sint gebawet: word order as *sein beschaffen und gewurket* (above).

verwandelt, see under *irdisch* (above).

Martin Luther, Matthew x, 5–10. New Testament, First Edition 1522:

Dise tzwelffe sandte Jhesus, vnd gepott yhn vnd sprach, Geht nit auff die strasse der heyden, vnd zihet nit yn die stedte der Samariter, Sondern gehet hyn tzu den verloren schaffen aus dem haus Israel, geht aber vund predigt, vund sprecht, das hymelreych ist nahe er bey komen, macht die schwachen gesund, reynigt die außsetzigen, weckt die todten auff, treybt die teuffel aus, umbsunst habt yhrs empfangen, umbsonst gebet es auch, habt nicht gollt noch sylber, noch ertz ynn eweren gurttelen, auch keyn tasche zur weg fart, auch nit zween rocke, keyn schuch, auch keynen stecken, denn eyn arbeyter ist seyner speyse werd.

Definitive Edition, 1546:

Djese zwelffe sandte Jhesus, gebot jnen, vnd sprach, Gehet nicht auff der Heiden strassen, vnd ziehet nicht in der Samariter stedte, Sondern gehet hin zu den verloren Schafen, aus dem hause Israel. Gehet aber vnd predigt, vnd sprecht, Das Himelreich ist nahe her bey komen. Machet die Krancken gesund, Reiniget die Aussetzigen, Wecket die Todten auff, Treibet die Teufel aus, Vmb sonst habt jrs empfangen, vmb sonst gebet es auch. Ir solt nicht gold noch silber, noch ertz in ewren Gürteln haben, auch keine Taschen zur wegfart, auch nicht zween Röcke, keinen Schuch, auch keinen Stecken. Denn ein Erbeiter ist seiner Speise werd.

As printed today:

'Diese zwölf sandte Jesus, gebot ihnen, und sprach: Gehet nicht auf der Heiden Straße, und ziehet nicht in der Samariter Städte, sondern gehet hin zu den verlorenen Schafen aus dem Hause Israel. Gehet aber und prediget, und sprechet: Das Himmelreich ist nahe herbeigekommen. Machet die Kranken gesund, reiniget die Aussätzigen, wecket die Toten auf, treibet die Teufel aus. Umsonst habt ihr es empfangen, umsonst gebet es auch. Ihr sollt nicht Gold, noch Silber, noch Erz in euren Gürteln haben; auch keine Tasche zur Wegfahrt, auch nicht zween Röcke, keine Schuhe, auch keinen Stecken. Denn ein Arbeiter ist seiner Speise wert.'

Although everywhere admired, the language of the reformer's classical translation inevitably became more and more archaic with the passing of the centuries. New translations were undertaken, but the influence of the classical version was so dominating that no one succeeded in producing a contemporary rendering genuinely independent of Luther's diction until Hermann Menge published his translation in 1926. This work, which has been reprinted many times, is entirely in the idiom of the present day. To read Luther's classical translation and Menge's modern version side by side must be one of the best ways of learning to appreciate what has been basic in the evolution of German style in the last four hundred years.

Hermann Menge:

'Diese Zwölf sandte Jesus aus, nachdem er ihnen folgende Weisungen gegeben hatte: 'Den Weg zu den Heidenvölkern

schlagt nicht ein und tretet auch in keine Samariterstadt ein,
geht vielmehr zu den verlorenen Schafen des Hauses Israel.
Auf eurer Wanderung predigt: 'Das Himmelreich ist nahe
herbeigekommen!' Heilt Kranke, weckt Tote auf, macht
Aussätzige rein, treibt böse Geister aus: umsonst habt ihr's
empfangen, umsonst sollt ihr's auch weitergeben! Sucht euch
kein Gold, kein Silber, kein Kupfergeld in eure Gürtel zu
verschaffen, nehmt keinen Ranzen mit auf den Weg, auch
nicht zwei Röcke, keine Schuhe und keinen Stock, denn der
Arbeiter ist seines Unterhalts wert.'

BIBLIOGRAPHY

A synopsis of Early NHG grammar on historical lines and passages from
representative authors are conveniently accessible in K. Brooke, *Introduction
to Early New High German*, Oxford, 1955. A. Götze, *Frühneuhochdeutsches
Glossar*[2], Berlin, 1971, is a dictionary of Early NHG words not in use in
recent German.

8

THE RISE AND NATURE OF THE MODERN STANDARD LANGUAGE

We have seen that the most remarkable feature of the MHG period was the development of the *Dichtersprache*. This idiom was the achievement and prerogative of the leading feudal circles. But during the 13th century courtly society, which had fostered the *Dichtersprache*, disintegrated. We may take the beginning of the interregnum after the death of Frederick II in 1250 as the starting point of a new epoch marked by far-reaching social changes brought about in large measure by the expansion of urban centres. Hitherto German had been chiefly used for poetry, it had been mainly a medium of purely artistic expression. Prose had hardly been cultivated at all, for the language of administration and learning was Latin (see below 'The Role of Latin'). But now the vernacular was coming into its own as the language of administration in the widest sense, including law and business. This was truly an epoch-making change and the first decisive step on the way to modern standard German.

The language of the first documents in German from this period is appropriately termed *Urkundendeutsch*. Though in most cases clearly continuing the earlier scribal tradition, *Urkundendeutsch* has a marked regional character which reveals itself in the phonetics, accidence and vocabulary. In view of the immense increase in administrative documents of all kinds in German after 1300, it is convenient to call the language of these later documents *Kanzleideutsch*. This, too, had pronounced regional features. In the 14th century, for instance, six main types of *Kanzleideutsch* may be distinguished: Swiss, Swabian, Rhenish-Franconian, Central Franconian (Central German), Bavarian-Austrian, Bohemian. But deeds and documents are not the only witnesses to the evolution of the German language in the 14th century. Apart from some poetry, there is a fair amount of prose, mainly of a religious nature. In particular the Mystics cultivated the language for evangelistic purposes; it was they who gave German prose a soul.

All these texts bear a regional stamp. All the same, unifying trends have been detected, not yet in matters of vocabulary, but in orthography and morphology. The chanceries undoubtedly influenced each other in the direction of uniformity. The Imperial Chancery, which was not permanently established in any one centre, was naturally in a position to play a special role here, but its importance should not be overrated since the separate provinces rather than the country as a whole were the important administrative units. In the religious texts similar tendencies have been observed. Indeed, a regional form of written German current in the East Central German area is actually referred to as 'daz mittelste dûtsch' in a translation of the Gospels issued at Halle in 1343. These various forms of literary German will in the last analysis have rested on the speech of the upper classes in the different regions. Since the language was tending towards unification in morphology, it is certain that educated speech will have been, more or less, keeping abreast of these developments.

The unifying tendencies of the 14th century continued in the 15th at an accelerating pace. The basic conditions are evident: a growing population and a further extension of urban life with increased trade and commerce. The general prosperity led to a rise in the level of culture, one reflex of which was a heavy demand for reading matter. Literacy not presupposing a knowledge of Latin must have quickly become rather widespread as is shown by the rapid increase in the production of German manuscripts in the 15th century. Then in 1445 the printing era opened and the printers must soon have become aware that there would be a good market for German books written in a language acceptable over a wide area.

On what linguistic basis was this progress towards uniformity being achieved?

We must go back to 1300 at least. By this date, a large part of the German-speaking area lay east of the Elbe and Saale on territory previously inhabited by Slavonic peoples (see pp. 170ff.). The German inhabitants were colonists drawn from various parts of the country west of the Elbe and Saale. In the north, the colonial dialects were Low German, in the south they were High German with a strong Central German bias. But these were naturally not traditional dialects like Saxon or Bavarian, they were recent amalgamations arising from a fusion of dialects brought in by the settlers. In particular the southern part of the colonial area, the part east of the Saale, offered good prospects for settlement with the result that a lively west-to-east movement in the direction of Silesia went on for a long time. All this gave the German of the area an especially flexible character. Nowhere else in the German-speaking world were conditions so favourable for linguistic compromise: a neutral territory adjacent to the traditional Central German area through which it drew newcomers from the north and south as well.

As time went on, the territory east of the Saale—the Mark Meissen—formed, under the House of Wettin, a state which in size and influence almost rivalled that of the Habsburgs. As a consequence of political and cultural superiority, the linguistic forms established in writing and educated spoken use east of the Saale began to gain currency in the west, especially in the central districts. The compromise character of the language, which naturally aided its acceptance, is clearly seen in the vowel system. The MHG diphthongs *uo, ie, üe* have become the simple long vowels *u* etc. according to Central German practice, while the MHG monophthongs *î, û, iu* have become *ei* etc. as in Bavarian. This mixture is the hall-mark of the modern standard language, too.

At the same time as East Central German was expanding, another 'Common German', this time with a Bavarian basis, was developing in the south-east on the territory of the Habsburg state. We find this language actually termed 'gemeines Deutsch' in 1464 and, encouraged by the pre-eminence of the Habsburgs, it was in use from Vienna to Nuremberg. In 15th-century Germany there were thus two major areas of educated German, each feeling its way towards unity within itself and at the same time, inevitably, influencing one another.

Such was the position when the Reformation came amid a tremendous outburst of patriotic feeling. At the centre of events stood the Reformer himself, Martin Luther, whose work was

destined to have more influence on the German language than
that of any other person. Luther was a Thuringian. It was
natural that he should use a language of the East Central
German type. In fact, in his *Tischreden*, he expressly states that
he follows the Saxon Chancery (i.e. Meissen, the chief chancery
in Kursachsen) so that 'Ober- und Niederländer' may understand him. Of course, neither the language of the Saxon
Chancery specifically nor the East Central German 'Common
Language' were uniform in the sense that spelling and morphology were absolutely fixed. Luther's own orthography was,
by modern standards, inconsistent in the extreme, as may be
seen from the specimens on pp. 106 f. This is true of the morphology as well, though not to the same extent. However, it is
not clear how far Luther was responsible for his own forms.
His works circulated in print and the printers' readers were
probably the final authority in such matters. But there is, of
course, no reason to suppose that Luther was himself any more
consistent than the correctors.

Luther's prime importance lies in the enormous circulation
of his works. One-third of all publications in Germany between
1518 and 1523 bears Luther's name. This was but a foretaste.
His New Testament appeared in 1522, the whole Bible in 1534.
Compared with the prodigious success of this work, all previous
publishing paled into insignificance. In the years 1534 to 1574
some 100,000 copies of the Luther Bible left the press in
Wittenberg alone. To these must be added the untold copies
produced by other printers. This was unparalleled in the history
of publicity. Never before had any man exercised such influence
through the medium of writing. Borne by the mood of the
Reformation, Luther's work came into the possession of a
major part of the German people which made it certain that a
language of the East Central German type would one day
become the undisputed national standard.

The Reformer's publications were, of course, not acceptable
to the Catholics, but the literary superiority of Luther's Bible
was such that versions made afterwards were heavily indebted
to it. Nevertheless, a comparison between such versions and
Luther's work throws much light on linguistic conditions in the
16th century. We have referred above to the rivalry between

the two main literary languages, East Central German and Bavarian German. At the Reformation Bavaria and Austria remained Catholic and this at first strengthened the already existing linguistic divergencies. We can illustrate these with examples from the Catholic version of the Bible in literary Bavarian made by Luther's great opponent Eck, published in 1537. Where Luther has *rein, gut, König, gleuben, gehen, arbeiten* and *erbeiten*, Eck has *rain, gůt* (i.e. *guot*), *Künig, glauben, gan, arbeiten*. Luther has *ich war, ich hatte*, Eck *ich was, ich hett*. Luther writes *der Gesang, die Luft*, Eck *das Gesang, der Luft*. Luther retains the final *-e* in *Auge, Name, Schätze*, but Eck will have nothing to do with this 'Protestant *e*', he has *Aug, Nam, Schätz*. In nearly every case Luther's forms have become the modern standard. The same applies to the vocabulary. Luther's *Kahn, Lappen, Ufer, Ziege* are rendered *Nachen, Blätz, Gestad, Geiß* by his southern contemporaries. They change *beben* to *bidmen* (Luther himself wrote *eyn großer erdbeden* in the 1522 New Testament (Acts XVI, 26); later editions have *ein großes Erdbeben*), *gleiten* is replaced by *wanken* or *schlupfen/schlifpen* (cf. NHG *schlüpfen*). But Luther had the powerful Centre on his side and soon afterwards the North, too, as his language made headway there. The importance of Bavaria and Austria was bound to decline. After a period of hesitation Switzerland came out of her High Alemannic isolation and also accepted Luther's German.

In the Protestant parts Luther's language was authoritative. But his language only became familiar to the majority of his readers after they had learnt it. For the first time, Germans were beginning to feel that literary language was something to be acquired by study. The earliest guides to such study were the spelling books of the 16th century. At this time the first primers to help foreigners learn German also made their appearance. But they were not able to teach a national language, since regional types maintained themselves throughout the century, though East Central German was the leading type. The regional *Schriftdialekte* were in all essentials now determined by the printers, hence the term *Druckersprachen*. The printers, ever anxious to extend the market, played an important part in bringing about a degree of unity in formal matters. In this respect they were usually more progressive than the authors themselves. For instance, the manuscripts from the pen of Hans Sachs are more archaic than the contemporary printed versions.

Early in the 17th century it was apparent that the question of the literary language was entering a new phase. The leading position of the East Central type, now further enhanced by the political hegemony of Kursachsen and Kurbrandenburg, was about to be confirmed as the national literary language. The material basis was already present. What was still lacking was a definition of the standard language and a prescriptive statement of orthography and accidence obligatory for the whole German-speaking area. It was the poet Opitz who first attempted to remedy this deficiency. Opitz drew up rules for poetic composition which he published in his *Buch von der deutschen Poeterey* in 1624. In this work Opitz prescribed the actual forms of the words, e.g. he forbade the apocope and syncope of *e* as in Upper and West Central Ger. *Speis, Leut, gschwind, solchs,* and his more conservative forms *Speise* etc. have prevailed. At this stage such matters were of high importance. Opitz held that educated speech, free from dialect influences, was the only acceptable basis for poetic diction. This may well have been felt aesthetically desirable, but how was it to be achieved? Opitz had given no grammar of his ideal literary language. How could one decide in every case whether a form was to be classed as dialectal or not seeing that there was no definitive guide?

It was Schottel who finally produced an acknowledged grammar, the first serious attempt to codify the standard literary language; this was his *Ausführliche Arbeit von der teutschen Haubtsprache,* 1663. Here Schottel was no longer concerned with regional types, not even with East Central German as the dominant representative. He was concerned solely with a national literary language, *die Hochteutsche Sprache,* which should stand above all regional literary forms as it stood above the spoken dialects. This does not alter the fact that his national language remained substantially East Central German.

The next eighty years witness the steady consolidation of the national language. It could not have been otherwise. The pressing needs of administration, business and education, the spirit of the times, then the Enlightenment and the kindling of a national consciousness in spite of particularism—all these factors had a share in moving the literary language in the direction of the greatest possible uniformity. Saxony continued to be in the fore in cultural matters; Leipzig became the centre of the book trade. During the course of the 18th century, with the work of Gottsched and Adelung, both partisans of Saxon usage, the grammatical unity of the literary language was achieved. Gottsched's *Deutsche Sprachkunst* appeared in 1746, Adelung's *Umständliches Lehrgebäude der Deutschen Sprache* in 1782. These were the authorities; now one could spell properly, now one could decline and conjugate properly.

There remained, however, the question of vocabulary. Which words could one use in writing and which should one avoid? Which were entitled to literary status, which were merely dialectal? These questions were by no means rhetorical. It turned out that, in a large number of cases, any decision was arbitrary. It was a fact that a fair part of the German lexicon had a regional character. For so many concepts there simply were no nationally recognised terms. Adelung endeavoured to define the position in his monumental dictionaries *Versuch eines vollständigen grammatisch-kritischen Wörterbuchs der Hochdeutschen Mundart, 1775–86* and *Grammatisch-kritisches Wörterbuch der Hochdeutschen Mundart, 1793–1801*, but his views were of necessity sometimes interim views. Usage is for ever changing. The formal structure of a literary language—the orthography, the accidence—can be stabilised more or less, but the vocabulary, the semantics, the living and developing idiom know no bounds.

THE NATURE OF MODERN GERMAN

After the normalising work of Gottsched, the language was almost immediately raised to great heights by the classical writers. Above all, they enriched the language stylistically and the language they wrote is to all intents and purposes the language employed today. The most important development since the grammatical standardisation of literary German has been the adoption, more or less, of this language as the habitually spoken form by the majority of German speakers.

Two hundred years ago, nearly all spoken German was dialectal. Only a small elite could actually speak the literary language and most of these could doubtless use dialect as well if required. Except in Saxony, the difference between the literary language and the ordinarily spoken form was quite appreciable, in extreme cases (e.g. Switzerland, North Germany) the literary language was virtually a foreign tongue to those who spoke the local dialects.

This situation was radically altered in the second half of the last century. The growth of conurbations brought together people from the most different dialect regions. Under modern conditions—full literacy, compulsory schooling—the common speech of the city dwellers became essentially High German, i.e. literary German. The local colouring was usually prominent as well, but there was everywhere a clear tendency to speak as much like the literary form as possible. This was also a socially superior way of expressing oneself and as such was bound to make progress. This tendency has greatly increased during the present century thanks especially to such influential mass media as the cinema, the radio and the television. The standard language is now spoken in hundreds of small townships where a century ago only broad dialect was heard. The standard forms have been penetrating into the countryside, especially during the last few decades, so that today the dialects are everywhere on the wane (see p. 133).

Standard German, as spoken, is called *Umgangssprache*. It is misleading to translate this term 'colloquial'; it is better to define it as 'non-dialect speech'. *Umgangssprache* is, however, far from uniform. It is much less homogeneous than the English spoken in England, for instance. It is not yet possible to speak of a national *Umgangssprache*, since the regional variations are still so considerable. The difference between the ordinary conversational styles heard in Berlin and Munich is probably as great as between London and New York; the difference between Berlin and Vienna is certainly greater. We are here concerned with differences between spoken varieties of the standard language, we are not concerned with dialect, though of course each variety of *Umgangssprache* contains local elements, many of which are ultimately of dialect origin. The differences between the *Umgangssprache* of any two places involve, apart from pronunciation, both vocabulary and idiom. We give some examples from Berlin and Vienna, leaving aside the question of pronunciation.

The names of fruits and vegetables are very often different: Berlin *Apfelsine*, Vienna *Orange* 'orange', B. *Pflaume*, V. *Zwetschge* 'plum', B. *Aprikose*, V. *Marille* 'apricot', B. *Tomate*, V. also *Paradeiser* 'tomato', B. *Kartoffel*, V. *Erdapfel* 'potato', B. *Blumenkohl*, V. *Karfiol* 'cauliflower', B. *grüne Bohne*, V. *Fisole* 'runner bean', B. *Petersilie*, V. *Petersil* 'parsley'. Culinary terms can be confusingly diverse: B. *Eierkuchen*, V. *Palatschinken* 'pancake', B. *Schrippe*, V. *Semmel* '(bread-) roll', B. *Hefe*, V. *Germ* 'yeast', B. *Kloß*, V. Knödel 'dumpling', B. *Hackfleisch*, V. *Faschiertes* 'minced meat', B. *Schweinebraten*, V. *Schweinsbraten* 'pork for roasting', B. *Lunge*, V. *Beuschl* 'lights', B. *Tunke*, V. *Sauce* 'gravy', B. *Mostrich*, V. *Senf* 'mustard', B. *Quark*, V. *Topfen* 'curds', B. *Sahne*, V. *Obers* 'cream', to which we may add such untranslatable continental specialities as B. *Napfkuchen*, V. *Gugelhupf*, B. *Pfannkuchen*, V. *Faschingskrapfen*. Accordingly, a *Speisenkarte* drawn up in Berlin looks remarkably unlike a Viennese *Speisekarte*.

Scores of other everyday things and concepts have differing names: B. *Decke*, V. *Plafond* 'ceiling', B. *Diele*, V. *Vorzimmer* 'vestibule', B. *Eimer*, V. *Kübel* 'bucket, pail', B. *Kissen*, V. *Polster* (m.) 'cushion', B. *Klammer*, V. *Kluppe* 'peg' (for hanging out washing), B. *(Koch)topf*, V. *Reindl* 'saucepan', B. *Bürgersteig* or *Gehsteig*, V. *Trottoir* 'pavement', B. *Sonnabend*, V. *Samstag* 'Saturday', B. *Treppe*, V. *Stiege* 'stairs', B. *Harke*, V. *Rechen* 'rake', B. *Umschlag*, V. *Kouvert* 'envelope', B. *Bonbon*, V. *Zuckerl* 'sweet', B. *Netzgardine*, V. *Netzvorhang* 'net curtain', B. *Kopf-schmerzen*, V. *Kopfweh* 'headache', similarly B. *Zahnschmerzen* etc. For euphemistic reasons *Stuhl* 'chair' came to be avoided in Vienna and the more refined *Sessel* lit. 'armchair' took its place. To render 'armchair' V. then went to the French *Fauteuil*, hence B. *Stuhl*, V. *Sessel* 'chair', B. *Sessel*, V. *Fauteuil* 'armchair'. Vienna does not ordinarily distinguish between 'foot' and 'leg', V. *Fuß* corresponding to B. *Fuß* and *Bein*; this may be due to Slavonic influence, cf. Czech *noha* 'foot, leg'.

The differences concern nouns in particular, but there are many cases where adjectives and verbs differ as well. We give a few typical illustrations.

Adjectives: B. *artig*, V. *brav* 'good' (of behaviour), B. *niedlich*, V. (approx.) *herzig* or *putzig* '(approx.) nice and pretty and small', B. *verschossen*, V. *geschossen* 'faded' (of materials), B. *pitschenaß*, V. *patschnaß* 'dripping wet', B. *mächtig*, V. *geil* 'rich' (of food)—Caution! In Berlin *geil* means something quite different—For 'funny, peculiar' B. has *komisch* and *ulkig*, V. only *komisch*. For 'bad' B. uses mainly *schlecht* and *schlimm*, V. commonly uses *arg* as well, with idiomatic complications.

Verbs: B. *meckern*, V. *raunzen* 'grumble', B. *fegen*, V. *kehren* 'sweep'—B. *Schornsteinfeger*, V. *Rauchfangkehrer* 'chimney-sweep' —B. *plätten*, V. *bügeln* 'iron', B. *zu-, aufschließen*, V. *zu-, aufsperren* 'lock, unlock', B. *kleben*, V. commonly also *picken* 'stick', B. *vorsagen*, V. *einsagen* 'prompt' (one's neighbour at school), B. *Staub wischen*, V. *abstauben* 'dust'. In Berlin the commonest verb for 'use' is *gebrauchen;* it is replaced in Vienna by *verwenden*. In Berlin the verb *machen* usually translates both 'to make' and 'to do'; in Vienna the commoner verb is *tun*.

Here a few sentences in further illustration of typical differences: B. *ich denke*, V. *ich glaube* 'I think so', B. *der Jung spielt auf der Straße Fußball*, V. *der Bub spielt auf der Gasse Fußball* (or *tut auf der Gasse Fußball spielen*) 'the boy plays football in the street', B. *das Mädchen sieht gesund aus*, V. *das Mädel schaut gesund aus* 'the girl looks well', B. *die Miete ist eben hoch*, V. *der Zins ist halt hoch* 'the rent happens to be high', B. *der Müllkutscher hat in der Kneipe gesessen* (or *saß in der Kneipe*), V. *der Mistbauer ist im Wirtshaus gesessen* 'the dustman was sitting in the pub.', B. *wir haben ein Bücherregal in der Ecke zu stehen*, V. *wir haben eine Bücherstellage in der Ecke* (or *im Eck*) *stehen* 'we have book-shelves standing in the corner', B. *ich bin erkältet* (*habe eine Erkältung*), V. *ich bin verkühlt* (*habe eine Verkühlung*) 'I've a cold', B. *sie werden sowieso wieder dreckig*, V. *sie werden eh' wieder schmutzig* 'they'll get dirty again anyhow'. It will be noticed that both use familiar constructions not admissible in formal literary style: B. *wir haben ein Bücherregal zu stehen*, V. *der Bub tut . . . spielen*.

How much do these considerable variations affect mutual

comprehension? Generally speaking, very little; for most of the words are known to both parties, though many of them have nuances of meaning which are not the same in both places. The Berliner and the Viennese understand each other, but the natural, spontaneous idiom of the one makes a very outlandish impression on the other. For instance, the word *dreckig*, used in the last example above, is quite normal in Berlin. It is there the first word, so to speak, for 'dirty', but it is vulgar in Vienna. Occasionally a phrase commonly used in one place causes amusement in the other. The Berliner says *er wird hochgehen* 'he'll go up' (the ladder, hill), but to a Viennese this means 'he'll be nabbed' (by the police). It can happen that a phrase usual in one city cannot be understood at all in the other. V. *es steht nicht dafür* 'it isn't worth the trouble' doesn't suggest a thing to Berlin ears; it must be 'translated' *es lohnt sich nicht.* Quite a number of the individual words are difficult, too. Unless the context makes it clear, the uninitiated Berliner wouldn't be able to make anything of most of the Viennese culinary terms quoted above. Nor are the Viennese names for fruits and vegetables, in most cases, understood in Berlin at all. Vice versa, some of the Berlin names would be equally puzzling to a Viennese.

If a Berliner and Viennese meet, they automatically feel for common ground as regards idiom and vocabulary, each consciously avoiding expressions which may be assumed to be unfamiliar to the other. Occasional lapses are soon put right. We quote an instance heard not long ago. Two women, B. and V., were talking about the domestic round. B. used the word *Spind*, but V. did not understand and interrupted as though she had not heard properly. B. sensed the difficulty, paused a moment and then said *Schrank*, whereupon V. audibly whispered to herself *ah ja! Kredenz.* And then the conversation flowed on. The speaker's ordinary term for 'kitchen cupboard' was *Spind*, which she altered to *Schrank* as she realised that this would be better known, and finally the listener, quite unconsciously, 'translated' this into her own local term, the one she was most familiar with, *Kredenz.*

It is occasionally difficult to find common ground. Take the verbs for 'shrink' (of materials): B. *einlaufen*, V. *eingehen*. It does not normally enter into the consciousness of either of the parties that their particular word is not universal. If we ask a Berliner what he thinks about the sentence *das Kleid ist eingegangen*, we must expect to be told, perhaps with some vehemence, that such a sentence is nonsense seeing that *eingehen* means 'die' and is applicable to animals, plants or unsuccessful newspapers, but certainly not to dresses. If we ask a Viennese to comment on *das Kleid ist eingelaufen*, we may expect to be informed that this is impossible German since *einlaufen* means what it says, namely 'run in', and obviously no dress does that. When confronted with the alternative possibility, the reaction is one of incredulity.

What has been said so far about mutual comprehension refers, of course, to average, polite conversational language. We should perhaps add that, in the realm of slang and substandard speech, mutual comprehension is often out of the question. In fact, the German spoken on the lowest social levels in Vienna is not immediately understood by a Berliner at all, and the situation the other way round is not very different. On these levels pronunciation is particularly significant; as before, the words and idioms can be very different: B. *Fresse*, V. *Goschen* 'gob', B. *Quanten*, V. *Haxen* 'feet' (vulgar), in V. also 'legs' (cf. V. *Fuß* above), B. *doof*, V. *deppat* 'daft', B. *hau ab!* V. *putz di!* 'clear off'! B. *wa?* V. *gel?* 'isn't it?' (i.e. equivalents of the standard *nicht wahr?*).

It is true that to some extent the Berlin-Vienna contrast reflects a wider German-Austrian contrast which makes the differences more drastic. But within Germany itself the amount of diversity is still most remarkable. There is, in particular, a superabundance of nouns. Look in the large dictionaries for the German words for 'string' or 'butcher' or 'floor cloth' or 'charwoman'. In each case there are at least half-a-dozen regional synonyms.

This lack of standardisation by contrast with English—or French—is a product of German particularism. English and French adopted as the literary standard words based, in the main, on the educated speech of London and Paris, old and influential capitals of centralised states. Berlin, on the other hand, only sprang into prominence at the beginning of the last century. For hundreds of years Germany had no permanent capital, only a number of provincial capitals. Separate kingdoms existed within Germany until 1918. Austria and Switzerland were outside the German Reich altogether. These conditions retarded the development of a uniform German vocabulary and the various regions continue to use many of their own local expressions, especially those pertaining to everyday things, and introduce them into writing and print.

We can illustrate this aspect by considering the synonyms for 'charwoman'. In this we shall be assisted by P. Kretschmer, *Wortgeographie der hochdeutschen Umgangssprache*, 1918. Kretschmer's book is based upon replies to questionnaires sent to a large number of localities throughout the German-speaking world and in it we find a store of information on the regional distribution of many German words, including the terms for 'charwoman'. We learn that *Putzfrau*, for example, is usual in the Cologne area, *Bedienerin* in most of Austria, *Aufwartefrau* is typical of North and Central Germany, but with *Aufwärterin* as well in several places within this area, *Zugehfrau* occurs in Augsburg and Aschaffenburg, *Zugeherin* in Bavaria generally. There are various other names, each from a different region, e.g. *Aushilfsfrau, Eingeherin, Zuspringerin, Lauferin* or *Lauffrau*, the last from the Württemberg district where *laufen* is popularly used for *gehen*. Each of these terms is thus proper to a certain locality or localities. In a few places two names are in use, more or less side by side, for instance in Bern *Putzfrau* and *Aushilfsfrau*, but on the whole one term only is in use in any given place. This term is thus 'official' in its own area. Not only is it used in speaking, it may also be used in writing. If one advertises for a charwoman one would use the local term. If necessary, this term would be used in local legislation. There is no question of any of these words being classed as dialect words. Dialect signifies a form of language not ordinarily acceptable in writing. But we are clearly not dealing with dialect here, but with varying regional usage where one word is pretty well as good as another. Nevertheless some terms are more widely used than others. Especially at the present time there is a tendency for such terms to spread at the expense of the more local ones, a tendency encouraged by the national press and other publications intended for the widest circulation since these prefer to use the terms known to the majority of people. In the present case, perhaps *Putzfrau* (the term used in Berlin) may be regarded as the main form.

How do the Germans themselves cope with this exceptional diversity? They normally use the word current in their own locality, but from talking to people from other areas and through reading, they become acquainted with at least the commonest synonyms. There may be some feeling, too, for a main form.

This remarkable diversity in the vocabulary is not new in the history of German. In times gone by, the amount of diversity was, if anything, even greater. Nowadays, thanks to the influence of the literary language, it has been possible in many cases to adopt one of a number of regional synonyms as the acknowledged standard term.

In the process of standardisation Luther's work has been very important. We saw above (p. 113) how elements of Luther's vocabulary, which are now part and parcel of everyday German, were not understood in his own day by, for instance, the Upper Germans. The general acceptance of Luther's words does not mean, however, that the Bavarian synonyms have been entirely replaced. In fact, most of them survive to this day, principally in local use. In any language, each individual word has its own history. Let us look back to the nouns quoted on p. 113 and consider what has happened to each of them in modern German. Luther's *Ufer* has by now entirely replaced *Gestad* as a normal term for 'bank' (of a river, of the sea), but the southern word has remained in literary use, especially in the form *Gestade*, as a poetic word. Luther's *Kahn* has to all intents and purposes replaced *Nachen*, so that the latter only survives locally, as a technical term. Similarly *Ziege* has virtually driven *Geiß* out of ordinary literary use, though the word is still usual in sportsman's parlance to denote the female of various species, e.g. *Gemsgeiß*. It also occurs in some standard compounds, e.g. *Geißblatt*, and in more or less petrified contexts like '*Der Wolf und die sieben Geißlein*'. Finally, *Lappen* is today understood everywhere, but its many synonyms, such as *Fetzen, Lumpen, Tuch*, are proving most obdurate; *Blätz* lives on in restricted local use.

Words like Luther's *Ufer, Kahn, Ziege, Lappen* were already well known in Central and partly also in Northern German at the beginning of the 16th century. Luther occasionally used words which had much less widespread validity than this and still they have won general acceptance. An outstanding example of this is the word *Hügel* 'hill'. This word is only found once or twice in writings before Luther; it is entirely absent from the medieval records. It was certainly not understood in the south in the 16th century, since Luther's contemporaries render it by different words, notably by *Büh(e)l*, common in the south. Other terms for hill are *Haug, Buckel, Koppe, Hübel*. In the Low German area the form corresponding to HG *Hübel* is *Hövel*, cf. Standard Dutch *heuvel*. Faced with a variety of local forms, Luther chose the one most familiar to himself.

Even though *Hügel* is now the undisputed standard word, it is not very frequently used, at any rate not by comparison with *Berg*. We have perhaps learnt to equate *Berg* with 'mountain', but this is only one possible meaning. Anybody who has seen the *Berge* which make up the *Siebengebirge* will realise that *Berg* can also mean nothing more than 'hill' and in the flatter parts of the country this is its usual meaning. Furthermore, 'mountain' is a rather bookish word. 'Hill' is the homely word and in this respect, too, it has more in common with *Berg* than *Hügel*. It is productive in the same way: 'uphill, downhill'/*bergauf, bergab*. For the great majority of Germans only *Berg*, not *Hügel*, is a vital word; *Berg* conjures up a multitude of associations, *Hügel* is far less vivid. Engl. 'mountain' and Ger. *Hügel* go together as essentially literary and technical words. Significantly, neither of them occurs to any appreciable extent in toponymy. 'Mountain' is hardly a place-name element in England; *Hügel* is certainly not found in any traditional names in the German-speaking area, whereas its unsuccessful literary rivals are common, e.g. *Kitzbühl*. Even though a genuine German word, *Hügel* remains in a sense a foreigner in most parts of the country. It has, in fact, been in general use for a much shorter time than 'mountain' has in English; the word came to us from French with the Normans.

The process of developing standard terms from a number of competing synonyms has continued since Luther's time and is, as we have seen, still far from completed. Consider the word *Schmetterling* 'butterfly'. It is more than likely that Goethe, while still a small boy, had never heard this word, though he would get to know it later from reading. The reason is that until about 1780, the term *Schmetterling* as an ordinarily spoken word was confined to Saxony. Here it had been well known for some time and was one of half-a-dozen synonyms which, since the beginning of printing, had been competing for general recognition. Thanks no doubt to the supremacy of Saxony, *Schmetterling* was by 1750 becoming the most favoured literary word. In dialect or near-dialect we may still hear some of the synonyms: *Müllermaler, Sommervogel, Vlinder, Milchdieb, Butterfliege*. One synonym *Falter* is, however, also literary, often technical, cf. *Tag- und Nachtfalter;* it includes moths.

The search for a term which could gain universal approval has often led to the creation of new words, particularly compound words. The dialects have a number of different root words for 'sow', but the literary creation *Mutterschwein* is neutral, transparent and at once acceptable to all. (*Sau* is, of course, a common word in German, but it is not so precise as 'sow' in English; it tends to mean 'pig' in general.) Similarly the dialects have a number of words for bitch, for which the literary language has created *Hündin*. This explains why *Hündin* is such a colourless word when compared with Engl. 'bitch'. Referring to anatomy only, it has none of the nuances inseparable from the English word. Another literary creation is *Pflugwende* 'turn of the plough', for which the dialects offer a plethora of synonyms, but no parallel. There are at least six different root words in regular use today for 'string': *Band, Kordel, Schnur, Spagat, Strick, Strippe*. It is in keeping with a general trend that a seventh synonym, the compound *Bindfaden*, is bidding fair to become the accepted main, if not yet standard, term.

THE SITUATION IN NORTH GERMANY

The reasons for the demise of Low German as an official language and its decline as a literary medium have already been touched upon (pp. 78 f.). Had historical circumstances been otherwise, linguistic evolution in the north would doubtless have taken a different course. If the north had maintained its traditional cohesion and prosperity into modern times, it would most likely have developed into an independent state with its own Standard Low German as the official language, which would have differed as much from Standard High German as Dutch does.

There had been a good deal of printing in Low German— about 350 titles date from before 1500. But in the next century competition from High German publications began to curtail seriously the output in Low German. Luther's New Testament and then the whole Bible appeared in Low German versions in 1523 and 1534 respectively. At the same time, however, Luther's original text was widely used in North Germany, due especially to the influence of princes and towns favourable to the Reformation. In 1621 the last Low German Bible was published, in 1635 the last New Testament.

As we have seen (p. 78), Low German was progressively abandoned as an official medium during the course of the 16th century. As the various towns and provinces went over to High German for administrative purposes, the schools followed suit somewhat later. Schools in Brandenburg were all using High German in 1550, in Magdeburg by 1580. Other places were slower to change. Brunswick and Westphalia did not go over to High German until 1630, Mecklenburg and Pomerania followed about 1640, Lübeck, Hamburg, Bremen, Schleswig-Holstein 1650, Oldenburg 1670. In Ostfriesland the change-over has been dated to 1680, but here Dutch books had been in use since the middle of the century.

All these developments spelt the doom of Low German as a literary language. It was destined to live on mainly as a spoken medium in the form of its dialects, which evolved under the ever-increasing influence of the literary High German. Certainly Low German continued to be written, but when the language ceased to be employed officially, the degree of standardisation which had already been achieved in written Middle Low German was lost. Henceforth all writing in Low German was perforce dialect writing. We have a sample on p. 144.

High German influence was naturally strongest in the towns.

The upper classes and the educated were the first to change to spoken High German. The use of High German in the north was clearly associated with class interests, which then expressed themselves in a contempt for Low German. Of this there is documentary evidence. Georg Torquatus, a clergyman and native of Magdeburg, tells us in his *Annalen*, written between 1567 and 1574, that the leading circles in the town had come to regard Low German as 'sächsische Barbarei'. As was noted above (p. 78), the last official ordinance to be issued in Magdeburg in Low German is dated 1570. But the change to spoken High German did not happen overnight, so to speak. It took place over a number of generations, during which time mixed varieties of spoken language came into being, collectively known as *Missingsch* or *Messingsch*, basically Low German but with a plentiful admixture of High German elements. While the educated classes were moving towards High German speech, the middle strata were acquiring *Missingsch*. This they used among themselves, reserving Low German—*Platt*—for their dealings with the lower orders and the country population. This was still, by and large, the position in the last century. It is reflected in the speech of the characters in Fritz Reuter's novels.

We may say that the North German countryside in particular remained faithful to Low German until the present century. But since the advent of the popular press and then the cinema and the radio, speech habits have greatly altered. Today, Low German is being abandoned on every hand. Many now regard it as a boorish, outmoded form of speech and consciously eschew it. To the mind of the ordinary speaker, Low German is merely an outlandish dialect of Standard (High) German. The Low German dialects are thus sharing the fate of the High German dialects which are all now retreating in one way or another before the advance of the standard language. But it will be some time yet before *Plattdeutsch* in its various dialects disappears altogether. It may be supposed that its influence will long continue in the host of words and expressions which colour the speech of all Germans from these parts. It will also continue in the pronunciation of High German as heard in the north. We should remember, for instance, that the distinction between

p, *t*, *k* (voiceless) and *b*, *d*, *g* (voiced) is only found in North
Germany. Most English people who have learnt German
unconsciously make the same distinction because it is also a
feature of English, but it is a fact that in Central and Southern
Germany, in Austria and Switzerland, *b*, *d*, *g* are voiceless in all
positions. We may note here, too, that the use of the glottal
stop is most marked in North Germany. Its use decreases as
one goes south, to disappear altogether in Bavarian and
Alemannic German.

THE LOW GERMAN ELEMENT IN STANDARD GERMAN

During the centuries many words from Low German have
found their way south into the High German dialects and some
of them have become an integral part of the vocabulary of the
modern standard language. An early example is *schlank*
'slender, slim', first appearing as MHG *slank* about 1160. In
origin it is MLG *slank*. This loan word advanced slowly, but
surely. Luther uses it, though not in his Bible; Adelung in
1798 still regarded it as dialectal, but today it is a standard
term heard everywhere. Its old competitor, a purely High
German word *rahn*, survives only to a limited extent in dialect
and is quite unknown to the great majority of German speakers.
Another early example is *hoffen* 'hope'. It is first recorded about
the same time as *slank*, becoming more frequent in the next
century as it spread south and by the end of the Middle Ages
it had completely ousted the traditional High German word for
this concept (*ge*)*dingen*. Everything points to *hoffen* being an
adaptation of MLG *hopen* to the High German phonetic system.
It is known that this sometimes happened and we have already
noted an example of a similar borrowing the other way round:
MLG *sik* from MHG *sich* (p. 83).

But, generally speaking, the Low German words were
taken into High German more or less in their Low German
form and precisely this enables us to identify them. A good
example is *fett* 'fat', met with in Central German texts from the
14th century. This is a Low German word originally, the
earliest known form being OLFr. *feitit*. This may be directly
compared with shifted OHG *feiȝȝit*, whence MHG *veiȝet*,
NHG *feist*. Thus *fett* and *feist* are doublets, but the Low

German form has become the standard term for 'fat', while the genuine High German form *feist* has a place in the standard language only because it has acquired a derogatory ring 'obese, fat and greasy'. Spreading south about the same time as *fett* was another Low German word *Lippe* 'lip'. Luther uses it, but the word had to be explained to his Upper German contemporaries. Their word was *Lefze*, a term in use today only in the sense 'lip of an animal'. Another word from the north is *plötzlich*, first occurring in various forms in High German texts from the 14th century on; it subsequently quite replaced the older word *gähling*, cognate with *jäh* 'precipitate'—a reminiscence remains in the little used literary word *jählings*.

Over a large part of the Low German area original *ft* has been changed to *cht*. Thus in Low German dialect—and in Dutch—*Lucht* 'air' contrasts with High German *Luft*. Several words in Standard German show this change, which immediately marks them out as northerners. For instance, *Schacht* in Low German dialect means any kind of shaft, but in Standard German it means only pit-shaft, the shaft of a tool etc. being *Schaft*. An explanation is not far to seek. *Schacht* is a technical term from Westphalia, the North German mining area; it has been in use since the end of the 13th century. North Germany was the land of the pit-heads, in South Germany mining was still open-cast. Another example of a doublet is the pair *sacht* and *sanft*. Low German has dropped *n* before the consonant group, a regular phonetic feature in the north. In its native districts *sacht* means soft in a wide sense, like *zacht* in Dutch, but in Standard German the meaning is 'gentle, quiet'. The other nuances are covered by *sanft* (and *weich*). Engl. *soft* is, of course, ultimately identical with *sacht* and *sanft*. *Schlucht* 'gorge, ravine' is yet another northerner of this type. The word did not, however, reach the High German area until modern times, but it has nevertheless succeeded in pushing its High German equivalent *Schluft* right into the background. This form is today entirely unknown to most Germans as it occurs only as a local topographical name, much as *Klinge* or *Tobel*. It is perhaps surprising that a Low German word rather than a High German term from the Alpine region of the south should become the generic expression for 'gorge, ravine'. But

maybe its very neutrality gave it an advantage over its High
German rivals.

It goes without saying that many Standard German words
referring to seamanship are of Low German origin, notably
Boot (itself a loan from Engl. *boat*). The names of seafish are
often Low German: *Butt* flatfish (*Steinbutt* turbot, *Heilbutt*
halibut). And then the sea itself. Ger. *See* 'sea, lake' was originally masculine, but in Low German the gender was changed
to feminine. The word is also used in Standard German with
this gender, but only when the meaning is 'sea,' the older,
masculine gender being reserved for the meaning 'lake'. Today
the essentially North Ger. *die See* competes with *das Meer*.
To some extent usage is defined, e.g. *die Ostsee* 'the Baltic',
but *das Mittelmeer* 'the Mediterranean'. But regional variations
are found. The North says *wir gehen an die See*, the South says *wir
gehen ans Meer* 'we're off to the seaside' (on holidays, for instance).

THE ROLE OF LATIN IN GERMANY

Even the most desultory account of the evolution of literary
German would be incomplete without some reference to the
once common use of Latin as a literary medium in Germany.

Before the Germans learned to write German, they learned
to write Latin. When the illiterate Franks burst into Roman
territory, they were faced with new problems of government,
at any rate in those parts where they formed no more than the
ruling minority (pp. 184 f.). They had perforce to rely on Gaulish
officials who naturally used Latin, the language of the Roman
administration. With the emergence of the Frankish feudal state
with its relatively complex organisation, written documents,
such as title deeds to land and property, legal codes, ordinances,
inventories, receipts etc., became necessary everywhere and so
Latin came to be employed in the purely German parts as well.
Its prestige would be greatly enhanced after the conversion of
the Frankish court to Roman Christianity in 496. As the con-
quests of the Franks brought one German tribe after another
under their domination, the use of Latin spread to all parts of
Germany as the sole language of administration (in which the
church officials played a leading part) and as the medium of

all serious writing. We saw (p. 9) how the writing of German first began in the glossing of Latin manuscripts. Original works in German eventually followed, but Latin remained the principal literary language until well on into modern times.

German began to challenge Latin in the administrative sphere in the 13th century. About 1225 Eike von Repgow translated the *Sachsenspiegel*, a book of common law, into Low German. This work came to be regarded as authoritative and exercised great influence; High German versions were made at once. The first imperial document in German dates back to 1240 and others followed, though not becoming frequent until about 1275. About 2,500 documents in German are known from the period prior to 1300—as against an estimated half a million in Latin. At the beginning of the 14th century most of the urban chanceries were using German; the others had followed suit by the middle of the century. There were social reasons for these changes. The use of Latin had been closely associated with traditional feudal interests and with the Church. But now the lower gentry and especially the influential burghers of the towns were replacing the feudal aristocracy as the leading force in society.

The Church however remained; the Church was the special guardian of Latin and continued to be hostile to the use of the vernacular in certain spheres. As part of the constant struggle against heresy the ecclesiastical authorities often inspired legislation forbidding the publication of religious matter in German. In 1369 Charles IV issued a general ban on all such books. In an age when so much thinking was done in terms of religion, the attitude of the Church was a hindrance to the development of German prose in an important sphere. As late as 1486 we find the Archbishop of Mainz making it clear in a censor's edict that German bibles would not be welcome in his diocese.

The first fruits of Gutenberg's art confirm the ascendancy of Latin. Gutenberg printed his first book, the Latin Bible, in 1445; not until 1461 did a German book, Boner's *Fabeln*, appear. Even when the Reformation had given such an impetus to publishing in German, far more Latin titles were being issued than German ones, though they would not reach the mass circulation of some of the German books. Seventy per cent of the titles published in Germany in 1570 were still in Latin. In 1681 the German titles appear in the majority for the first time, in 1691 the Latin titles appear in the majority for the last time. Forty years later, the Latin titles had sunk to under a third of the total.

In Germany as elsewhere the Renaissance gave Latin a new lease of life. The German Humanists and their followers indulged in a veritable cult of the language. They corresponded in Latin, they issued their polemical tracts in Latin, they even published original verse in Latin. This was strikingly the case in the 16th century, for the fervour of the Reformation not only led to a great increase in the use of German as a literary language, it also led to the intense cultivation of Latin in certain provinces of intellectual activity. At a time when, in other spheres, the use of Latin was declining, the language firmly maintained its position in the world of learning. An exceptional man like Paracelsus broke with tradition when he stayed to lecture in German at Bâle University between 1526 and 1528, but the turning point was not reached until Thomasius, one of the leading intellectuals of his time, began to teach through the medium of German at Leipzig University in 1681. He found many imitators and so the decisive break with Latin was made.

The use of Latin for so long meant a corresponding neglect of German and exercised a retarding influence on the development of literary German. When the native language finally ousted Latin, ample traces of the latter are seen not only in the many learned words adopted from Latin, but also in the cumbrous style of the German. We see the writers of the time literally struggling with the German language to make it capable of expressing concepts previously formulated in Latin only. A tendency to write in a style with involved periods, which was common until recently and is still not entirely obsolete, is part of the legacy of Latin.

BIBLIOGRAPHY

The rise of the modern standard language is treated in the general histories of German referred to in the 'General Bibliography' (p. 265).

A survey of the relationship between written and spoken German since the earliest times is given in W. Henzen, *Schriftsprache und Mundart*[2], Bern, 1954. This work includes a careful study of the development of the modern standard language.

E. A. Blackall, *The Emergence of German as a Literary Language 1700–1775*, Cambridge, 1959. A monograph presenting the results of much original research.

F. Tschirch, *1200 Jahre deutsche Sprache*[2], Berlin, 1969, illustrates the evolution of German style with biblical texts selected from all periods of the language.

K. von Bahder, *Zur Wortwahl in der frühneuhochdeutschen Sprache*, Heidelberg, 1925, considers the origins of a large number of words used in the standard language and discusses the factors which led to their adoption as the standard terms.

P. Kretschmer, *Wortgeographie der hochdeutschen Umgangssprache*[2], Göttingen, 1969. A copious collection of regional synonyms used in non-dialectal speech with notes on their history and distribution.

9

THE GERMAN DIALECTS

When thinking of German dialect, we must take care not to be influenced by our conception of dialect in England. By comparison with German standards, dialect in this country is not only very rare, but hardly dialect at all. In fact only in some parts of Lowland Scotland do we today find deviations from the literary norm which bear any comparison with conditions in many parts of the German-speaking world. In England, dialect speech has in fact either disappeared altogether or has been so reshaped by the standard language that its forms differ but little from the standard. But in the German-speaking countries standardisation has still far to go. Certainly the trends are all towards levelling out, particularly in Germany itself. The number of dialect speakers is constantly declining and the dialects themselves are being modified by the standard language at an ever-increasing rate. But all the same, dialect speaking is a reality and an important factor over wide areas of Germany, of Austria and, above all, in Switzerland and Luxembourg.

In what ways do the dialects differ from Standard German? They naturally differ in respect of phonetics; they also differ, sometimes very greatly, in vocabulary and grammar. In many cases the sum total of the differences is so great that the dialect is not immediately comprehensible at all to one who knows only Standard German, though with some experience it can usually be fairly soon understood by any German speaker. By the same token, many of the dialects are not mutually comprehensible, but dialect speakers naturally use the Standard Language when conversing with strangers. The variations in dialect speech found throughout the German-speaking area are well-nigh unlimited. Let us begin with some material which will give an idea of the nature of the phonetic differences. Map 127 of the *Deutscher Sprachatlas*, 1956, distinguishes 47 pronunciations of the Standard German word *was* and 20 pronunciations of its Low German equivalent *wat*. These are distributed, roughly speaking, as follows. The form *was* is characteristic chiefly of Swabia and the northern fringe of the High German area from Cassel to Dresden. The form *wos* is typical of Bavaria and Austria, but also occurs widely in Thuringia and Hessen. Furthermore, there are within these areas a number of intermediary pronunciations between *was* and *wos*. Theoretically the number of possibilities is infinite, but the *Sprachatlas* distinguishes the following: three *a*-sounds, front, back and neutral, likewise three *o*-sounds, and then a vowel mid-way between *a* and *o*. In some dialects the vowels are lengthened, e.g. *waas, woos*. Some have developed other vowels, e.g. *wäs, wes, wös, wus*, some again have developed diphthongs, e.g. *waos, waus, waös, wäus, woas, woes, wois, wous*. In a few places final *s* has been dropped, occasionally it has been lengthened: *wass, woss*. Although not indicated here, the pronunciation of the initial *w* will vary also. It is usually labiodental, but in some areas it is bilabial, in others it is pronounced as an English *w*. In an area just east of the Vogelberg, forms are found which have changed *w* to *b*, e.g. *bas, bos, bäs, bais, bous*. In the Low German area diversity is almost as great. Here the forms are characterised by the unshifted final *t*, hence *wat, wot, wät*, etc., though it is occasionally lost: *wa*. Forms with diphthongs are found, e.g. *waot, woat*. The change of *w* to *b* is present in a small area west of Coblenz around Arnsberg, e.g. *bat*.

Such a range of diversity is not at all unusual, in fact many words show even greater differences. Let us take another simple word like *Wort*. Maps 112–115 of the *Deutscher Sprachatlas*, 1954, plot no less than 338 forms of the word *Wort* in the dialects of Germany, Austria and Switzerland, not to mention a further 36 in Northern Germany for which Frisian or Danish influence is certain, or at least very likely. Leaving these on one side, we find that the evolution of a simple word like *Wort* has often resulted in forms which are quite unrecognisable to the uninitiated. Here are representative examples from the High German area:

WORT, *woort, woart, woaert, woaurt, woert, woärt, woört, woirt, woiert, wourt,*
wouart, wouert, wouirt, wouort, wart, waert, woert, waoert, wauort, wert, weart,
weirt, weort, weoart, weört, wiauert, wiort, wört, wöert, wöort, wöurt, wöuert,
wurt, wuart, wuert, wuirt, wuiert, wuört, wuort, wuoart, wuoert, würt, wüert, worrt,
woarrt, wortt, wurtt, wuorrt, woret, wot, woot, woat, wooat, woaet, woaot, woet,
wooet, woit, wojt, wout, wöt, wöat, wöaut, wat, waet, waot, waouet, waut, wäut,
wäuet, weot, weut, weuet, wiot, wut, wuut, wuat, wuet, wuät, wuäot, wuot, wuoat,
wüat, wüot, wott, woott, woatt, wooatt, woett, wött, wöitt, watt, waott, weuatt,
wuatt, wewert, wewart, wewet, wewat, worwat, weowwert, wewwat, worscht,
woarscht, woerscht, woirscht, wourscht, wouscht, wöscht, wörscht, waoscht, wauoscht,
wurscht, wuascht, wuoscht, worcht, wocht, woarcht, woacht, woicht, warcht, wacht,
waocht, wuacht, bort, boort, boart, boat.

We may, however, discern some measure of order among this
plethora of forms. First, there are the many variations of the
vowel. These reflect local developments of the original *o.* Of
the consonants, *r* is by far the most unstable. It may become
strongly fricative and voiceless, yielding such forms as *worcht*
or *worscht,* and then may be lost altogether, hence such forms as
wocht or *waoscht* (a form *woscht* is not recorded, perhaps fortuitously). In many places *r* has become vocalised, as in *woat,*
wooat, waet, and this development has doubtless led to a number
of the diphthongs recorded above. In a few cases a secondary
glide consonant *w* appears, e.g. *wewart, weowwert.* A parasitic
vowel has emerged between *r* and *t* in the one example *woret.*

The diversity of the High German area is paralleled in Low
German with forms like *wod, wood, woad, woaed, woid, wojd, waed,*
waid, waod, waud, weud, wud, wuod and others. In this area,
however, *r* has been lost everywhere, though some of the
diphthongs will be witnesses to its one-time existence. Here
of course the unshifted *d* answers to *t* in the High German.

It should be noticed that many features of dialect pronunciation are often heard even in the educated pronunciation of
Standard German. In the example *Wort,* for instance, the pronunciation of *r* is very variable. A great number of speakers
roll it (uvular *r*), but some trill it. Many, however, substitute
a vowel, hence pronunciations like *woat* (above) may also be
heard in educated speech.

The remarkable diversity of the German dialects is further
exemplified by the differences in local vocabulary. Some dialect
words are used over large regions of the country—and as a

consequence often appear in print as regionalisms—while others are confined to small areas or even to single villages, and are not ordinarily met with in writing at all. Many monographs deal with the distribution of dialect words and, by way of illustration, we take a recent study by Maria Ptatschek, *Lamm und Kalb* (*Bezeichnungen weiblicher Jungtiere in deutscher Wortgeographie*), 1957. This work is a collection and interpretation of the German names for 'ewe lamb' and 'heifer calf'. We here limit ourselves to the latter, and turn first to the index which lists the names for 'heifer calf'—in printed German usually *Färsenkalb* or *Kalbin*—substantially as follows:

Bamberle, Bätschel, Budele, Busele, Faikalb, Fasel(kalb), Färse(nkalb), (MHG) galte, Gissekalb, Hammele, Häns-che, Husele, Johl(kalb), Kalbe(n), Kalbin, Kalm(kalbl), Kälbermietzel, Kalmmockele, Kausekalb, Keek, Kiehbamberle -budele -hammele -husele -mietzel -mockele, Kiese(nkalb), Kießke, Kischkalb, Kisse, Kiwwekalb, Köj, Kuahbusel -kalm, Küahlekalb, Kühche(skalb), Kiesch, Kuhkalb, Kühle, Kuhmetschel, Kükualew, Küscher, Kusen, Mäxche, Meise(nkalb), Metzchen, Metzekalb, Mockele, Mohle(kalf), Mohlenösken, Mölla, Mollack, Mootschang, Motsche(nkalb), Mutterkalb, Nismänneken, Nöß(kalb), Quie(nkalf), Sterke-(nkalf), Thiesen(kalb), Tochterkalb, Ziecherl, Ziehkalb -mockele, Ziglkalbl, Zillkallef.

If we now consult the references in the text, we see that almost all the above names exist in a great variety of forms. For instance, the terms *Färse/Färsenkalb* fall into three groups corresponding to the three areas in which they are found, all of which are in North Germany and the dialects consequently Low German.

The first is a very small area near the mouth of the Ems. All the forms here have the diminutive element *k*: *Färske, Veerske, Verske, Veeske.*

The second area is somewhat larger. It comprises the rural districts around Aachen. The forms reported are *Fäesch, Fäsch, Feäsch, Fäech, Viäsch, Väsch.*

The third area is very much larger. It comprises the districts within roughly a hundred miles of Berlin. These are the forms: *Färse(nkalf), Ferse(nkalf), Färsche(n), Fersche(n)*. It is in this third area only that the compound forms occur. They arose because in certain places *Färse* shifted its sense to 'heifer' and then the second element became necessary to denote the heifer calf.

The position in these dialects is exactly reflected in Standard
Ger. *Färse* 'heifer' and *Färsenkalb* 'heifer calf', where Low Ger.
-kalf has been merely rewritten *-kalb*. That these words have
become literary German at all is exclusively due to the influence
of Berlin. It is natural that usages originating in its rural environment should frequently appear in Berlin and subsequently become widely diffused. So far these terms have made
little headway in the south. In Austria, for instance, the most
usual term is *Kalbin*.

All these various names for the heifer calf are not of equal
age. Most of them have only been recorded in recent times, but
the first date of recording is not an absolute guide to the actual
age of the word. Especially words of this nature may be missing
purely fortuitously from the older records of the language.
Some of them must have been in use before the beginning of
written records, as we shall show; on the other hand, many
are definitely recent and secondary.

Comparative evidence may sometimes enable us to postulate
the certain existence of a word for a period earlier than the one
in which it is first recorded. For a good example of this we may
take the word *Färse* mentioned above. This name is first
recorded in the early 13th century; the medieval spelling is
verse. There is no record of the word before this date. All the
same, an investigation into its affinities shows that not only
must it have existed at the time of the earliest literary
monuments in German, but also that it must have been in use
for at least something like a millennium before that.

What evidence is there for this conclusion? Regional NHG
Farre means today a mature bull, but in Early NHG the sense
'young bull' is attested. This is also the meaning of Middle
Dutch *var*, clearly the same word. It is undoubtedly ancient,
witness OHG *farro* with the meaning 'bull' without further
qualification. However this may be, the sense 'young bull' is
adequately attested and this, together with the form of the
word, makes it obvious that it could be somehow related to
Färse. But just how is it related? Let us look first at OHG *farro*.
Comparative evidence indicates that OHG *-rr-* could arise
from Prim.Gmc. *-rz-*, in which case the Prim.Gmc. form would
be **farzan*. Now Prim.Gmc. *-z-*, in its turn, is known to have

arisen from -s- by 'grammatical change' (Verner's Law), so that we may postulate a still earlier *farsán*. We now consider *verse* again. It is apparent that this word could derive from a Prim.Gmc. *fársjô*, which would automatically give *fers(i)a* for the oldest literary period (umlaut of *a*), whence *verse*. And this must be the form we want. Prim.Gmc. *farsán* m. and *fársjô* f. are obviously closely related words differentiated solely by the regular different terminations for masc. and fem. and by the position of the accent. Without a doubt these words referred to the young animal. They have every appearance of being part of the Indo-European inheritance for the base *far-* recurs in various IE languages, notably in Greek *póris* calf, Gmc. *far-* corresponding to Gk. *por-*.

The list of names for heifer cow, above, contains several other terms which are certainly of great antiquity. We have only space to draw attention to two or three of these. *Nöss*, in other places *Noss*, continues OHG *nôz* cattle, which corresponds to Old Engl. *néat*, Old Fris. *nât* and Old Norse *naut* do., and presupposes Prim.Gmc. *nautan*. The term *Kusen* can be shown to be secondary from *Kuse* (-*n* from oblique cases), which occurs in MHG *kuose*. This name has an exact parallel in Icelandic *kusa*, further the closely related Swedish *kossa* and Norwegian *kussa*, the latter also attested in the Old Norse period. All these words have meanings similar to the German. Clearly this term, too, goes back to Prim.Gmc. times and it is reasonable to see in it an *s*-extension of the base which otherwise gives the form *Kuh*, etc. A similar *s*-extension was identified in the words *Färse* and *Farre*, discussed above. It rather looks as though this -*s*- had a diminutive function. Finally we mention *Mohle* which is plausibly linked with OHG *mâla* young cow, a German name found in the *Lex Salica* (early 9th century). Its affinities, however, are unknown. These examples will suffice to show that the German dialects, taken together, preserve an enormous number of ancient words lost in the standard language. It goes without saying that the lexical treasures of the German dialects are of inestimable philological value. Much remains to be done before they are fully exploited.

In the sphere of grammar, differences between the dialects may also be considerable. The inflexional endings in the dialects are often at variance with those in the standard language. Some notion of these differences may be seen from the examples in the sections below. As a general statement, it may be said that the dialects tend to be more analytical in structure than the standard language. The case system is often more decayed, in fact a three-case system is usual, the genitive, apart from isolated survivals, having disappeared as a syntactical case. Possession is expressed periphrastically by *von* or by a dative construction: literary Ger. *der Hut des Vaters* becomes *der Hut vom Vater* or *dem Vater sein Hut* with, of course, the appropriate dialect modifications. It is noteworthy that this latter construction at any rate is ancient; it occurs in the Second Merseburg Charm, *c.*750: *demo Balderes volon sín vuoʒ*, i.e. *dem Fohlen Baldurs sein Fuß*. In the absence of a genitive, prepositions like *trotʒ, während, wegen* govern the dative (if there is one). Another notable feature of the dialects is the loss of the preterite, its functions being taken over by the perfect. Standard Ger. *ich sah* becomes *ich habe gesehen*, Standard Ger. *ich hatte gesehen* becomes *ich habe gesehen gehabt*. Dialects which have not lost the preterite entirely retain it only in the case of the most commonly used words, especially the preterite of *sein*. Semantically, the preterite and perfect have fallen together and this dialect development is reflected in the literary language too, where the more succinct preterite is the normal past tense, the perfect being a stylistic alternative. It should be remembered that Ger. *ich sah* and *ich habe gesehen* are entirely synonymous, whereas Engl. *I saw* and *I have seen* express somewhat different aspects of meaning. A further characteristic of the dialects, this time an ancient trait, is the use of the present tense to express future time, hence *wir gehen morgen* rather than *wir werden morgen gehen*. The latter is, historically speaking, a secondary development; in their earliest stages none of the Germanic languages had a special future tense. Like all spoken language, dialect speech tends to avoid dependent constructions. For example such a bookish sentence as *gestern kam ein Fremder, welcher ein Ferkel kaufen wollte* becomes in Bavarian dialect *gesting is a Fremda kemma, der hätt a Fakki kaafen mögn*, i.e. transposed into NHG: *gestern ist ein Fremder gekommen, der hat ein Ferkel kaufen mögen* (=*wollen*).

All the above features are also typical of at least the homely and intimate speech of the urban and other areas where dialect proper is no longer spoken. It may be emphasised that foreign learners should master them too, otherwise their German conversation is bound to be stilted and unnatural.

Specimens of Modern German Dialects

There is a far-reaching correspondence between the boundaries of the modern dialects and the boundaries of the administrative divisions of the Late Middle Ages. Clearly the latter have decisively affected the former. All the same the modern dialects, in so far as they are spoken on traditionally German territory, still fall into the three great divisions of High German, that is Middle Franconian, Bavarian and Alemannic, while in the north the Saxon (and Lower Franconian) dialects continue the Low German of the Middle Ages. Only in parts of Germany east of the Elbe, where the language was formerly Slavonic, have new dialects arisen which combine elements of the traditional groups. This is particularly the case in East-Central Germany, where colonists from different parts were thoroughly mixed and where, as a consequence, new dialect syntheses arose. Hence the dialects of this region have a composite character.

It is not practicable to attempt here an outline of dialect grammar, as the differences between the regions are so multifarious. The reader can, however, form some idea of the general character of many German dialects from the section on Pennsylvania German below, while the specimens of dialect which now follow—one from each of the four traditional groups—will illustrate the nature of the differences between the main regions.

For strictly scientific purposes dialect texts need to be transcribed in a consistent phonetic script, but in practice most dialect contributions for general reading are published in an orthography which is a compromise between a phonetic representation of the actual sounds of the dialect and the spelling of the standard language. Our specimens—short poems which have appeared in various local collections—are no exception to this rule.

Franconian—Odenwald

> Der Hannes aus 'm Ewerndorf
> gäiht an der Mihl vorbei;
> do gauzt a grouβer Millerschhund—
> de Hannes wurmt des glei.

> Der Hannes gäiht weirer mit seim Beil
> —der Hannes will in Wald—
> des Oundier äwer reiβt sich lous.
> Der Hannes rift: 'Boll, halt!'

> Der Boll, der fällt de Hannes oun
> un springt gar an em nuff;
> doch der verstäiht kaan Spaβ, nimmt 's Beil
> un girr em Boll aans druff.

> Der Boll is dout. Der Miller nimmt
> de Hannes ins Gericht.
> 'Werim schläigschte de Boll dann dout?'
> der Miller zornig spricht.

> ' 's war Noutwehr'.—'Recht. Was hoschte dann
> nit 's Helm genumme, Hans?'
> 'Ja, wann des Dier statt mit de Zäihn
> gebisse hett mim Schwanz!'

Mihl Mühle	*an em nuff* an ihm hinauf
gauzt bellt	*girr* gibt
glei gleich	*aans* eins, d.h. einen Schlag
weirer weiter	*werim* warum
des Oundier das Untier	*schläigschte* schlägst du
äwer aber	*hoschte* hast du
Boll Bulle, d.h. Bullenbeiβer	*'s Helm* den Stiel (des Beils)
fällt . . . oun fällt . . .an	*mim* mit dem

Bavarian—Carinthia

'*Du mei flochshaarats Dirndle,*
i hob di so gern,
und i khunnt wögn dei Flochshaar
a Spinnraderl wern.'

'*O du liagater Bua du,*
häär auf mit dei Khirn.
wonns long a so furt rödst,
so khriagst ma noch Birn'.

'*Es is so, es bleibt so,*
i khonn nix dafiar,
und so long miar Gott 's Löbm schenkcht
khäärt mei Herz nur diar!'

'*I bin a orms Maderl,*
hob nix ols a Mihl,
a Kholb und zwo Khiahlan,
und dos is holt nit viel.'

'*Brauch nix, mei liabs Herzle,*
kha Khuah und kha Mihl,
die Liab, dos is 's Anzge,
is olls, wos i will.'

'*Wonns a so manst, mei Buable,*
so glabet i 's schier.
No, do host zärscht a Busserl,
und donn khäär i diar'.

flochshaarats flachshaariges	*khäärt* gehört
Dirndle Mädchen	*orms* armes
khunnt könnte	*Maderl* Mädel
wögn wegen	*zwo Khiahlan* zwei Kühlein
Spinnraderl Spinnrad	*holt* halt, d.h. eben
wern werden	'*s Anzge* das Einzige
liagater Bua lügenhafter Bursche	*olls* alles
häär höre	*wonns a* wenn du es auch
Khirn Girren	*manst* meinst
wonns wenn du	*glabet* glaubte
Birn Birnen, d.h. Schläge	*zärscht* zuerst
Löbm Leben	*Busserl* Küßlein

Alemannic—Swiss (Yberg)

> *Ghörsch es i dr Tüffe lüte?*
> *'s chunt es böses Fahri zritte,*
> *'s chutet scho dur d Bärg und Flüehne,*
> *gleitig rüefed a dä Chüehne!*
> > *Ho Loba!*
>
> *D Wulche chönd mit Blitz und Dunnder,*
> *d Bärg und d Nosse schlüffid drunder,*
> *au dr Drusbärg häd e Chappe,*
> *'s Wätter stübt ehm drüber appe.*
> > *Ho Loba!*
>
> *Jez lat's a mit Dunndre, Blitze,*
> *'s pfifft dur d Rus, um d Felsespitze;*
> *'s isch as wie ne Hellerache—*
> *ghörsch nid drus all Tüfel lache?*
> > *Ho Loba!*
>
> *Alls e Gluet und alls es Tobe,*
> *'s wätterlaichnid unde, obe,*
> *'s cha mit üs nu gleitig ände,*
> *Herr, mier sind i Dine Hände!*
> > *Ho Loba!*

Readers unfamiliar with Swiss German will perhaps not object to a word-for-word translation into Standard German:

Hörst du's in der Tiefe läuten? / es kommt ein böses Unwetter zugeritten / es braust schon durch die Berge und Flühe (jähe Felsabhänge) / schnell ruft an die Kühe / Ho Loba! (Rufname, eig. Kuh)

Die Wolken kommen mit Blitz und Donner / die Berge und die Nosse (Felsspitzen) schlüpfen drunter / auch der Drusberg hat eine Kappe / das Wetter staubt ihm drüber ab (der Sturm jagt drüber hinab) / Ho Loba!

Jetzt läßt's an mit Donnern, Blitzen / es pfeift durch den Runs (Schlucht), um die Felsenspitzen / es ist als wie in einem Höllenrachen / hörst du nicht alle Teufel lachen? / Ho Loba!

Alles eine Glut und alles ein Toben / es wetterleuchtet unten, oben / es kann mit uns nun schnell enden / Herr, wir sind in Deinen Händen / Ho Loba!

Low Saxon—Ostfriesland

> *Dat Spinnweil schnurt, de Moeder spinnt,*
> *Bi't Für spöölt still hör lüttje Kind.*
> *Dat Für brannt hell, hell schint dat Lücht,*
> *De Rook stigt up, de Funke flügt.*
> *Dat Kind slöpt in, de Sandmann kummt,*
> *Acht Ühr de olle Tornklock brummt.*
>
> *'Buskerl geiht um, min sötet Kind,*
> *Man gau toe Bed, eher hei di find'.*
> *Dat Kind wakt up, rift de Oogen ut,*
> *'Is, Moeder, hei denn all darbut?'*
> *'Hörst neit, dat Nabers Jan all rehrt?'*
> *'Hett hei denn all?' fragt 't Kind verfährt.*
> *'Kumm gau, hier is din Awendbrot,*
> *Ick treck di ut, dann hest gin Not.*
> *Nu foll din Hand un bed din Christ;*
> *Dann leg ick di in 't warme Nüst'.*
> *Dat Spinnweil schnurt, de Moeder spinnt.*
> *Un is vergnögt, warm slöpt hör Kind.*

Spinnweil Spinnrad	*all darbut* bereits draußen
bi't Für beim Feuer	*Nabers* Nachbars
spöölt spielt	*rehrt* weint
hör lüttje ihr kleines	*verfährt* in Angst versetzt
Rook Rauch	*ick treck di ut* ich ziehe dich aus
olle Tornklock alte Turmuhr	*gin* keine
Buskerl Butzemann	*foll* falte
min sötet mein süßes	*bed* bete
man gau aber schnell	*Nüst* Nest
hei er	
rift de Oogen ut 'reibt die Augen aus', d.h. reibt sich die Augen	

BIBLIOGRAPHY

The *Handbuch zum Deutschen Sprachatlas*, by W. Mitzka, Marburg, 1952, gives a general account of the *Sprachatlas* (mentioned above) and comments on the results shown on its maps. The publication of these began in 1926 and is continuing. As the *Sprachatlas* is concerned primarily with sounds, the need was felt for a comparable series of maps which would plot the geographical distribution of synonyms. This need is being met by the publication, begun in 1951, of the *Deutscher Wortatlas*. Both atlases are published by the Dialect Institute attached to Marburg University.

W. Mitzka, *Deutsche Mundarten*, 1943. A comprehensive survey of the dialects with chapters on the history and methods of dialect research. E. Schwarz, *Die deutschen Mundarten*, Göttingen, 1950. In many ways a supplement to Mitzka's book. A most useful and practical book is R. E. Keller, *German Dialects*, Manchester, 1961, which gives accounts of the phonology and morphology of representative modern dialects, illustrated by texts of substantial length. All these works contain bibliographies.

A popular, eminently readable book on Bavarian German is J. Lachner's *999 Worte Bairisch*, Munich. It first appeared in 1930 and has often been reprinted.

The work by M. Hornung and F. Roitinger, *Unsere Mundarten*, Vienna, 1950, will be found a convenient guide to the peculiarities of the Austrian dialects.

The Linguistic Situation in Switzerland and Luxembourg

We have noted above that dialect speaking is especially significant in Switzerland and Luxembourg. We may now briefly consider the situation in these places.

SWISS GERMAN

The Swiss dialects form, broadly speaking, the High Alemannic sub-division of Alemannic. The mountainous country with its many remote valleys has been an ideal terrain for dialect proliferation. When the Swiss dialects were first comprehensively studied at the beginning of the last century, it became apparent that they were indeed remarkably diverse. Since then, however, the development of communications has led to important changes. As the outlying districts were brought into contact with wider areas, their linguistic peculiarities at once began to diminish and often disappeared. The influence of Standard German through the printed word and, more recently, through the wireless, has done much towards unifying Swiss idiom. But the standard language is not replacing Swiss German as the spoken medium. On the contrary, something like a Swiss koine *Schwyzertütsch/Schweizerdeutsch*, very different from Standard German, is emerging and proving viable. There were in Bâle and Zürich a couple of generations ago large and influential colonies of Germans, who spoke Standard German. One expected that Standard German would now make headway in Switzerland, at least in these cities. But this did not happen. The descendants of these Germans preferred *Schwyzertütsch;* in other words, they were assimilated. There is no doubt that *Schwyzertütsch* is felt to be an expression of German-Swiss nationality and that a certain opposition to Germany and things German, especially unpleasant ones, is implicit in this. On the other hand the Swiss can, of course, speak the standard language and it is used in parliamentary debates, in the courts, in the church, in the universities and the higher forms of schools. In public meetings, both Standard German and Swiss German may be heard. When the Swiss speak Standard German, their accent at once betrays their nationality. Moreover, the variety of Standard German used in Switzerland contains a very large number of regionalisms.

Schwyzertütsch is essentially a spoken language. It has made no serious progress as a written medium. The Swiss already have an adequate literary medium in the standard language and do not need another. Still, *Schwyzertütsch* sometimes has its uses in writing. On the pedestrian crossing next to the busiest corner in Bern you can see spelt in steel studs the warning *LÜEG RECHTS!* 'Look Right!' What more proof could one want that *Schwyzertütsch* is the native language of the German Swiss?

BIBLIOGRAPHY

A comprehensive account of the structure of a Swiss dialect and at the same time an illustration of its surprising richness and originality may be found in A. Weber, *Zürichdeutsche Grammatik*, 1948. R. E. Keller, *German Dialects*, pp. 30–115, gives an account of the German of Zürich and Bern.

LUXEMBOURG GERMAN

The linguistic situation in the Grand Duchy of Luxembourg must be unique. Some 300,000 persons, or 98% of the native inhabitants of the country, speak as their native idiom a now fairly uniform German dialect *Luxemburgisch* or, as they call it themselves, *Letzebursch*. These people read German newspapers and German books just like speakers of other German dialects, for Standard German is also an official language in Luxembourg. But it is not the only one. The main official language, the language which greets you on signs, notices and over shop windows is, by reason of a long tradition, French. Look along a street in Luxembourg City and you think you are in France, but glance at a bookshop and you seem to be in Germany. Then listen in to a local conversation—and you are at a loss to know where you are, so different is Luxembourg German from Standard German.

From time to time efforts have been made to develop LuxG as a literary language and as an official medium. This tendency was particularly marked just after the last war when many publications in LuxG appeared, including parliamentary debates, which, like all other discussions in Luxembourg, are carried on in the local tongue. But a reaction soon set in. In 1950 there were 23 publications in LuxG, but the number had dropped to 7 in 1954. The salient factor is that the Luxembourgers, having already German and French as literary languages, are content that their third medium—the one that comes naturally to them—should remain an oral one. All the same they take a patriotic pride in LuxG as the hallmark of their nationality, for both Standard German and more so French are felt to be foreign.

LuxG is a Franconian dialect, closely allied to the speech of the Moselle valley. Luxembourg has for long been politically orientated towards France and French has been extensively employed as the official language. As a consequence the dialect has escaped the levelling influence of Standard German, though under modern conditions NHG overshadows this as any other dialect. As a frontier dialect, LuxG has been much influenced by French throughout the centuries. In its structure LuxG is markedly analytical and word order, as a result, is more rigid than is usual in German.

BIBLIOGRAPHY

R. E. Keller, *German Dialects*, pp. 248–98, provides an excellent introduction to the study of LuxG. This account may be supplemented by R. Bruch, *Grammaire Luxembourgeoise/ Luxemburgische Grammatik*, Luxembourg, 1955. This concise, authoritative guide, edited bilingually, is addressed in the first place to those who already speak the language. But if used in conjunction with the first mentioned work, the foreign learner will rarely find it a disadvantage that the words and sentences in LuxG, quoted in illustration of the grammar, have as a rule been left untranslated. The book contains a full bibliography.

PENNSYLVANIA GERMAN

The German-speaking communities in Pennsylvania are referred to on p. 181. In the following, we give a short account of their language.

Pennsylvania German as it is technically called—locally *Pennsilfaanisch*(*-Deitsch*) or Pennsylvania Dutch—has a long history. It began as early as 1683 when the first settlers, mainly from the Rhenish Palatinate and Switzerland, settled in Germantown in East Pennsylvania. Up to 1775 the then border territory west of Philadelphia was almost exclusively German and the literary language of the inhabitants was Standard German. Between 1775 and 1820 the dialects of the original settlers began to coalesce to give a new, rather uniform dialect which in the main resembles the speech of the eastern Palatinate. Although English was the official language, it could make little headway as a colloquial medium in the rural areas of German-speaking East Pennsylvania. Indeed, for several generations, the Germans assimilated many non-German immigrants, hence we find among the native speakers of Pennsylvania German people with such surnames as Buffington, Burns and Mac-Pherson. But in the 1830s greatly increased immigration into Pennsylvania turned the German majority into a minority. English became more and more the literary language of the Germans, though it was not until about the beginning of this century that the mass of the German farmers became really bilingual. There has been a decline in the number of speakers since this time and the speech of the younger generation, at any rate, is plentifully interlarded with anglicisms.

As literary German was being superseded by English, efforts were made to develop Pennsylvania German as a literary medium and a modest amount of success was achieved. The language has been regularly written since about the middle of the last century and is the vehicle of a typical folk literature consisting mainly of poems, sketches and stories. Otherwise it can hardly compete with English as a written language, so that the Pennsylvania Germans are in an analogous position to, say, the Frisian minorities in Holland and Germany. They may habitually speak their own language, but their main, and, as often as not, sole literary medium is the state language. This is also substantially the situation in the Celtic fringes of Britain.

Outline of Pennsylvania German

SOUNDS AND SPELLING

Although PG has been in written use for over a hundred years, a uniform orthography has not been agreed upon. The various systems fall into two categories: an English type and a German type. One of the latter is used here as we follow Buffington and Barba, *A Pennsylvania German Grammar*, 1954, the fullest introduction to the language which has appeared so far.

The following spelling conventions are to be noted:
PG *ae* = NHG *ä*, PG *gg* (only medially) = approximately NHG *j*.

NOUNS

PG retains the three genders, though nouns occasionally have a gender different from that of their NHG equivalents: *die Dann* thorn, *die Haar* hair (NHG *der Dorn, das Haar*).

PG nouns no longer have any distinct case endings. The formation of the plural is likewise much simpler than in NHG. Four main patterns are observed:

Plural in *-e*, all genders: *der Daag* day, *die Nacht* night, *es Dier* animal; pl. *Daagge, Nachde, Diere*.

Plural in *-er* with umlaut where applicable, neut. and masc.: *es Buch* book, *es Loch* hole, *es Schtick* piece, *der Deich* pond, *der Mann* man; pl. *Bicher, Lecher, Schticker, Deicher, Menner*. Here belong also diminutives in *-che: es Kindche* (*cf.* NHG *Kindchen*), pl. *Kindcher*.

Plural in *-s*, all genders, mostly English loans: *der Schtor* shop (Amer. store), *die Schtori* story, *es Peement* pavement; pl. *Schtors,*

Schtoris, Peements. Similarly *der Kall* fellow, pl. *Kalls* (cf. NHG *Kerls*).

No special plural ending, masc., fem., occasionally neut.: *der Hund* dog, *es Bee* leg, pl. *Hund, Bee.* There is frequently umlaut: *der Zaah* tooth, *der Wagge* cart, *die Maus* mouse, *die Kuh* cow; pl. *Zeeh, Wegge, Meis, Kieh.*

Possession is expressed by the usual circumlocutions: *em Voggel sei Nescht* or *es Nescht vum Voggel* the bird's nest.

ARTICLES

The articles have only two cases: the common case (really the old nominative having the functions of the accusative as well) and the dative. The definite article declines as follows: sg. com. m. *der*, f. *die*, n. *es*, dat.m.n. *em*, f. *der;* pl.com. *die*, dat. *de.* The indefinite article: com.m.f.n. *en*, dat. m.n. *me*, f. *re.*

ADJECTIVES

These are declined for the common and dative cases. As in NHG there are three declensions (strong, weak, mixed), but owing to the regular loss of final *n* in PG the plural form always ends in *-e.* The inflexional forms of *gut* 'good' are:

Strong sg.com.m. *guder*, f. *gudi*, n. *gut*, dat.m.n. *gudem*, f. *guder;* pl. *gude.*
Weak sg.com.m.f.n. *gut*, dat. and pl. *gude.*
Mixed — com. as in strong declension, dat. as in weak.

NUMERALS

1 *eens*, 2 *zwee*, 3 *drei*, 4 *vier*, 5 *fimf*, 6 *sex*, 7 *siwwe*, 8 *acht*, 9 *nein*, 10 *zehe*, 11 *elf*, 12 *zwelf*, 13 *dreizeh*, 14 *vazeh*, 15 *fuffzeh*, 16 *sechzeh*, 17 *siwwezeh*, 18 *achtzeh*, 19 *neinzeh*, 20 *zwansich*, 21 *eenunzwansich*, 30 *dreissich*, 40 *vazich*, 50 *fuffzich*, 60 *sechzich*, 70 *siwwezich*, 80 *achtzich*, 90 *neinzich*, 100 *en hunnert*, 1000 *en dausend.*

PRONOUNS

The personal pronoun has three cases: nom., acc. and dat., as follows:

Sg.nom.	*ich*		*du*		*er*	*sie*	*es*
acc.	*mich*		*dich*		*ihn*	,,	,,
dat.	*mir*		*dir*		*ihm*	*ihre*	*ihm*

Pl.nom.	*mir*	*dihr*,	*ihr*,	*nihr*		*sie*	
acc.	*uns*		*eich*			,,	
dat.	,,		,,			*ihne*	

The three forms of the 2nd pl.nom. are regional variants. The unemphatic forms of *mir*, *dir* and *dihr, ihn, ihm, ihre, ihr, nihr, ihne* may be indicated in writing: *mer, der, en, em, re, er, ner, ne.*

The nom. pl. *mir* is a secondary form of *wir*, widespread in German dialects; it arose as explained in the chapter on Yiddish (under 'Pronouns'). The forms *dihr* and *nihr* developed from such groups as *seid⁀ihr* and *sin⁀ihr*, see the verb 'to be' below.

The reflexive pronoun is as in NHG: *sich*.

The possessives are:

sg. *mei* my, *dei* your, *sei* his, its, *ihre* her; pl. *unser* our, *eier* your, *ihre* their.

VERBS

The PG verb is more analytical than its NHG counterpart. With one exception, see *sei* 'be' below, all PG verbs have lost the preterite indicative, though the preterite subjunctive survives in some 15 common verbs. Strong and weak verbs are distinguished solely by the manner of forming the past participle. There is no present participle. Inflexions are as follows:

Infin. *schreiwe* write
Pres.sg.1 *schreib*, 2 *schreibscht*, 3 *schreibt;* pl. *schreiwe*
Imper.sg. *schreib*, pl. *schreiwe*   Past part. *geschriwwe.*

In certain districts the older 2nd pl. indic. and imper. *schreibt* is used.

Similarly the weak verb *mache* make, apart from past. part. *gemacht.*

Examples of verbs with strong past participles: *verliere* lose, *verlore; drinke* drink, *gedrunke; nemme* take, *genumme; lese* read, *gelese; graawe* dig, *gegraawe.*

The verbs 'TO BE' and 'TO HAVE' in PG:

Infin. *sei, hawwe*

Pres.sg.1 *bin, hab,* 2 *bischt, hoscht,* 3 *iss, hot;* pl. *sin, hen* (2 also *seid, hett*)

Imper.sg. *sei, hob,* pl. *seid, hen (hett).*   Past part. *gewest, ghatt*

Subj.sg.1,3 *waer, hett,* 2 *waerscht, hettscht;* pl. *waere, hedde* (2 also *waert, hett*)

The pret. indic. of *sei* survives : sg. 1,3 *waar,* 2 *waarscht;* pl. *waare* (2 also *waart*).   It is commonly used to form the past durative, see below.

Compound tenses are formed with the same auxiliaries as are in use in (dialectal) NHG, e.g. *ich hab gschriwwe* I have written, *ich hab gschriwwe ghatt* I had written, *ich bin gebliwwe* I have stayed, *ich bin gebliwwe gewest* I had stayed. Similarly the future: *ich wa schreiwe* I shall write (*wa* = NHG *werde,* the remaining forms being sg.2 *wascht,* 3 *watt;* pl. *warre* (2 also *watt*). In practice, however, future time is normally expressed by the present tense, e.g. *ich schreib glei* I'll write straightaway (NHG *ich schreibe gleich*), the compound future expressing chiefly probability, hope etc., as often in NHG. Passive constructions are common, thus *es watt gschriwwe* it is (being) written. PG makes frequent use of a durative: *ich bin am Schreiwe* I am writing, and an emphatic: *ich duh gaar net schreiwe* I'm not writing at all. Both these constructions may be heard locally in colloquial German: *ich bin am Schreiben, ich tue gar nicht schreiben.*

The surviving subjunctives are used mainly as in NHG, e.g. *ich hett gschriwwe* I would have written, *ich waer gebliwwe* I would have stayed (NHG *ich hätte geschrieben, wäre geblieben*). It is, however, also employed in ways not found in Standard German, for example in indirect speech: *er saagt, ass er sei Fraa sehne deet* he says that he sees his wife. Transposed into NHG this would give *er sagt, daß er seine Frau sehen täte.* Though historically a preterite subjunctive, PG *deet* here functions as a present.

THE VOCABULARY OF PG

The vocabulary of PG is seen to be typically that of a south-west German dialect with some borrowings from literary German and a considerable admixture of English elements.

It follows that PG contains many words which either do not occur in Standard German at all or are regional only, e.g. the nouns *Bauerei* farm, *Gaul* horse, *Hinkel* chicken, as opposed to usual NHG *Bauernhof*, *Pferd*, *Küchlein/Küken*, or the verbs *blaffe/gauze* bark, *drickle* dry, *schwetze* speak, which have exact correspondences in the related German dialects, but the normal NHG words are *bellen*, *trocknen*, *sprechen*. In Standard German, *Gaul* and *schwätzen* have pejorative nuances not at all implicit in the corresponding Pennsylvanian. Words now mostly felt to be old-fashioned in Germany may continue unimpaired in PG, e.g. *Sack* pocket, *Schnuppduch* handkerchief. *Sack* and *Schnupftuch* are not heard very much in German today, the ordinary words being *Tasche* and *Taschentuch*. The PG word for potato is *Grummbier*, cf. regional NHG *Grundbirne*. The form *Bier* 'pear' is more original than *Birne*, where *n* has been taken over from the plural, cf. MHG *bir*, pl. *birn*, OHG *bira;* the source is an early Romance form **bira/pira*, Monastic Lat. *pira*.

THE ENGLISH ELEMENT

Inevitably English words are being adopted more and more by the Pennsylvania Germans and in the present conditions of bilingualism the impact of English upon PG is simply enormous.

Here are a few common examples of English loans; it will be noticed that they have been thoroughly assimilated to the PG phonetic system, in all essentials that of the Franconian dialect of the Rhenish Palatinate: *der Koschdemer* customer, *der Schmok* smoke, *die Kraut* crowd, *die Tscheel* jail, *es Kaundi* county, *es Sobber* supper; *dresse* dress, *ringe* ring (a bell), *schmoke* smoke, *tschumpe* jump; *reddi* ready; *ebaut* about. Naturally, hybrids occur: *der Groossdaadi*, *die Groossmammi*. Occasionally a German word takes on a new meaning through association with a similar sounding English word: *des iss es Meedel, ass ich net gleich* this is the girl that I don't like. Loan translations are frequent: *der Riggelweg* railway, *mitaus* without, *scheeguckich* nice-looking. Very many English idioms re-appear in German garb: *es iss uff zu dir* it's up to you, *ich bin alrecht* I'm alright, *mir sin kalt* we're cold, *was Zeit iss es?* what time is it? These contrast with more genuine German phrases such as: *es ist deine Sache, bei mir ist alles in Ordnung, uns ist kalt, wie spät ist est (wieviel Uhr ist es)?*

It cannot be said that many of these loans have been actually necessary. But such things really illustrate the inevitable weakness of a mainly oral medium like PG in face of the overwhelming attraction of the major language.

Specimen of Pennsylvania German

From Buffington and Barba, *PG Grammar* (see Bibliography).

Do reecht die Eva nuff un robbt eener vun de Ebbel ab un gebt em Aadam die Helft devun. Un wie sie der Abbel gesse hen ghatt, do hen sie sich uff eemol arrig gfarricht un gschemmt un hen sich gschwind hinnich de Hecke verschlubbt. Zum Unglick iss dann graad der liewe Gott in der Gaarde kumme un hot gerufe: 'Aadam! wu schteckscht du dann?' Un wie er weit un breet nix gsehne hot vum Aadam un aa ken Andwatt grickt hot, do hot er glei gedenkt: 'Harriyesses, die sin mer am End doch an mei Abbelbaam gange.'

Noochderhand sin der Aadam un die Eva hinnich de Hecke rauskumme un hen so arrig geziddert, ass der liewe Gott glei gewisst hot, was do los iss. Nadierlich waar er arrig bedriebt un hot gsaat: 'Aadam, fer was hoscht du mir net gfolligt? Des hett ich gaar net vun dir gedenkt, ass du mich so bedriegge deedscht. So ebbes iss mir in meim ganse Lewe noch net bassiert!'

'Ach, liewer Gott, ich bin net schuld draa, ich kann nix defor,' hot der Aadam geandwatt, ''s iss die Eva gewest, die iss schuld draa—die hot der Abbel abgerobbt! Ich hab sie gewannt un's hot nix gebatt.'

'Ich kann aa nix defor,' hot die Eva gheilt. 'Do iss ken Mensch schuld draa als wie graad selli falsch Schlang—die hot mich verblaudert.'

do da

neffreeche hinaufreichen

abrobbe abpflücken

Abbel Apfel

esse essen, pp. *gesse*

arrig 'arg', sehr

farrichde fürchten

hinnich hinter

verschlubbe 'verschlüpfen', verstecken

Gaarde Garten

sehne sehen, pp. *gsehne*

aa auch

griegge kriegen, pp. *grickt*

Harriyesses Herr Jesus

geh gehen, pp. *gange*

noochderhand nachher

rauskumme herauskommen, pp. *-kumme*

nadierlich natürlich

bedriebt betrübt

saagge sagen, pp. *gsaat*

follige folgen

des dies

bedriegge betrügen

duh tun, pret.sg.2 *deedscht*

ebbes etwas

draa dran

wanne warnen

badde nützen

heilen 'heulen', weinen

selli jene

verblaudere 'verplaudern', hineinreden

---

die Eva . . . em Aadam: the article with proper names is a feature of southern German dialects.

gesse hen ghatt: lit. *gegessen haben gehabt.* This word order is paralleled in many German dialects, though *gegessen gehabt haben* is widespread in other areas. The standard language normally has, of course, the simple pluperfect *gegessen hatten.*

weit un breet: cf. MHG *wît, breit.* Whereas MHG *î* and *ei* have fallen together in NHG to give *ei* (*weit und breit*), some dialects have kept the sounds distinct. For PG we may formulate the sound changes as follows: MHG *î* > PG *ei*, MHG *ei* > PG *ee.*

un wie er weit un breet nix gsehne hot vum Aadam: the NHG verb would normally come to the end of the clause, i.e. *von Adam gesehen hat* (or *sah*), but the Pennsylvanian order is normal in German dialects and common in colloquial speech everywhere. It is now appearing more and more in simple written style.

noochderhand: Standard German has used *vorderhand* 'for the time being' since the first half of the 18th century, but its 'opposite' *nachderhand* remains confined to certain dialects. One might in principle compare *Frühling*, which has replaced *Lenz* as the ordinary word for springtime, but its opposite *Spätling* 'autumn' has been unable to shake the position of *Herbst* and remains a little known, purely local expression.

ass: this aphetic form of *daß* also occurs in Germany; it is standard in Yiddish (*az*).

fer was: NHG *für was* is commonly heard in dialect and in much colloquial speech either beside, or instead of, *warum.*

ebbes: this alternative development of MHG *etewaz* 'etwas' is very widespread in German dialect, cf. *epes* in Yiddish ('Germanic Component').

badde: this impersonal verb occurs commonly in western German dialects, occasionally appearing in print as *batten.*

als wie: a favourite combination in many dialects and in unaffected colloquial speech, but avoided in careful style. It is, however, occasionally classical, e.g. in Faust:

> *Da steh' ich nun, ich armer Tor!*
> *Und bin so klug als wie zuvor.*

seller m., *selli* f., *sell* n. (= NHG *selb-*) 'that' has replaced *jener* as in several German dialects.

Our second specimen is a rendering of Old Mother Hubbard, here called *Alt Mammi Schwank,* by John Birmelin (1873–1950).

> *Die alt Mammi Schwank,*
> *Sie geht an der Schank*
> *Un sucht ihrem Hundel en Gnoche:*
> *Do waar nix zu finne*
> *Wie Schtaab un Schpinne,*
> *Es Hundel hot gschnuffelt, geroche.*

> *Noh geht sie ins Wattshaus*
> *Fer'n Kessel voll Bier,*
> *Un kummt sie, do batzelt*
> *Er hinnich der Dier.*

> *Des Hundel iss oweds*
> *Als wacker gebliwwe,*
> *Hot Bicher gelese*
> *Un alsemol gschriwwe.*

(*noh* < *dernoh* darnach, *Wattshaus* Wirtshaus, *batzelt* purzelt, *hinnich der Dier* hinter der Tür, *des* dieses, *oweds* abends, *als* immer, *wacker* wach, *alsemol* manchmal).

BIBLIOGRAPHY

A. F. Buffington and P. A. Barba, *A Pennsylvania German Grammar,* Allentown, Pennsylvania, 1954. A comprehensive general textbook containing graduated lessons, reading material and glossaries. An appendix deals with the relationship of PG to other German dialects.

An informative account of the external history of PG is given by R. C. Wood 'Pennsilfaanisch' in W. Stammler, *Deutsche Philologie im Aufriß,* vol. I, 1952, cols. 785–807.

10

THE EXTENT OF THE
GERMAN-SPEAKING AREA THROUGH
THE CENTURIES

We begin with the main German-speaking area.

STATISTICS

German is spoken as the first language by over 93 million people living in a continuous linguistic area made up of the following territories: the German Federal Republic (including the Saarland) 61 million, the German Democratic Republic (including East Berlin) 17 million, West Berlin 2 million, Austria rather more than $7\frac{1}{2}$ million, the Italian province of Bolzano (the northern half of South Tyrol) at least 200,000, the major part of Switzerland somewhat over 4 million, Liechtenstein 25,000, the major part of the French provinces of Alsace and Lorraine over $1\frac{1}{2}$ million, Luxembourg 350,000, the eastern fringe of Belgium especially in the districts of Eupen and Malmédy 60,000, North Slesvig in Denmark about 30,000.

RECENT LOSSES IN THE EAST

Before 1945 the area occupied by native speakers of German was considerably greater than it is now. As a result of the Second World War, Germany lost East Prussia together with Danzig and the Memel Territory, and the frontier with Poland was shifted back to the Oder-Neisse line with Stettin and Swinemünde falling to Poland. The area between the pre-1939 Polish-German frontier and the present Oder-Neisse line with a population of some 7 millions was almost entirely German. East Prussia with Danzig and the Memel Territory had a population of close on 3 million, of whom 95% were Germans. In addition, German was the mother tongue of at least 1 million persons living in pre-1939 Poland, mainly in the districts of the Polish Corridor. Such Germans as had not already fled or been evacuated from these areas were, for the most part, deported to Germany after the conclusion of hostilities. An area around Königsberg, renamed Kaliningrad, and the Memel Territory are now part of the U.S.S.R.; the other districts are Polish. The few Germans remaining east of the Oder-Neisse are unlikely to retain their language for long; they will eventually be absorbed by the Polish majority. In Czechoslovakia, the areas adjoining the frontiers with Germany and Austria were either entirely German-speaking or mixed, i.e. partly German, partly Czech. As mentioned on page 178, enclaves of German speech existed far inside the country. Owing to centuries of German and Austrian political ascendancy, the German language enjoyed great prestige in Bohemia and Moravia. The descendants of German settlers maintained the German language even in the predominantly Czech-speaking towns. About 10% of the population of Prague spoke German as the first language. Altogether German was the native language of some 3¼ million Czechoslovak subjects in 1938. But since 1945 this situation has been radically altered. The Germans within the pre-1938 frontiers were expelled en masse. Those few who were allowed to opt to stay may be expected to become assimilated in the near future.

Map 4 shows the extent of the eastern areas lost to German since 1945.

GERMAN IN THE SOUTH TYROL

To the south and west the linguistic frontiers were not so affected by the outcome of the war, but conditions have not been static here either.

The South Tyrol was allotted to Italy by the Allies in 1919 in spite of the protestations of the almost exclusively German-speaking population of the northern half of the area. The German speakers numbered 230,000 in 1921. Italy demanded this territory not only because it is an important source of hydro-electric supply, but also because Italy required a strategic frontier on the Brenner. During the Fascist period, Italianisation was actively encouraged. German had to give way to Italian in the schools, the German population was even called

German replaced by Polish (on U.S.S.R. territory also by Russian and Lithuanian.)

German replaced by Czech (In the East by Slovak.)

MAP 4

Eastern areas lost to German since 1945

upon to adopt Italian names. Government-supported indust-rialisation caused a large movement of Italian proletarians into the towns in the area, especially into Bozen/Bolzano, the chief centre. In 1920, Bozen had 20,000 mainly German-speaking inhabitants. Within two decades the number was 50,000, the newcomers being monoglot Italians. The marked anti-German policy of the Italian administration in South Tyrol was ob-viously distressing to the Nazi government and led to diplo-matic exchanges. In 1939 it was agreed that German speakers south of the Brenner could opt for resettlement in the *Reich* by 31st December, 1942; about 165,000 Germans in South Tyrol are stated to have chosen this course and, in spite of war-time difficulties, many were actually transferred to Germany.

Post-war administrations have not shown the intolerance of the Fascist period and the area now enjoys a measure of local autonomy. The German language has official status and is taught in the schools besides Italian. All the same, the con-tinuing immigration of Italians is undermining the position of German. The balance of forces is such that it is the German speakers who have to learn Italian, not vice versa. Many are bilingual already and, as often happens in analogous cir-cumstances, bilingualism here is most likely the prelude to assimilation. And indeed the number of German speakers is on the decrease.

In the South Tyrol dialect speaking is usual; the dialects themselves are an organic part of the Austro-German dialects spoken north of the state frontier. In earlier times, the lin-guistic boundary between German and Italian ran consider-ably further south than at present. In the Early Middle Ages, Tirolean German perhaps formed a continuum with Lango-bardic, the Old High German dialect of Lombardy.

SWITZERLAND

The rather more than 4 million Swiss who speak German as their native language constitute about 65% of the total popula-tion of Switzerland. Close on one million or 18% use French, about 600,000 Italian, less than 45,000 Romaunsch (see Map 5). In Switzerland there are no bilingual areas officially, so that, for example, German Swiss moving into the French part

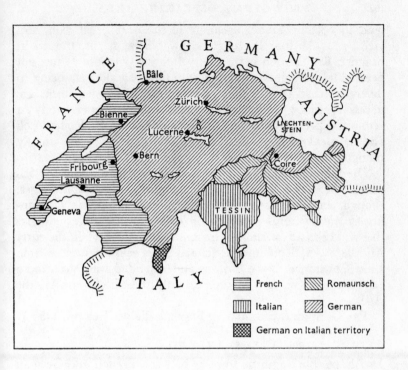

MAP 5

Languages in Switzerland

161

tend to become French-speaking in the next generation, and vice versa. All four languages enjoy official status, though in practice Romaunsch is in a very inferior position. It has not been able to achieve a literary standard, the dialects being so divergent that at least four, sometimes five written forms are necessary. Since printing under these circumstances is rarely an economic proposition, very little is published in Romaunsch and its speakers inevitably turn to German. They are usually bilingual.

The Germanisation of the S.E. of Bern began about the 5th century and was largely completed during the Middle Ages, though some of the most southern valleys remained Romance-speaking until the 16th or 17th centuries. German has likewise been advancing in the east of the country. In the early Middle Ages, Romaunsch dialects were spoken almost from Lake Constance to the Grisons and extended into Vorarlberg (Austria), where they lingered on until the close of the Middle Ages.

The German Swiss commonly speak dialect (see pp. 145 f.).

ALSACE-LORRAINE, SAARLAND

In Alsace, the linguistic frontier between French and German has been relatively stable since the Middle Ages; in Lorraine, however, French has been slowly advancing. As may be seen from Map 6, Alsace is almost entirely German-speaking, whereas Lorraine has a considerable French minority. In both provinces dialect speaking is customary. The dialects of Alsace belong to the Alemannic group, those of Lorraine are Franconian.

Alsace was first joined to France in 1648, Lorraine in 1766. By the middle of the last century French was coming to be regarded as the language of polite society in Alsace-Lorraine and was making headway in the towns. These developments were reversed when the territory was annexed by Prussia in 1871 after the Franco-Prussian War. The language of administration was henceforth German and education, which now became free and compulsory, was conducted through the medium of German wherever German was the usual language. But Prussia wished to Germanise the territory entirely and

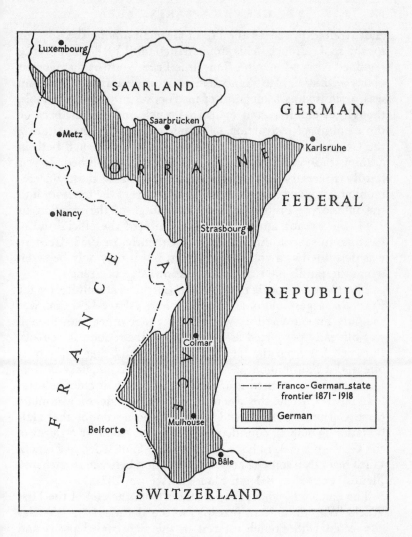

MAP 6

German and French in Alsace-Lorraine

endeavoured to spread the use of German among the 15% or so who spoke French. This aim persisted until 1918 when France regained Alsace-Lorraine. This time France pursued a vigorous policy with a view to Frenchifying the whole territory. German was permitted as a medium of instruction in primary schools, though all children had to learn French and French became the medium of instruction in higher education. Then, during the German occupation of 1940–44, the use of French both in administration and education was promptly abolished. It was hardly necessary any longer since the Nazis most unceremoniously moved many French inhabitants of the territory into the interior of France. Taking advantage of the reaction in 1944, the French administration prohibited the official use of German in schools altogether. Subsequently, in 1953, German was permitted as a voluntary subject, but it may only be taken when the pupils have acquired a knowledge of French.

The German speakers of Alsace-Lorraine constitute by far France's largest national minority and Alsace-Lorraine was the only French territory where a language other than French was officially permitted as a medium of instruction in schools. But such has been the fate of this borderland that today over one and a half million persons, whose native language is German, are being trained to regard French as their chief cultural language. Clearly the attempt is being made to assimilate these German speakers and there can be no doubt that Gallicisation is making considerable headway. About two-thirds of the German speakers have at least some knowledge of French. Until recently a somewhat similar situation between French and Flemish existed in Belgian Flanders (see pp. 187 f.).

The Saarland, whose special status from the end of the First World War until 1957 (except for the decade 1935–45) was connected with French interest in the rich coal deposits and the iron and steel plant, must be described as entirely German-speaking.

LUXEMBOURG, BELGIUM AND DENMARK

Apart from a single Walloon-speaking village in the north near the Belgian frontier, the language of the Grand Duchy of Luxembourg is entirely German. In speaking, dialect is the

normal form (see pp. 146 ff.). In Belgium, the eastern fringe north
of Luxembourg is German-speaking. Here lie the districts of
Eupen and Malmédy, the former exclusively German, the
latter having an important Walloon-speaking area (the town
of Malmédy and its environs). These districts went to Belgium
by the Treaty of Versailles in order to give Belgium control of
the rivers Vesdre and Amblève. Of the 60,000 German
speakers in the area, very many know French as well, and the
number is increasing. Luxembourg German is spoken by a
small and dwindling number in the Arlon district. (See Map 8.)

Holland has no German minority problem. Here matters
have been more settled. Moreover the linguistic situation is
radically different from elsewhere; the nature of the Dutch-
German linguistic boundary is discussed on pp. 188 f.

Finally, there is the German minority in Denmark. The
30,000 strong German minority living in villages and small
towns in North Slesvig just over the Danish border are doubtless well content with their lot. Their economic position is good
and their language fully recognised by the Danish constitution.
We have seen evidence for officially inspired assimilation of the
German-speaking minorities, e.g. in Italy and France, but
this does not seem to be the case at all with the Germans in
Denmark—there is also a Danish minority just south of the
frontier in Germany! Yet it seems that even here the state
frontier must eventually become the linguistic divider. Germans living in Denmark are in daily contact with Danes and
naturally learn Danish. Their interests, especially the all-
important economic ones, tend to be with Denmark and it is to
be supposed that this small minority will eventually be Dani-
cised. Likewise the Danes living south of the border will ultimately be Germanised; in fact the process of Germanisation
has been continuing here for a long time. In the early Middle
Ages, Danish was spoken as far south as the Eider, the Danes
having advanced south to occupy land deserted by the Jutes
and Angles on their migrating to Britain in the fifth and sixth
centuries. Since the beginning of modern times at least, Danish
has been slowly retreating north. (See Map 2.)

THE NON-GERMAN-SPEAKING DISTRICTS OF AUSTRIA AND GERMANY

A review of the present boundaries of the German-speaking world would be incomplete without some reference to the non-German districts of Austria and Germany.

In certain rural areas along the southern frontier of Austria, notably in Carinthia, the native language is Slovene, locally often known as *Windisch*. These Slovene speakers are cut off from Slovenia proper by the formidable barrier of the Kara-wanken mountains which form not only the political, but also a natural frontier. Not more than 20,000 people on Austrian soil, chiefly south of the Drau and Gail, use the Slovene language. Further east, in Burgenland, a similar number speak Croat as their first language—similar enclaves stretch south-ward through Hungarian territory to the north-east boundary of the main Croat-speaking area on the lower Drau (Drava)—while a few thousand others in Burgenland have Hungarian as their mother tongue. All these groups are bilingual and are in fact being assimilated, much as the German-speaking groups on the other side of the frontier are also losing their national identity. In Germany a few thousand Danish speakers live in Schleswig just south of the state frontier. In North Friesland and, to a minute extent in East Friesland, the first language in some districts is Frisian (see Chapter 12). Following the general fate of most minorities in Europe today, these groups are losing ground, and all the quicker since they are so small. A remarkable exception is the only other enclave of non-German speech in Germany, that of the Lusatian Wends, and the circumstances warrant special mention.

The territory of the Lusatian Wends (or Sorbs) begins about 50 miles south of Berlin (see Map 7). The towns in the area are the creations of German colonists and have always been mainly German-speaking. Wendish predominates only in a few rural districts, especially north-west of Bautzen; in others there are more monoglot Germans than Wendish speakers. The Wends are the descendants of the Slavonic population which, in the early Middle Ages, extended eastward to the Saale (see p. 170). But during the course of the Middle Ages, the

MAP 7

Lusatia and the Wendish enclave

Slavonic tribes lost their independence to German princes and were finally Germanised, except for the present enclave where, in a rather poor region of swamp, forest and low-lying hills, the remnant of the Wends has managed to preserve its national identity.

Wendish falls into two somewhat divergent dialects, a northern dialect spoken in the Cottbus district and a southern dialect spoken in the area around Bautzen. Both these dialects have given rise to literary languages, known respectively as Lower and Upper Wendish (or Lusatian). The earliest text is a New Testament from 1548. The first census returns in 1832 showed the number of Wendish speakers to be somewhat less than 130,000. Following the general increase in populations in the 19th century, the number of Wendish speakers rose to 170,000 in the 1860s, but then began to decline since the rate of assimilation on the borders of the enclave greatly increased during the last decades of the century. By this time the population had become more or less bilingual. At present probably some 70,000 know Wendish, rather more than half using the southern dialect. This figure contains a high proportion of older people.

Official policy in the last century favoured Germanisation, especially through the schools, where the use of the Wendish language was discouraged or forbidden. It had no official status, no more than Frisian had. During the Weimar Republic official policy was less obviously anti-Wendish; it may be described as a policy of toleration without recognition. Inevitably, the number of Wendish speakers continued to decline. Then, with the coming to power of Hitler in 1933, Germanisation took on a most threatening aspect, culminating in measures taken in 1937 openly aimed at the extirpation of Wendish national culture. All Wendish organisations, whether religious or secular, including the scholarly *Maćica Serbska* of world-wide renown, were dissolved by government decree and their property confiscated. All publications in the Wendish language were forbidden. Wendish-speaking clergy and school teachers were transferred to purely German areas. With such actions as these an element of terrorisation entered into the process of Germanisation, before which the majority of the Wends capitulated. Many parents made a point of speaking to their children only in German, and young people generally, even if they knew Wendish, used German wherever possible. The Wendish language was as good as banished from public places. There were villages where, before Hitler came to power, German was so rarely heard that people turned round to stare if they heard German spoken on the street. But in these same villages at the end of the war, only 12 years later, people would look round if they heard Wendish being spoken.

Since 1945 a policy without precedent anywhere in Germany has been followed with the aim of preserving the Wendish language. Legislation in 1948 and 1950 ended all forms of discrimination against Wendish. Lusatia was declared a bilingual area where Wendish can be used officially for all purposes on an equal footing with German. The school system has been reorganised so that Wendish-medium education, both primary and secondary, is available to all Wendish-speaking children. Generous government grants—'cultural reparations' they are sometimes called—have made possible the production of books in both Upper and Lower Wendish on a scale undreamt of before. Periodicals and a daily newspaper appear— the latter only in Upper Wendish, so far. Very many of the speakers of Lower Wendish are illiterate in their mother tongue —a similar situation exists among the Gaelic speakers of Scotland—but literacy in Upper Wendish is much more usual. Altogether Wendish culture is more vigorous in the south, thanks partly to the relative tolerance of Saxony. But the north, as part of Brandenburg, was almost defenceless against Prussian regimentation.

Will the new policy save the language? All depends on whether Wendish-medium education and official encouragement generally spread the habitual use of Wendish among the rising generation sufficiently to make good the losses of the Nazi period. The serious decline in the total number of those speaking Wendish has been slowed down, but not yet arrested. On the other hand, post-war developments have given the Wendish people a new pride in their heritage and there are signs that they, the smallest of the Slavonic nations, may succeed at the eleventh hour in preserving their identity as a

separate people. At the same time, thanks to their being bilingual, they can fully participate in the wider life of the country.
The present trends in Lusatia are of unique interest to all who
care for the problems of linguistic and cultural minorities in this
modern age.

GERMAN VERSUS SLAV IN THE EAST

The earliest known home of the Slavonic peoples is the region
between the Don, the Carpathians and the upper and middle
reaches of the Vistula. Between the Slavs and the sea to the
north lay the so-called Baltic tribes : the Prussians and Lithuanians. It seems most likely that the Balts had been neighbours of
the Slavs for a long time. At any rate the languages of the
Baltic group—Lithuanian, Latvian and the now extinct Old
Prussian—have very much in common with the Slavonic
languages. Both groups are Indo-European of an archaic,
highly inflected type. The similarities between them are perhaps best explained by assuming a period of prolonged contact
between two originally distinct groups. All the same they are
often classed together as Balto-Slavonic as though descended
from a single original group. To the west of the Slavs lay the
Germanic tribes.

About the beginning of the 5th century Slavonic tribes are
seen to be expanding westwards into territories apparently
deserted by Germanic peoples. This movement led to the
occupation in the 6th century of Moravia, Bohemia and Upper
Austria; the leading Slavs here were the Czechs. The ancestors
of the modern Slovaks, who live to the south and east of the
Czech-speaking area, formed an integral part of this immigration. The linguistic and national distinctiveness of the Slovaks
is a feature which came into existence later. At the same time
as Moravia and Bohemia were being occupied, another large
group, the Sorbs, colonised the area north of the Ore Mountains
from the Queis (Kwisa), Bober (Bóbra) and Oder in the east
to the Saale in the west. Their northern border ran east-west
a little south of Berlin, which throughout Slavonic times was
never more than a fishing village. East of the Sorbs were the
Poles; to the north other Slavonic tribes took possession of the

vast tract from the Vistula to the Elbe. Slavs were now established along the whole southern coast of the Baltic up to the
Kieler Föhrde, and they actually crossed the water to form
settlements on the southern coasts of Danish islands. The
tribes in the area bounded by the Elbe, the Baltic and the
Vistula delta, north of the Sorbs and Poles, may be divided into
two main groups: in the western part Polabians (*po* 'on',
Laba 'Elbe'), in the eastern part Pomeranians or, more technically, Pomoranians (*morje* 'sea'). All the above Slavonic
peoples are described as West Slavs; they were known to the
Germans under the collective name of 'Wends'.

Thus, in the 6th century, the once purely Germanic lands
east of the Elbe and Saale became entirely Slavonic. Whatever
Germanic population may have remained behind must have
been assimilated. Then the Slavs crossed the Saale in large
numbers and settled far inside Thuringia and North Bavaria.
They likewise crossed the Elbe further north and formed
settlements on the western bank. These movements continued
into the 7th century. But in these districts, the immigrants did
not replace the Germans entirely; the population remained
mixed. In some of these places the Slavs probably settled with
the express permission of the Germans, but such Slavs would
not be entirely independent.

When the westward movement of the Slavs came to a halt, the
main frontier between German and Slav remained fairly static
until the beginning of the 9th century. After the final defeat of
the Saxons in 804—achieved with the help of the powerful
Slavonic Obodrites—Charlemagne turned his attention to the
east. Certain Slavonic tribes had supported the Saxons and
Charlemagne led several expeditions against them. From the
middle of the 9th century, the Germans and Slavs were continually waging war upon each other. Now the tide was turning.
Before it had been the land-hungry Slavonic tribesmen who
advanced westwards, but now it was German feudal princes
who cast covetous eyes on the lands towards the east. Henry I
set about the conquest of the east in earnest. By 929 he had
reached Meissen, where he built a castle, and soon his authority
reached to the Oder. He divided the newly subjected territory
into marches (*Marken*). Otto I began the Christianisation of the

Slavs and established bishoprics from 948 onwards. But rebellions, the first in 955, weakened the grip of the German overlord and restored *de facto* Slavonic independence as far as the Elbe and Saale. It was not until the reign of Lothar of Supplingenburg (1125–37) that the losses of the second half of the 10th century were recovered. The northern part of the Slavonic territories preserved its independence a little longer than the southern half, but in 1160 Henry the Lion overthrew the Obodrites in Mecklenburg and afterwards obliged the Slavs in Pomerania to acknowledge his overlordship. In the south, German authority reached the Oder, but now in the north it stretched beyond to the delta of the Vistula. Not only did German barons now vigorously re-assert their rule over Slavonic territory, they proceeded to secure their authority by an assault on Slavonic life and culture. The Slavs were driven from the best land which was given to German peasants imported into the territory. In the course of the 12th century, Germans settled in large numbers at many points between the old German-Slav frontier on the Elbe/Saale and the Oder. They played a leading part in the foundation of towns in the Slavonic territories. The settlement of Germans in the east continued undiminished in the 13th century, both in the towns and on the land, and this provided the basis for the Germanisation of the area.

We can give some data on the gradual extinction of Slavonic, our main source being R. Trautmann, *Die slavischen Völker und Sprachen*, Leipzig, 1948. Slavonic almost certainly died out first in the old areas of mixed German and Slavonic speech west of the Saale and Elbe. Even so, Slavs are regularly mentioned here in the 11th and 12th centuries. As late as 1227 'rustici Sclavi' are recorded near Erfurt. In the 13th century German colonisation of the very sparsely inhabited region of the Ore Mountains drove a wedge between Czechs and Sorbs. By the Thirty Years' War, Sorb was quite extinct between the Saale and the Elbe. But it survived east of the Elbe in Lusatia. Details of the linguistic situation here are known since the middle of the 16th century, when the Sorb-speaking territory is seen to be almost surrounded by German, only in the north-east on the Oder was it still in touch with Polish. This last territorial link with the Slavonic world outside was cut during the 18th century. The Sorb enclave in Lusatia survives to the present day, as described earlier in this chapter.

There is likewise some information on the demise of Slavonic in the north. Arkona on Rügen was the cult centre of the Baltic Slavs. The rich sanctuary here was destroyed in 1168 and the inhabitants of the island came under German rule. Tax rolls from 1314 and 1318 show that the population of Rügen was still almost entirely Slavonic, yet according to an old report the last Slavonic speaker on Rügen died in 1400. This rapid decline may indicate that repressive measures came into operation against the use of Slavonic. Such proscriptions are known to have been issued by the Germans in other parts of the eastern territories. Here and there in the north, Slavonic lingered on until the beginning of modern times, and in one place, the so-called Lüneburg Wendland, on the lower reaches of the Jeetze, north of Salzwedel, it survived until the first decades of the 18th century. This was long enough for the language to become the object of antiquarian interest. Collectors, partly under the influence of Leibniz, did what they could to record the language for posterity by compiling glossaries and taking down sentences or short texts, much as antiquarians in this country were at the very same time noting down scraps of the Cornish language before it became entirely extinct. The Slavonic dialect of the Lüneburg Wendland is technically known as Dravaenic Polabian.

Dravaenic Polabian is virtually all that remains to us of the speech of the most western of the Slavs. But further east, in Pomerania, between the Oder and the Vistula, Slavonic maintained itself better. It is certain that the area was still predominantly Slavonic in 1300 and, in spite of continuing Germanisation, the eastern part at any rate always had a mixed character. The native Slavs are here called Kashubs and a modest literature has appeared in their language, beginning in 1586 with a translation of Lutheran hymns. The Kashubs were very numerous until the middle of the 18th century, but then a rapid decline set in due to assimilation and emigration. But this decline did not lead to the complete Germanisation of the area. After about 1850 Polish influence, already traditionally strong—the area was under Polish administration from 1466 to 1772—began to increase steadily, and many Poles settled in the area, especially after the creation of the Polish Corridor. Today the Kashub language is quite extinct in Germany. In 1938 it was used by only 3,000 persons living mostly in the *Kreis* Bütow (Bytów). Other Pomoranian dialects, very close to Kashub, were spoken in recent times by small numbers at various points; the best recorded of these lingered on north of Slupsk until the first decade of this century. Comparison of the Pomoranian dialects with Dravaenic shows that the Pomoranian and Polabian dialect groups were more closely related to each other than to any other West Slavonic language.

The Slavonic past of the territory beyond the Elbe and Saale is everywhere apparent in the toponymy. Looking at the village names on a sign post in Mecklenburg, one could easily imagine oneself to be in a Slavonic country. Names with such characteristic Slavonic endings as -ow (Slav. *-owo*), -au (Slav. *-awa*), -itz, -in predominate: Pankow, Treptow, Prenzlau, Zwittau, Müritz, Strelitz, Schwerin—notice the un-Germanic stress on the final syllable as in Berlin. Other examples of Slavonic names are Potsdam lit. 'under the oaks' (Polab. *damp* 'oak') and Leipzig (Sorb *Lipsk*) which contains *lipa* 'lime tree'. A dozen names at least are based on *glina* 'clay', such as Glienicke in Berlin and Gleina in Thuringia. A very old Slavonic toponymical term survives in Rostok. The name denotes a 'broadening', here in reference to the wide estuary of the Warnow near which the town is situated. Breitling, the name for this estuary today, may be regarded as the German for Rostok, just as Mecklenburg translates Polab. *Wili Grad* 'Great Fort', the town's original name.

GERMAN BEYOND THE VISTULA

The German advance to the Baltic coast in the 12th century led to the growth of German influence in the Baltic generally. German merchants, with Lübeck as their centre, were very active in the Baltic Sea by the middle of the century. In 1201 they founded Riga. By this time they also dominated the coast from the delta of the Vistula to the Gulf of Finland and were preparing to colonise the whole area. In 1202 a religious order,

the Knights of the Sword, was formed to christianise (and con-
quer) the Baltic lands. The Knights of the Sword were the
military force necessary to effect German colonisation. They
achieved a large measure of success, but their expansion
inland was decisively checked by the Russians in 1242. From
this century date the many German-speaking enclaves in the
Baltic countries which survived until recently (see p. 178).

Up to the 13th century the Prussians who, as we have seen,
were a Baltic people akin to the Lithuanians and Latvians,
lived in undisturbed possession of their homeland, the coastal
area between the Vistula and the Memel. But in 1230 the
Knights of the German Order broke into the land and began
a long war of conquest against the heathen Prussians. By all
accounts this was a most savage campaign in which great
numbers of Prussians were wiped out. German peasants were
brought in to take over the holdings of the former owners and
by 1283 the remnant of the Prussians could resist no longer.
When the rule of the Order came to an end in 1525, the
Prussian language survived only in Samland, the peninsula just
north of Königsberg between the Frische and Kurische Haff.
Here were peasants still unable to understand German and for
these a catechism, in Prussian and German, was twice printed
in 1545, followed in 1561 by Luther's Catechism, also in a
bilingual edition. Apart from two glossaries amounting to less
than a thousand words, these catechisms—some 30 pages of
text—are the chief remains of the Prussian language, which
is presumed to have become extinct by 1700.

After the subjugation of Prussia, the German Order turned
to the conquest of Lithuania. But now powerful allies came to
the assistance of the Lithuanians and prevented further German
progress eastwards. The combined opposition of Lithuanians,
Poles and Russians brought German expansion to a halt.
Subsequently, the German Order became a vassal of the Polish
king, but the province of Prussia remained German-speaking
until its dissolution in 1945.

THE SOUTHERN FRONTIER

To the south the linguistic frontier was less dynamic than in the
east. All the same, German was here too encroaching on

Slavonic, though more slowly. German has ousted Slavonic from what are now the provinces of Upper and Lower Austria; here the replacement of Slavonic by German began in the 9th century, when Bavarian peasants were settled in the March on the Enns. In Burgenland, German today faces Hungarian. The Leitha has been the historic frontier between German and Hungarian since the middle of the 10th century. The Hungarians, who appeared in Europe about 900, seem to have taken over chiefly Slavonic territory and their north-western migration combined with the German movement south-east along the Danube valley to divide the West Slavs from the South Slavs (Slovenes, Croats). In Styria and Carinthia, German has been gradually replacing Slovene since the Middle Ages, but further east German has recently been the loser to Italian (see p. 160).

The Bavarians probably entered Austria in the middle of the 6th century. Germanic peoples had been moving through the Danube valley since the fall of the Roman *Limes*, but the mountainous parts were probably still in the hands of the Rhaetians. German undoubtedly ousted Rhaeto-Romance from many of its strongholds. Today Rhaeto-Romance dialects are found everywhere on the southern flank of the German-speaking area from the East Tyrol to Switzerland, except where, in a few places, Italian has broken through the Rhaetian girdle.

South of the old German-Romance linguistic frontier below Bozen/Bolzano were two enclaves of German dialect speech, technically known as *Zimbrisch*, but called *Tautsch* by the natives. The first enclave, the so-called Seven Communes, lay about 20 miles south-east of Trient/Trento, the second enclave, the Thirteen Communes, a little south of the first, about 20 miles north-east of Verona. *Zimbrisch* has been rapidly declining since the first glossary of the dialect was published in the middle of the 18th century. Before the war not more than 50 persons in the village of Giazza (Thirteen Communes) still used the dialect. It is likely that the 'Cimbrians' were brought in from Bavaria. The Seven Communes were probably German as early as 1100, the Thirteen Communes about 1300.

However that may be, they were perhaps not the first Germans in the area. In 568, the Germanic Langobardi—

subsequently called Lombards—moved into Italy from the
Central European Plain, to which they had immigrated a
couple of generations before after a sojourn in Lower Austria.
They now spread thinly over most of Italy, but their main
centres were in the north. It is not possible to say in which
localities Langobardic was spoken. It is known that Trient
belonged to the Lombard kingdom. The town of Mezzolom-
bardo is not far east of Trient and Bozen, so perhaps this area
once held a substantial Langobardic population. It is known
that German was in use south of the Brenner Pass by 650.
It is conceivable that Langobardic and Bavarian German were
actually in contact in this region. Langobardic is an Old High
German dialect, which implies contact with other southern
Germans. But we assume that Langobardic acquired its High
German characteristics before entering Italy. At all events, the
Lombards were in touch with the larger German world to the
north, and not to the disadvantage of the latter. The origin
of the oldest German book, the Latin-German Dictionary
known as the *Abrogans*, has been traced to Lombardy and it is
ultimately from the repertoire of a nameless Lombard *scop*
that comes the best surviving example of ancient German
heroic song, the celebrated Lay of Hildebrand.

German in Eastern and Central Europe and in the Balkans

Beginning in the great period of colonial expansion in the 12th
and 13th centuries, German settlers penetrated into lands far
to the east and south of Germany proper. They were either
traders or craftsmen attracted to the towns, or else peasants
prepared to clear forests and bring uncultivated land under the
plough. In many places their descendants maintained their
German mother tongue down to the most recent times. The
same applies to another, rather special group of German
speakers involved from the earliest times in the eastward movement—the German Jews. Their speech, however, developed in
an exceptional way to acquire the status of an independent
language (see Chapter 13).

Until about a generation ago, or less, German was still

widely spoken in Russia and the Baltic States, in Central
Europe and in the Balkans. The first mentioned went back to
the time of Catherine the Great, when peasants mostly from
south-western Germany received land in Russia, notably in
the region of the Middle Volga. After the 1917 Revolution, a
Volga German Republic emerged and in 1939 the number of
Germans was estimated at a million and a quarter. But many
of these were removed from the area during the Second World
War and resettled in various places, so that the old cohesion was
broken and the way wide open for rapid assimilation. The
German Balts, some 200,000 in number, were mainly town
dwellers, whose ancestors arrived by sea. They were traders and
artisans, not peasants. Their main centre was Riga with a
German population of 45,000. Most of the German Balts were
transferred to the *Reich* in 1939–1940, and so the *Deutschbal-
tentum*, whose history went back well over 7 centuries, has now
ceased to be.

Many of the enclaves in Central and Southern Europe were
likewise ancient, being founded in the period of early German
colonial expansion. For example, the enclave known as the
Zips, centred on Käsmark/Kežmarok in Slovakia, was certainly established by the middle of the 12th century. The
enclave around Iglau/Jihlava in Moravia came into being a
century later. Larger groups were found in the Balkans. The
most vigorous from the cultural point of view and the most
exemplary from the German nationalistic standpoint were the
Transylvanian 'Saxons', nearly a quarter of a million strong,
on Rumanian territory. They organised their own German-
medium schools and printed their own German-language
newspapers. An even larger group of some 700,000 Germans,
the 'Danube Swabians', lived in close proximity to each other
in a group of enclaves on the fertile soil of the Banat and Bačka.
Those on the Rumanian side of the frontier were culturally
more active than those in Yugoslavia where, since the beginning of this century, assimilation had been proceeding apace.
The German colonisation of Transylvania began in 1141 and
continued for a century and a half. But as comparative dialect
studies have shown, the original settlers were not Saxons; they
must have come from the Rhenish districts south of Cologne

to the Moselle. Nor have the 'Danube Swabians' much to do with Swabia. Most of them came from the Rheingau and Odenwald, the earliest arriving after the Turkish Wars to occupy deserted land.

In spite of their geographical isolation, these and other similar groups never lost contact with the country of their origin. Though each spoke its own peculiar dialect, all used Standard German for literary purposes and in education. Altogether about a million and a half would speak 'colonial' varieties of German dialect in the enclaves in Central and South-Eastern Europe in 1939. But as a consequence of movements of populations during and especially after the Second World War, the majority of these enclaves have disappeared or been greatly reduced in size and influence. It looks as though it is only a matter of time before these Germans are assimilated. Only in Rumania are the old centres more or less intact.

German as a Second Language

German has been widely used as a second language in Scandinavia and the Baltic area and in Central Europe. In the north, German influence became predominant at the time of the Hanseatic League (p. 79) and German is still widely understood in the Scandinavian countries. But during the present century, and especially since the Second World War, German has generally been replaced by English as the first foreign language in Scandinavia. Formerly much scientific work, especially by Danish and Swedish scholars, appeared in German. Nowadays almost all of them publish in English.

German has for long had considerable standing in Poland, though in the face of competition from Russian. In Bohemia and Moravia, German was at one time so firmly entrenched as the language of the ruling classes—in origin immigrant Germans—that it would have been no surprise if the Czech language had succumbed. But Czech did not die out, though it absorbed very many German elements. The last century witnessed a great conflict between the Czech and German languages as part of the struggle of the Czechs for national independence. The position of Czech became unassailable after the foundation of the Czechoslovak Republic in 1918 and was confirmed again after the expulsion of the Germans in 1945. Most educated Czechs have an excellent command of German, but the position is doubtlessly now changing, as, since the war, Russian has become the first foreign language taught in schools. Elsewhere in Central Europe—Hungary, Slovenia, Croatia—German has for centuries been the best known foreign language and has accordingly exerted a good deal of influence on the vocabulary and even the structure of the languages spoken in these countries. But since the war, German has been ousted by Russian as the first foreign language. Political developments have largely cut off these Central European countries from the German-speaking area. One may well say that the German era in Central Europe came to end in 1945.

German Overseas

Germany was the last of the European powers to acquire overseas possessions and these were lost during the First World War. Thus German never became to any appreciable extent the second language of Africans or Asians as have, for instance, English or French, nor did German become the basis for any pidgin. Some German words, however, found their way into the Pidgin English of Melanesia. These words came, of course, from the former German possessions in New Guinea and on neighbouring islands. The names of several tools are German: *hobel* plane, *maisel* chisel, *sangge* pincers, *hama* hammer, though this last could be from English. Other examples: *esel* donkey, *gabel* fork, *gumi* rubber, *tapel* slate (*Tafel*). There is the verb *tilim* divide out; apportion (*teil-* + Engl. *him*). Ger. *Mark* is believed to be the source of Pidgin *mak* shilling: *Yu pei haumas mak?* How many shillings have you paid? (see J. J. Murphy, *The Book of Pidgin English*[8], 1966).

German has, however, been carried overseas by emigrants to the areas of predominantly white settlement such as Australia and America. But only where the German-speaking immigrants constituted a large majority in a given area could the language survive. German was preserved for a time by a small community of wine-growers in South Australia, but assimilation is the rule there today. Here and there in South and Central America German-speaking enclaves exist, though they are too small to hope to survive for long. Only in the United States are there German-speaking communities large enough to resist complete assimilation—at least for the time being. These communities are found mainly in East Pennsylvania, the total number of speakers being about 250,000. A brief description of Pennsylvania German is given on pp. 148–156.

11

DUTCH AND AFRIKAANS

The term Dutch is not altogether a happy one. By Dutch we understand, of course, the inhabitants of Holland and their language. Leaving aside the detail that Holland is also the name of a province (or rather two: North and South Holland), we notice that the Dutch language is not confined to Holland alone, but extends southward covering the northern half of Belgium and overspilling into the French *arrondissements* of Hazebrouck and Dunkirk (see Map 8). In these parts, however, the language goes by the name of Flemish.

The Dutch themselves may call their language *Hollands*, a name reflecting the key position of the double province in the evolution of the standard language, or they may call it *Nederlands*, which appropriately links with *Nederland*, the name for the whole country. The Flemings, as we have said, normally call their language *Vlaams*, i.e. Flemish. But in linguistic works, both Dutch and Flemings refer to the language as *Nederlands*. As there are important historical differences between the language of the Dutch and the Flemings, it is often necessary to distinguish them, in which case the terms *Noordnederlands* and *Zuidnederlands* are most appropriate. These may be rendered into English as 'North Netherlandish' and 'South Netherlandish', for Netherlandish (or Netherlandic) has been used in imitation of *Nederlands*. But there is no gainsaying that these neologisms sound clumsy and artificial beside the familiar, homely words Dutch and Flemish.

Dutch is the oldest name for the language. Its Flemish form is *Diets*, the corresponding northern form being *Duits*, older *Duutsc*, the source of Engl. *Dutch*. The word is known to continue Old Franconian **theudisk* 'tribal, pertaining to the people' from **theod* 'tribe, people' (cf. in these senses OSax. *thiod*, *thiudisk*, OHG *diot*, *diutisk* > NHG *deutsch*). The word first occurs in the Latinised form *theodiscus*, late in the 8th century.

MAP 8

Linguistic boundaries in Belgium

It is most likely that the use of the word to denote the language developed in the area we are now discussing. At this time the most easterly of the Franconians who, as we shall presently see, comprised the bulk of the Germanic settlers in this region, were becoming romanised. Consequently, as a designation of language, the term Franconian, Old (Low) Franc. *frenkisk*, was ambiguous, since it could now mean both 'French' Franconian or German Franconian. An unambiguous designation was called for; *theudisk* 'tribal, pertaining to the people', hence in the present context something like 'traditional, inherited', came to denote the language of the German Franconian in conscious contrast to the language of the Roman Franconian, i.e. French. Subsequently the term was extended to embrace all German dialects, a natural development in view of the leading role played by the Franconians in the early political unification of the German tribes.

EXTERNAL HISTORY

Three Germanic tribes are known to have taken possession of land in the area where Dutch is now spoken: the Frisians, the Saxons and the Franks. The Frisians were settled along the coast, perhaps as far south as Dunkirk. Subsequently they were, to a large extent, absorbed by the other tribes. The Frisian language, however, survives in one large enclave in the Netherlands, as described in Chapter 12. The Saxons, moving westward, invaded Frisian Territory at a number of points. It is probable that many of the Saxon invaders of Britain crossed the sea from the coastal region of Belgium and Zeeland. South of the Saxons came the Salian Franks. The beginning of their migration into the Low Countries is put at about the end of the 3rd century A.D. when they forced the Roman defences on the Lower Rhine. A hundred years later they were being given permission by the Roman administration to settle in an area on the present Belgian-Dutch frontier. Immediately afterwards their expansion continued as they pushed back the Saxons on their northern flank and spread along the Roman roads to the east and south-east, until they were halted, so it seems, on the fortified line running from Maastricht to the North Sea near Boulogne. But all the Roman possessions east of this line were irrevocably lost. Then, with the final recall of the garrisons to Rome in 402, the Franks could cross the fortified line and resume their movements east and south-east. There is some evidence that the Gaulish population welcomed the Germanic tribesmen as these broke up the lati-fundia. At any rate the Franks were able to advance beyond Paris and effected settlements even south of the Loire, as the many Germanic place-names in the region prove. But the deeper the Franks moved into Gaul, the thinner became the areas of settlement.

Where the Frankish settlements were small and isolated, the process of Romanisation could begin almost at once. But in the areas of thicker settlement, in the districts in touch with the Low Countries, Franconian speech persisted for centuries. It was from such areas that so many Germanic words found their way into French, and no doubt Frankish influence is significant for the division of France into the two great linguistic regions, *Langue d'Oc* in the south and *Langue d'Oïl* in the north. Yet none of the regions of Salian settlement south of the Maastricht-Boulogne line could maintain its Germanic charac-ter permanently. The same fate overtook the southern settle-ments of a related group, the Ripuarian Franks, who colonised Limburg and afterwards broke through the Maastricht-Boulogne line to the south. No texts in Franconian have come down to us from these former areas of Franconian settlement. Without a doubt the language had been long forgotten there when, about 1200, the linguistic frontier becomes clear from contemporary records. Apart from some losses to French in French Flanders (area of Boulogne to Dunkirk), the present-day boundary virtually coincides with that of 1200.

EARLY DUTCH

Very little is known of the dialects spoken in the Low Countries before the last quarter of the 12th century. Almost the only witness is a fragmentary psalter (some 25 psalms) from the 10th century. The language of this document is termed Old Low Franconian and is seen to be a Low German dialect close to Old Saxon. Like OSax. it shows no sign of the High German sound shift. On the other hand, it is marked off from OSax. by certain features, the most notable concerning the plural endings of the verbs. Whereas these have fallen together in OSax. to give a single plural ending, they still differ in OLFr. just as they do in OHG.

It is certain that the area of OSax. speech extended into the Low Countries (and for that matter the area of OLFr. extended some distance into Germany). The evidence of the modern dialects shows that the north-eastern provinces Groningen, Drente, Overijsel and the northern part of Gelderland are Saxon. But Saxon did not play a decisive part in the evolution of the Dutch language; the basis of Dutch is Franconian only.

Apart from the OLFr. psalter, the literary records begin about 1170; they become most abundant after 1250. The language had now reached its 'Middle' stage and is henceforth known as Middle Dutch, a term which is used for the language until about 1550, when Modern Dutch is considered to begin. Naturally, Middle Dutch is not a uniform language. Dialect-speaking was everywhere the rule. Non-literary writing is very often purely dialectal, while the language of all the works of literature shows local traits. All the same, attempts were made at an early date, for example in the work of Maerlant in the second half of the 13th century, to achieve at least a loose literary norm—*Diets*. As regards its general development MDu. may be closely compared with MLG, the two having reached a very similar stage of development. They contrast somewhat with MHG which in several points of accidence preserves a rather more archaic aspect. The four centuries or so covered by the MDu. period were, on the whole, times of continuing material prosperity and lively intellectual life in the Low Countries. During this period a rich and expressive literature of extraordinary diversity was produced. Bruges and Ghent, later Brussels and Antwerp, were the main centres. MDu. has accordingly a marked southern bias, and southern influence may be seen in the works of northerners as well.

MODERN DUTCH

At the beginning of the modern period the long hegemony of Flanders and Brabant was brought to an end by political

changes. The northern provinces had declared their independence in 1581, but after the fall of Antwerp in 1585, the southern
provinces again passed into Spanish hands. Tens upon tens of
thousands of refugees fled to the north, where in 1588 the Dutch
Republic was proclaimed. Then, while the south languished
under a foreign yoke, the free north attained a degree of general
prosperity unknown in history before. By 1650 the Dutch
Republic had become the world's carrier, the leading colonial
power, the chief centre of finance and trade. An intense artistic
and intellectual life accompanied these achievements. Amsterdam, The Hague, Haarlem, Leyden, all in the province of
Holland, were the focal points. Though preserving certain
southern elements from the older literary language, the usage
of the province of Holland now became the basis for written
Dutch. This was the avowed policy of the pre-eminent poet
Vondel, who took as his model the cultured speech of the
leading burghers of the Holland towns. His language, i.e.
Hollands, was soon being imitated everywhere. Dutch people
could now say they were using *Hollands* just as Spaniards may
call their standard language Castilian. Furthermore, Holland
Dutch—*het Algemeen Beschaafd* 'the General Cultured'—spread
as a spoken form too. Today it may be heard everywhere, though
the local tinge is often apparent, rather more so than in English.
Dialect speech, both Franconian and Saxon, may still be heard
in rural districts, but is rapidly declining.

   Linguistic matters, too, took a different turn in the south
after the final separation from the northern provinces. French
influence, which had been strong there as early as the 14th
century, now became even stronger due to an increasing
official use of French. The union with Holland in 1815 began to
change things, but after the defection of the south and the
formation of Belgium in 1830, the earlier policy was pursued
with determined vigour. Members of the well-to-do classes
in the Flemish areas often went over to French as their main
language. But the official persecution of the language led to
counter-measures by the Flemish Movement. The struggle was
long and acrimonious. Not until 1932 did legislation guarantee
the Flemish language precedence in the Flemish districts and
equality with French in State matters.

These events have left their mark upon the language. After some hesitation the Dutch of Holland was accepted as the literary norm for the southern provinces also, but since the school system was for so long French and as French had become the main official and literary language, the Flemings tended to read and write only or principally French, though continuing to speak Flemish—albeit plentifully interlarded with gallicisms. In these circumstances the dialects spoken in the south were hardly affected by *het Algemeen Beschaafd* as they were in the north. As a consequence, Flemish speech has remained essentially dialect speech down to the present time. But a big change is coming. The official use of the language and Flemish-medium education together with other factors, such as the press and radio, have led to a wide diffusion of the standard language and its use in natural speaking is on the increase. Only in French Flanders, where the language is not recognised as in Belgium, do the dialects continue more or less intact. The literary language of the French Flemings is mainly French, for them Flemish is first and foremost the patois.

THE DUTCH-GERMAN LINGUISTIC FRONTIER

It has been mentioned above that the dialects of the north-eastern provinces of the Netherlands are Saxon. They are, in fact, an organic continuation of the Saxon dialects on the German side of the state frontier. This frontier does not therefore correspond to any ancient linguistic boundary. Of course, there is a linguistic boundary today in the important sense that the official language on the one side is Standard Dutch, on the other side Standard German, as has been the position for close on four centuries. But against this the dialect on both sides is the same. Many German girls cross the frontier every morning to work in Dutch factories a few miles away. They mix easily with the Dutch employees. But these girls haven't learnt the Dutch language. It isn't necessary.

A Dutch farmer with land adjoining the frontier can, let us say, stroll up to the dividing wire and have a word with a German farmer working on the other side. These two can talk about their workaday business in the Saxon dialect with perfect mutual comprehension and no feeling that they are foreigners to each other. Yet the one will have a Dutch-language news-paper in his pocket, the other a German one. They will go home to listen to the news on the wireless. The one will tune in to Hilversum, the other to Hamburg. Now should these two meet and wish to talk about some matter of international importance, involving say, the Security Council, then the conversation will become halting. One of them will know the technical terms and associated phraseology only in Dutch, the other only in German. The differences can be considerable.

Further south the situation is the same. There it is the Low Franconian dialects of the Dutch side which extend unbroken across the state frontier into Germany where they ultimately merge with the Rhenish Franconian dialects, with which they form a continuum to Cologne and beyond.

STATISTICS

Dutch is the native language of at least 20 million persons. Of these, some 13½ millions live in the Netherlands, rather more than 6 millions in Belgium and a further 100,000 or so in the Flemish area of Dunkirk and Hazebrouck.

REASONS FOR THE RISE OF DUTCH

Since the Low Countries are, linguistically speaking, an integral part of the German system, we are prompted to wonder why this region, and this region alone, kept to its own regional language instead of adopting Standard German. North Germany, for instance, formerly used its own regional language for all purposes, but later went over to High German. Here the differences between the languages were certainly as great as between Dutch and High German and of the same order. Low German was swept aside, but Dutch survived. It is clear that the answer to our question is not a linguistic one. It is, in fact, economic and political. Since the 12th century the Low Countries have been a notably prosperous part of Europe. The soil is fertile and the geographical situation favoured the extension of trade. The region thus developed to a great extent independently of the rest of the German-speaking area. Such circumstances could not but encourage the growth of a written language based on the dialects of the region. By the time the

High German literary language reached the Dutch frontier it
found an equally influential rival already entrenched. Indeed,
the general historical situation in the early part of the modern
period favoured Dutch, for while Holland was becoming the
richest country in Europe, Germany was impoverished and
prostrate from the agony of the Thirty Years' War. In more
recent times, of course, Dutch has inevitably been influenced
by its mighty neighbour, especially in matters of word formation
and phraseology. But there has never been any question of
German replacing Dutch.

Germans often refer to Dutch as being a dialect of German,
by which they mean a dialect of modern standard German.
The main reason for this absurd statement is to be sought in
German chauvinism. It is, of course, purely a lay view, for it
is most unscientific. We summarise the essential facts. On
territory covered by closely related dialects there had arisen by
the end of the Middle Ages three literary languages: High
German, Low German, Dutch. Each was a natural product of
its own region. In early modern times, Low German was
replaced by High German, but not so Dutch. In terms of linguistic relationship German and Dutch are sisters. Dutch is no
more a dialect of German than English is.

Outline of Dutch Grammar

SOUNDS AND SPELLING

These are in part different from German. To begin with, *p, t, k*
are pronounced without aspiration, a feature which recalls
French; *r* is trilled, *ch* is always velar; in Holland *g* is commonly
pronounced like *ch*, but in Belgium initial *g* is an occlusive.
sch is pronounced *s* + *ch* in Holland, but *sg* in Belgium. Final
n is usually dropped in West Holland. *sj* is pronounced [ʃ]. *s*
and *z* are as in English, but final *b* and *d* are voiceless as in
German. *j* has the value of Ger. *j*, *w* is bilabial like Ger. *w* in
schwören, *v* is like Engl. *v*, but is only half-voiced in initial
position.

Vowels, written singly, are short in closed syllables: *kat* cat,
and before two consonants: *liggen* lie. Otherwise they are long,
except in unstressed endings: *zaken* things. In closed syllables

long vowels are written double: *zaak* thing. Notice *oe* spells [u:], *uu* or *u* spells [y:] when long, [œ] when short, *eu* spells [ø:], e.g. *voet* foot, *muur, muren* wall(s), *kus* kiss, *deur* door. The pronunciation of some of the diphthongs is not self-evident: *ei, ij* (in Belgium often *y*) spells [ɛi], *ui* [œy], *uw* [y:u], *ou* [ɔu], e.g. *Mei* May, *mij* me, *uit* out, *uw* your, *hout* wood.

Dutch words in this chapter are given in the so-called Reformed (or New) Spelling, the official orthography of both the Netherlands and Belgium. It discards a number of superfluous letters found in the older style. The differences are not great, but concern commonly occurring features, e.g. *Nederlands* 'Dutch', older *Nederlandsch*. The Reformed Spelling had been extensively used side by side with the older, then official orthography for over half a century before the decision of 1946.

NOUNS

Both in spoken Dutch and in the literary language nouns do not vary for case except for a limited use of the genitive, see below.

The plural is most commonly formed by adding *-en* to the singular: *stoel* chair, *vrucht* fruit, *boek* book, pl. *stoelen, vruchten, boeken.* Notice *kind* child, *koe* cow, pl. *kinderen, koeien.* The addition of an ending in Dutch may lead to spelling changes: *boot* boat, *man* man, pl. *boten, mannen.* Quite a number of nouns take the plural in *-s,* a formation which is ancient in the Saxon parts of the Netherlands, cf. OS. *dagos* days. Today it occurs, for example, with nouns ending in *-el, -em, -en, -er: tafel* table, *bezem* brush, *wagen* waggon, *kamer* room, pl. *tafels, bezems, wagens, kamers.* It is also used with some nouns denoting persons: *maat* mate, *oom* uncle, pl. *maats, ooms,* and after all diminutives: *boekje* little book, pl. *boekjes.*

Possession is ordinarily indicated by *van* of: *het geld van zijn zuster* his sister's money. In spoken Dutch, the non-literary construction *zijn zuster d'r geld* lit. 'his sister her money' is common, reminding us of the rather similar situation in German. A few everyday words may have a possessive inflection in *-s,* e.g. *vaders huis* father's house, *moeders tuin* mother's garden, as well as *het huis van vader, de tuin van moeder.*

In literary style a genitive, especially of feminine or plural nouns, is not unusual, e.g. *tegen het einde der eerste Meiweek* 'towards the end of the first week in May,' *het briesen der paarden, het brullen der koeien, het klagend en zoet geblaat der schapen* 'the snorting of the horses, the lowing of the cows, the querulent and sweet bleating of the sheep.' The genitive is often preserved in biblical language: *in het huis mijns Vaders zijn vele woningen* 'in my Father's house are many mansions.' In addition, there are numerous examples of the genitive in ordinary use, especially in set phrases: *het teken des kruises* 'the sign of the cross', *in naam der wet* 'in the name of the law'.

ARTICLES

In the definite article the old masc. and fem. have fallen together as *de*, the neut. is *het: de man, de vrouw, het kind*. Plural for all genders *de*. The genitive survives in formal literary style: sg.m.n. *des*, f. *der;* pl. *der*.

The indefinite article *een* is normally invariable, but genitives occur in formal style: m.n. *eens*, f. *ener*.

ADJECTIVES

Adjectives used attributively take an inflectional *e* in most cases: *de goede zoon* the good son, *een jonge moeder* a young mother, *dit oude bord* this old plate, *kleine ezels* little donkeys. But the adjective remains uninflected before a sg. neut. noun standing alone or preceded by *een: nieuw* (pron. [ni:u]) *brood* new bread, *een zwart varken* a black pig.

NUMERALS

1 *een*, 2 *twee*, 3 *drie*, 4 *vier*, 5 *vijf*, 6 *zes*, 7 *zeven*, 8 *acht*, 9 *negen*, 10 *tien*, 11 *elf*, 12 *twaalf*, 13 *dertien*, 14 *veertien*, 15 *vijftien*, 16 *zestien*, 17 *zeventien*, 18 *achttien*, 19 *negentien*, 20 *twintig*, 21 *een en twintig*, 30 *dertig*, 40 *veertig*, 50 *vijftig*, 60 *zestig*, 70 *zeventig*, 80 *tachtig*, 90 *negentig*, 100 *honderd*, 1000 *duizend*.

The development of intervocalic glide *g* in *negen* is of long standing; we met it in OSax. The initial *t* in *tachtig* (contrast Ger. *achtzig*) is a relic of an ancient prefix *ant-*, also attested in OSax. Both these features occur in Frisian as well.

PRONOUNS

The Dutch pronouns show a number of peculiar developments.

The commonest forms are:

Sg.nom.	*ik* I	*jij*, (polite) *u* you	*hij* he	*zij* she	*het* it
obl.	*mij*	*jou*, „ *u*	*hem*	*haar*	„
Pl.nom.	*wij* we	*jullie*, (polite) *u* you		*zij* they	
obl.	*ons*	„ „ *u*		*ze*	

In natural speech the pronunciation of the pronouns is
modified when unstressed, as in other languages. In the case
of *jij, mij, wij, zij*, this may be shown in writing: *je, me, we, ze*. It
will be noticed that *hij* is not included. When unstressed, *hij* is
pronounced [(h)i], but the spelling takes no acount of this. The
weakened form of *jou* is *je* and may be so written. *Het* is sometimes spelt *'t*. Unstressed *haar* is commonly pronounced [tər,
dər]. These pronunciations may be represented as *t'r, d'r*, but
they are normally not permissible in writing. They arose in
sandhi as follows. The sentence 'he has seen her' runs in quickly
spoken Dutch *hij heeft 'r gezien*, when *'r* is all that remains of
haar. In time, not *'r* alone, but also the preceding dental, which
really belonged to the verb, was felt to be the unstressed form of
haar, i.e. *t'r*. In voiced surroundings this became *d'r*.

In addition to *jullie*, in origin a compound (see 'Historical
Notes on the Pronouns' below), the simplex *je* may be used. The
use of *jij, jullie* and *u* (often written *U*, especially in letters) corresponds roughly to the use of Ger. *du, ihr* and *Sie*, except that
frequently in literary style and especially in religious language,
gij, unstressed *ge*, obl. *u*, is used for both sing. and plur. In
Flemish these words are at the same time the pronoun of
familiarity.

In spoken Dutch especially *haar* is often replaced by *ze*. If
persons are referred to, *ze* 'them' may be replaced by other
pronouns, as follows: *haar* when referring to female persons;
when referring to male persons *hun* may be used for the indirect
object, *hen* for the direct object and after prepositions, though
this last is an artificial literary form. The words *hun* and *hen*
are doublets, both originating from an old dat. pl. *hem*.

In conclusion we mention the pronoun *er* 'of them'; it is only
used in reference to a plural already mentioned: *hier zijn mijn
boeken, maar ik heb er niet veel* 'here are my books, but I haven't
many (of them)', a usage which recalls the French construction

with *en*. Historically Du. *er* is here the gen.pl. of the 3rd person pronoun < OLFr. *iro*.

Historical Notes on the Pronouns

We have now mentioned most of the pronominal forms permissible in Standard Dutch, only a few less common variants having been omitted. Some of the forms are not difficult to account for when we consider the ancient system, as seen in OSax. for instance, and if we bear in mind how drastically modern Dutch has reduced the number of cases. We observe, for example, that *hij, mij, wij* are diphthongised *hî, mî, wî* of the oldest period. From this we infer that *zij* presupposes **sî* which would replace *siu* by analogy with *hî* etc. The reader is here referred to the OSax. pronouns given in the chapter on 'Old Low German'; to all intents and purposes these were identical with the Old Low Franconian forms. Further, if we compare Du. *hem, het* with OSax. *imu, it*, we see that the initial *h* must be secondary. It will owe its existence to *hij* where *h* is ancient. We may postulate a similar origin for *haar* in view of OSax. *iru*. On the other hand the vocalism is problematic; the MDu. form is *hare* instead of the expected **here*.

But by no means all the above forms are self-evident or nearly so. In particular the second person has innovated and the evolution of the forms has been complicated. The Old Low Franconian position was as in OSax.: 2.sg. *thû*, pl. *gî*, which regularly became MDu. *du, ghi*. But owing to the courtly habit of using *ghi*—in imitation of French *vous*—for the singular as well, *du* gradually fell into disuse. The development began in the south; by the 17th century *du* was a literary rarity in the north too and could consequently find no place in the official States Bible (1637). Meanwhile MDu. *ghi* was evolving to ModDu. *gij* and its oblique case, old *iu*, now appears with regular diphthongisation as *jou*.

In a document of the second half of the 14th century there appears a new nominative form for the 2nd person: *je*, but not until nearly 100 years later does the corresponding stressed form *jij* occur. Shortly after 1600 these forms become very common in the north. They are clearly spoken forms which now come to the front as the initiative in literary matters is

taken over by the north. Henceforth, northern *jij, je* compete
with southern *gij, ge*. Perhaps the first occurrence of the new
type as the enclitic *je* gives a clue to its origin. One could
imagine some such late medieval form as **hebdgi* 'have you'
(cf. OSax. *hebbiad gî*) being progressively assimilated and
reduced in rapid speech, e.g. **hebdgi, *hebdji, *hebdje, hebje*, at
which point *je* (perhaps supported by *jou*) was extracted as the
pronoun, leaving only the stem of the verb. By analogy with *we,
wij* etc. the stressed form *jij* would be subsequently created. Felt
to be a form of *gij*, it was accordingly used with the 2nd pl. of
the verb: *jij* (or *je*) *hebt*. But when the pronoun followed the
verb, the latter remained without the personal ending, e.g.
heb je (or *jij*). This is the situation in the language today.

Since the language now used the same forms for both
singular and plural, various new pronouns arose to denote
the 2nd pl. These were compounded with MDu. *liede, lude*
'people'. The modern word *jullie* is a descendent of one of these,
its literal meaning being 'you (*je*) people'. The person of the
following verb varies; it may be either 2nd or 3rd pl.: *jullie
hebt, hebben* 'you have'. Further, need was again felt for a
distinctively polite form of address. Such a form was to hand.
There had become current in the epistolary style of the 17th
century the phrase *Uwe Edelheid* 'Your Grace'. It was often
abbreviated to *Uwe Edt* or *Uw Ed* and finally *U E*. This last
form passed into spoken use; it was eventually shortened to *u*,
which during the course of the 18th century became the commonly used polite form of address, singular and plural. Since
the original formula *Uwe Edelheid* was naturally followed by
the 3rd sg. verb, the same was the case with *u*. Nowadays,
however, when the origin of *u* is no longer spontaneously
apparent, there is a tendency to use *u* with the 2nd pl. verb—
there being now no original 2nd sg., see 'Verbs' below—hence
u hebt, beside older *u heeft* 'you have'.

There was no special reflexive in the earliest Dutch, but by
1500 Ger. *sich* was being imitated. This is now firmly established
as *zich*.

The possessive adjectives are: sg. *mijn* my, *jouw, uw* your,
zijn his, its, *haar* her; pl. *onze* (*ons* before n.sg.) our, *jullie* or
je, uw your, *hun* m.n., *haar* f. their. Unstressed *mijn, zijn* are

sometimes written *m'n*, *z'n*, similarly *jouw* may be written *je*. Unstressed *haar* is spoken *t'r*, *d'r*.

VERBS

The Dutch verb has reached a considerably more analytical stage than its German counterpart. In particular the subjunctive has gone, apart from stereotyped relics like *leve de koning* long live the king, cf. Ger. *es lebe der König*. A distinctive 2nd sg. termination has been lost owing to the replacement of the 2nd sg. by the 2nd pl. and then the position of the traditional 2nd pl. was weakened by subsequent developments, as described in the section 'Historical Notes on the Pronouns'. The forms now in use are as follows:

Infin. *schrijven* write
  Pres.sg.1 *schrijf*, 2,3 *schrijft;* pl.1,3 *schrijven*, 2 *schrijft*
  Pret.sg. *schreef;* pl. *schreven*
  Imper. *schrijf* (pl. literary only, *schrijft*)
  Pres. part. *schrijvend(e)*, past part. *geschreven*
(The longer form of the pres. part. is less usual, but not uncommon.)

  Principal parts (infin., pret.sg., past part.) of typical strong verbs: *verliezen* loose, *verloor*, *verloren; drinken* drink, *dronk, gedronken; nemen* take, *nam*, *genomen; lezen* read, *las*, *gelezen; graven* dig, *groef*, *gegraven*.

The paradigm of a weak verb:
Infin. *maken* make
  Pres.sg.1 *maak*, 2,3 *maakt;* pl.1,3 *maken*, 2 *maakt*
  Pret. sg. *maakte;* pl. *maakten*
  Imper. *maak* (pl. literary only, *maakt*)
  Pres. part. *makend(e)*, past part. *gemaakt*

The verbs 'TO BE' and 'TO HAVE' in Dutch:
Infin. *zijn* or *wezen*, *hebben*
  Pres.sg.1 *ben*, *heb*, 2 *bent*, *hebt*, 3 *is*, *heeft;* pl.1,3 *zijn*, *hebben*, 2 *zijt*, *hebt*
  Pret.sg. *was*, *had;* pl.1,3 *waren*, *hadden*, 2 (literary) *waart*, *hadt*
  Imper. *wees(t)*, *heb(t)*

Pres. part. *zijnde, hebbend(e)*, past part. *geweest (gewezen* only as adj. 'former'), *gehad*

(The infin. *zijn* and *wezen* are often interchangeable, but in some constructions only one of them is possible.)

Compound tenses are formed with the same auxiliaries as in Standard German except that *zullen* (= Ger. *sollen*) is used to form the future: *ik zal schrijven* I shall write. Other compound tenses: *het wordt geschreven* it is (being) written (*worden* = Ger. *werden*); *ik heb geschreven* I have written, *ik ben gebleven* I have stayed (*blijven* stay).

The Syntax and Vocabulary of Dutch compared with German

As neighbouring languages, sprung from a common source and affected during their formative period by the same influences, Dutch and German have all the essentials in common. There is not a single basic feature of Dutch syntax which does not have its counterpart, if not in Standard German, then at least in German dialect. The relationship in respect of vocabulary is likewise close. To be sure, a few words occur only in the Low Countries, but in the same way others are confined to circumscribed areas of Germany. In general, the lexicon of both languages has been elaborated upon the same basic stock. But in the course of their evolution Standard Dutch and Standard German have not always gone the same way. They have often diverged in details. Sometimes they have converged again. Where this has taken place, German influence will usually have been the cause, since in the modern period German has exercised a great attraction upon Dutch. The reader may form an idea of these trends by considering the following 'Specimen of Modern Dutch' and the 'Linguistic Notes' appended to it.

Specimen of Modern Dutch

From J. Brummelkamp,
Land- en Volkenkunde, 1949, p. 72.

Den Haag heeft zijn opkomst grotendeels te danken aan het feit, dat er sedert eeuwen de Regering is gevestigd. Talrijke gepensionneerden uit

Nederland en Indonesië hebben het als woonplaats gekozen. Als woonstad heeft Den Haag door de mooie omgeving ook veel voor op andere grote steden. In Den Haag staat het Vredespaleis, waar door het Hof van Internationale Justitie geschillen berecht worden tussen staten, die zich verbinden de uitspraak te aanvaarden. Binnen- en Buitenhof, waar Regering en Volksvertegenwoordiging zetelen, vormen schilderachtige delen uit het oude Den Haag. Hoewel het gunstig ligt en de grote badplaats Scheveningen er toe behoort, wonen toch nog heel wat forensen in Wassenaar en andere naburige plaatsen.

'The Hague owes its rise to a great extent to the fact that the Government has been established there for centuries. Numerous retired people from the Netherlands and Indonesia have chosen it as their home. As a residential town the Hague has many advantages over other large towns by reason of its beautiful surroundings. At the Hague is the Palace of Peace, where the Court of International Justice adjudicates disputes between states which bind themselves to accept the verdict. Inner and Outer Court, where Government and Parliament sit, form picturesque parts of the old-time Hague. Although it has a favourable position and the large resort Scheveningen belongs to it, even so quite a lot of people live out at Wassenaar and other neighbouring places.'

Linguistic notes:

Den Haag lit. '(at) The Domain', where *Den* is a relic of the older dative. Earlier meanings of *haag* are 'enclosure, hedge', cf. Ger. *Hag* and French *haie* which is a Germanic loan word.

heeft zijn opkomst . . . te danken lit. 'has its rise . . . to thank'; German would be *zu verdanken*. For *te*, see *toe* below.

opkomst lit. 'up-coming'. In German, *-kunft* is the abstract noun formed from the root of *kommen*, in Dutch it is *-komst* (infinitive *komen*). Both forms are ancient: OHG *kumft*, later *kunft*, MDu. *comst*. The *f* in German and the *s* in Dutch are secondary developments peculiar to each language. German does not use an exact parallel to *opkomst*—we should have to translate it by *Emporkommen*—but compare Ger. *Ankunft* arrival, *Zukunft* future, Du. *aankomst, toekomst*.

grotendeels, cf. Ger. *großenteils*.

feit is an old loan word from French *fait*.

er is aphetic for *der* (heard in dialect), an unstressed form of *daar* there, cf. OHG *dâr*, NHG *da*, but still *dar-* in certain combinations like *daran, daraus*.

sedert 'since', MDu. *do.* with excrescent *t* from earlier *seder*, a form historically identical with MHG *sider*, the change *i* > *e* being regular in this position in Dutch. This word stands in ablaut relationship to MHG *sîder* with the same meaning. The termination *-er* indicates that these forms are, in origin, comparatives; the positive form is seen in OHG, MHG *sît* since, NHG *seit*. Had MDu. *sedert*, however, evolved regularly we should have had ModDu. **zedert* like *zes* 6, *zeven* 7, from MDu. *ses*, *seven*. The phonetically irregular ModDu. *sedert* is explained as follows. Since MDu. *sedert* was, in practice, frequently preceded by words, the final consonant of which was voiceless, it could not in this situation evolve to **zedert* because its initial consonant was automatically kept devoiced by the preceding voiceless consonant in accordance with the principle of Dutch phonetics that two consecutive consonants must both be either voiced or voiceless. Then, for some reason, *sedert* established itself as the universally valid form. For another example of the effect of sandhi, see *toch* below.

eeuw, pronounced [e:u] 'century', is a regular development (insertion of *u* between *e* and *w*) of MDu. *ewe* long period, eternity, OLFr. *êwa* eternity, cf. OHG *do.* eternity, traditional law, MHG *êwe*, later *ê* do., marriage bond, NHG *Ehe*.

regering 'government' is derived from *regeren* 'govern' like Ger. *Regierung* from *regieren*, parallel formations coined in the 13th century. The infinitive ending MHG *-ieren* corresponds to MDu. *-ieren, -eren*. The suffixal element *-ier-* is the OFrench infinitive desinence *-ier*, to which the native ending *-en* was added. This distinctive termination became productive in assimilating foreign verbs, as in the present case. The prototype is Latin *regere*, but doubtless the Germanic creation was inspired by OFrench *reger* current at the time.

is gevestigd. Notice the word order is different from Standard German, where the finite verb follows the participle. German has no form corresponding exactly to Du. *vestigen* 'establish'; it has only *befestigen*, with rather divergent meanings.

talrijk is a calque on Ger. *zahlreich*.

pensionneren, cf. Ger. *pensionieren*. In German, verbs ending in *-ieren* do not now add the prefix *ge-* to the past participle, hence Ger. *pensioniert*. Dutch however regularly adds *ge-* to verbs of this type as well; this was possible in older German too.

en 'and', MDu. *en*, older *ende*, presupposing a still earlier *endi* as in OSax. It is an umlauted form of *andi*, cf. OHG *anti*, of which *unti* (> NHG *und*) was a variant.

woonplaats, cf. Ger. *Wohnplatz*.

gekozen from *kiezen* '(to) choose', pret.sg. *koos*, pl. *kozen*. This traditional Germanic word is in everyday use in Dutch, but it has now virtually disappeared from German, though it was once very common. It hardly survives except in the past part. *auserkoren* 'chosen' and even this is most frequently used as an adjective 'select, elect'; it has a parallel in Du. *uitverkoren*. In these forms *r* is ancient, having arisen in Common Germanic times out of original *s* (*z*) by 'grammatical change' (p. 26). The past part. *gekozen* in the present text is a modern form which came in analogically from other parts of the verb with *z* such as the infin. *kiezen* or the pret. pl. *kozen*. The original Germanic position was, however, still faithfully reflected in MDu. *kiesen, coos, coren, ghecoren*, with which we may compare MHG *kiesen, kôs, kurn, gekorn*. In German, *kiesen* has been replaced by *wählen*, an essentially southern word, unknown in Dutch.

woonstad, cf. Ger. *Wohnstadt*.

heeft . . . ook veel voor (*op andere grote steden*) lit. 'has . . . also much before (on other large towns)', i.e. 'has many advantages (over other large towns)'. The form *steden*, pl. of *stad* 'town', is the only example surviving in modern Dutch of a plural showing umlaut.

door de mooie omgeving, cf. Ger. *durch die schöne Umgebung*. The common word *mooi* 'beautiful' properly belongs to the Saxon area of Holland and also occurs in the adjacent parts of Germany. But it has for long been in standard use in Dutch where it competes with *schoon*, the word from the dominant Franconian element, in origin identical with Ger. *schön*. The word *mooi* occurs in MDu. and MLG. Its etymology remains a puzzle.

staat, infin. *staan*, cf. OSax., OHG *stân* beside *stên* > NHG *stehen*.

Vredespaleis, in German, *Friedenspalast*. The first element is *vrede*, in composition *vredes-*, cf. Ger. *Friede, Friedens-; paleis* is an old borrowing from French *palais*.

waar 'where'. As with *daar*, see above under *er*, the Dutch form is here more conservative than the German: OHG *hwâr*, later *wâr, wâ*, MHG *wâ* with the variant *wô*, NHG *wo;* an archaic form corresponding to the Dutch survives, however, in *warum* (going back to Late OHG *wâr umbe*).

het hof: neuter in Dutch, but masculine in German.

geschil 'dispute', cf. *verschil* difference, *verschillen* (to) differ, *verschillend* different. The root *schil-* presupposes OLFr. **skil-*. Such a root is not found in High German, but it does occur in Norse with the meaning 'divide', a meaning which naturally fits the Dutch as well. In High German 'divide' can be expressed by *scheiden* < OHG *skeidan*. From this we have *verschieden* different. Both Dutch and High German types are regarded as very ancient variations of the related bases *ski-, skai-;* in the one the base has been extended by *l*, in the other by a dental.

berechten '(to) adjudicate', based on *recht* 'justice'. German offers no parallel; it uses *entscheiden* or *urteilen*.

worden '(to) become', corresponding to NHG *werden*. Actually this would be the form expected in Dutch too, following MDu. *werden*. In some Dutch dialects, however, original *we-* changed to *wo-*, so that *werden* here became *worden*, and this local development has managed to establish itself as the standard form.

tussen 'between', historically identical with NHG *zwischen*. An old West Germanic numeral *twisk* 'twofold' survives in OSax. in the phrase *undar twisk* 'in between'. In OHG the phrase is *untar zwiskên*, i.e. the same word with a dat.pl. ending. An analogous phrase must have been in use in the Netherlands as well, since Du. *tussen*, MDu. *tusscen*, older *twusscen*, *twisscen* may be regularly derived from OLFr. **undar twiskun*, the first element being dropped as in High German.

staten, pl. of *staat* 'state', MDu. *staet* (*ae* is MDu. orthography for long *a* = ModDu. *aa*), like Late MHG *stât*, a borrowing, inspired by OFrench *estat*, from Latin *status*. The spelling *Staat* in modern German is due to Dutch influence, which also accounts for its irregular plural *Staaten*—we would expect a plural in *-e*. These forms became established in Germany at the beginning of the 17th century when the Dutch *Generalstaaten* were much in the news. (The now current spelling and form in Dutch is *Staten-Generaal*, the *a* being long by position.)

uitspraak 'verdict' is formally equivalent to Ger. *Aussprache*, but the senses do not agree here, and the Dutch must be translated by Ger. *Spruch* (*Richterspruch*, *Schiedsspruch*). But when the meaning is 'pronunciation' then Du. *uitspraak* and Ger. *Aussprache* coincide exactly.

te aanvaarden 'to accept'. For *te*, see *toe* below. The original sense 'approach' is preserved in MDu. *aenfaerden*, from which we postulate OLFr. **anafardian* from *ana* on, *-fardian* from **fard* journey, cf. OHG *anafartôn* approach, attack.

Binnen- en Buitenhof, a German translation would be *Innen- und Aussenhof*. The formations *binnen* 'inner, inside' and *buiten* 'outer, outside' are certainly ancient. They occur in MDu. and we may postulate OLFr. **bi innan*, **bi ûtan* to be compared with OHG **bi innan*, *bi ûzan*, MHG *binnen*, *bûzen*, which were Central German forms contrasting with forms without *bi* used in the south. In Standard German the southern forms have asserted themselves, hence NHG *innen*, *außen*, but Central Ger. *binnen* has also passed into the standard language mainly as a preposition, e.g. *binnen zwei Minuten* within two minutes, but the spatial sense is preserved in a few compounds, e.g. *Binnenland* interior (of a country). Forms analogous to the Dutch are common in the Low German dialects.

volksvertegenwoordiging, lit. 'People's Representation', from the verb *vertegenwoordigen* represent, corresponding in form to Ger. *vergegenwärtigen* represent to oneself, visualise. The concept 'represent (others)' is rendered in German by *vertreten;* Du. *volksvertegenwoordiging* is Ger. *Volksvertretung*. The Dutch word *tegen* 'against', contained in the above, is a contraction of an ancient **te jegen* from **te gegen;* it thus corresponds closely in form to Ger. *zugegen*. See further under *toe*, below.

zetelen '(to) sit, i.e. sit in session', the ordinary word for 'sit' being *zitten*, cf. Ger. *sitzen*. The verb *zetelen* is derived from *zetel* 'seat', in origin the same word as Ger. *Sessel*. But notice that German is unable to form a verb from this noun. In function, *zetel* in Dutch plays a similar role to *Sitz* in German.

schilderachtig 'picturesque'. This adjective is formed from the verb *schilderen* paint, cf. *schilderij* (painted) picture. The Dutch verb is the same as Ger. *schildern* describe, but the Dutch meaning is the primary one. Tacitus recounts that the ancient Germans painted their shields. When shields became coats-of-arms, painters were still needed, hence MDu., MLG *schilder*, MHG *schiltære* lit. 'shielder' signified such a painter. The present verb means then, literally, 'to (paint the) shield'. As for the adjectival ending *-achtig* in *schilderachtig*, this corresponds to High Ger. *-haftig*. In Dutch the aspirate is lost in composition and *cht* for *ft* is a Dutch innovation. It is, however, an ancient one, going back to the beginning of the tradition. It has been plausibly suggested that the change is ultimately due to the Celtic substratum in this area. At all events, we find that Du. *cht* regularly corresponds to High Ger. *ft*, e.g. Du. *lucht*, NHG *Luft*. The change seen in Dutch is also a feature over a wide area in North Germany and a few words showing the change have passed into Standard German. An interesting example is *Schacht* 'pit shaft' as distinct from genuine High Ger. *Schaft* 'shaft of an instrument', see p. 128.

het oude Den Haag, Ger. *das alte Den Haag*. It will be noticed that *Den Haag* is an invariable group. In Dutch, as in German, the names of towns are treated as neuters.

hoewel 'although', corresponds to Ger. *wiewohl*. Du. *wel* and Ger. *wohl* are ultimately identical, the former continuing *wela* as in OSax., the latter OHG *wola*, a variant of original *wela*—a similar change of *we-* to *wo-* was local in Dutch, see *worden* above. Du. *hoe* and Ger. *wie* are also related, though not identical. OLG *hwô* 'how' developed in two main ways. In the East Franconian part *w* was lost, giving **hô*, whence ModDu. *hoe*. Elsewhere evolution was regular, initial *h* being discarded, hence *wo* in most of the modern Low German dialects. These northern forms contrast sharply with the ablaut variant seen in High German, i.e. NHG *wie* < OHG *hwio*.

badplaats, cf. Ger. *Badeplatz*.

toe 'to' goes back regularly to OLFr. *tô*, cf. OSax. *tô*, OHG, MHG *zuo*, NHG *zu*. These were originally adverbs only. In addition there was the variant OSax. *ti*, OHG *zi* (also *za*) with the function of a preposition and commonly used with the verbal noun, i.e. the infinitive. Subsequently weakened forms of the preposition became current, e.g. MDu., MLG *te*, MHG *ze*. In Dutch this form has remained in use before the infinitive, cf. *te danken, te aanvaarden* above, whereas German has generalised *zu*.

behoren '(to) belong'. Notice that German is *gehören*. In both languages the basic sense is 'hear, obey'.

toch nog lit. 'though still', cf. Ger. *doch noch*. The form *toch* arose from *doch* in sandhi. In this case *d* was automatically devoiced whenever the word preceding it in the sentence ended in a voiceless consonant. Eventually this form separated out as the independent word *toch*. But it did not replace the basic form. Today *toch* and *doch* exist in Dutch side by side, but now somewhat differentiated in meaning and usage. For another example of a sandhi form, see *sedert* above. The word *nog* is so spelt to differentiate it in writing from *noch* 'neither, nor', the words being homophonous.

heel wat 'quite a lot' is an idiomatic phrase. Du. *heel* is the same word as Ger. *heil* 'whole, sound, unhurt'. German words corresponding in meaning to the Dutch are *ganz* or *sehr*, but *heil* is known in these senses too in the north. This northern usage has passed into Standard German in the term *heilfroh* very glad. Du. *wat* is the same word originally as NHG *was*.

forensen 'non-residents', i.e. people who work in a place, but live outside, sg. *forens*, a fairly recent term, based on Latin *forensis* 'external, outside'.

naburig 'neighbouring' from *nabuur* 'neighbour', cf. Ger. *Nachbar*. But German has no word formed after the style of *naburig;* the German translation here would be *benachbart*.

A further specimen of Dutch (*Matthew* x, 5–10) will be found at the end of this chapter.

DUTCH OVERSEAS

The Belgian colonisation of the Congo did not result in the expansion of Flemish in this part of Africa. When the territory was acquired in 1881 the state language was French only, Flemish being officially discouraged. Dutch colonisation, on the other hand, spread the language to distant parts of the world. New York was founded as New Amsterdam, though it passed into British hands as early as 1664. All the same, Dutch remained in common use in the town for over a century afterwards. In the rural environs it persisted much longer. Even at the end of the last century 'Jersey Dutch' could be heard from a few hundred old people in New Jersey State. The Dutch of these early settlers has supplied a few words to (American) English, e.g. boss, cookie, snooper (Du. *baas, koekje, snoeper*).

In three places Dutch was creolised. Firstly, in the former Dutch East Indies, as the so-called Language of the Sinyos and Nonahs (Du. *taal der sinjo's en nonah's* 'language of the gentlemen and ladies', *sinjo* being Port. *senhor* and *nonah* presumably a perversion of Port. *dona*, forms which derive from another creole language of the area, Malay-Portuguese). The language, basically Dutch, but with many Indonesian elements in both phonetics and grammar, is spoken mainly by people of mixed European and Indonesian descent. Now that the Dutch administration has left, the language is unlikely to maintain itself; its speakers will go over to the various Indonesian languages. Secondly, a creolised Dutch was the language of the coloured population of the former Danish Antilles. The European colonists here were chiefly Dutchmen and out of the pidgin used between them and the predominantly negro population arose a creole known as Negro Dutch (Du. *Negerhollands*). In 1917 the islands were sold to the U.S.A. Since then the use of English has become very general, so that the Dutch-based creole faces extinction in the near future. But far greater things were in store for Dutch in South Africa, where a creole form of the language was actually adopted by the Dutch settlers themselves. Their creole, now known as Afrikaans, is today a most important medium used by well over three million people. Afrikaans is an official language in every sphere and in the fullest sense of the word. It is thus the only creole language anywhere in the world to have achieved such status. In the next section we turn to a brief consideration of this unique development.

BIBLIOGRAPHY

There are a number of manuals and dictionaries of various sizes available for the study of Dutch. The concise reference grammar by E. Kruisinga, *A Grammar of Modern Dutch*, London, 1924, is an admirably lucid statement of the essentials.

An outline of the evolution and fortunes of the Dutch language forms part of C. P. F. Lecoutere and L. Grootaers, *Inleiding tot de Taalkunde en tot de Geschiedenis van het Nederlands*[6], Groningen, 1959. Well-known books dealing solely with the history of Dutch are the general synopsis by C.G.N. de Vooys, *Geschiedenis van de Nederlandse Taal in hoofdtrekken geschetst*[7], Groningen, 1970, and the volume by M. Schönfeld, *Historiese Grammatika van het Nederlands*[7], Zutphen, 1959, which gives a detailed account of the development of Dutch sounds, accidence and word formation.

For etymological questions, see J. Vercoullie, *Beknopt Etymologisch Woordenboek der Nederlandsche Taal*[3], Gent, 1925, or the larger J. Frank and N. van Wijk, *Etymologisch Woordenboek der Nederlandsche Taal*[2], The Hague, 1912, with a *Supplement* by C. B. van Haeringen, 1936.

AFRIKAANS

In 1652 a party of Dutch, led by Jan van Riebeeck, landed at the Cape of Good Hope to found a refreshment station for the Dutch East India Company. Van Riebeeck and the influential families among the new arrivals used a dialect of South Holland as their ordinary vernacular. In its new environment this dialect was modified at an astonishing rate. Apparently within a generation or so its formal grammar was drastically reshaped, nearly all inflexions being lost. The details of the process are naturally not ascertainable now, but the common assumption is that the new form of Dutch somehow arose owing to contact with foreigners at the Cape. One may, however, very well consider that such sweeping changes in the language must have been caused primarily by the use of pidgin, for this would be an everyday necessity in dealings with the many non-European slaves employed in Capetown. These slaves are known to have been brought in from different places and thus spoke a variety of languages, so that the pidgin would often be as necessary between slave and slave as it was between slave and master. Obviously the slaves would have little incentive to preserve their tribal languages and must soon have become the —first—habitual speakers of the pidgin.

It has recently been shown that for European children born in Africa this lingo became the primary medium. It was the children who 'murdered' Dutch, as G. G. Kloeke puts it (see Bibliography). But this important finding raises an equally important question: who taught these children to murder the language of their parents? As far as I can see, there can only be one main answer: the coloured women who acted as nurses in the European households. Van Riebeeck and his circle indeed imparted to the new creole its South Holland tinge, but it was the nameless coloured women who, by passing on their pidgin Dutch to the rising generation of Europeans, made it also a European colloquial, thus preserving it from the usually ephemeral fate of pidgin speech.

This remarkable transformation of spoken Dutch was, in essentials, completed in Capetown, as is proved by the basic uniformity of Afrikaans all over South Africa today. It would not be spoken by more than, say, a thousand souls when it began to spread as settlers moved further and further inland to establish isolated farming communities. Later immigrants, first the French who came in 1688, and then the Germans who started to arrive in considerable numbers in the next century, quickly adopted this African form of colloquial Dutch. Slaves, imported from the East Indies, gave up their Malay-Portuguese creole and the Hottentots, too, largely abandoned their native dialects in favour of the African Dutch. The descendants of these groups, the 'Whites' and the 'Coloureds', constitute the bulk of the Afrikaans speakers today.

But literary Dutch remained the written language of the speakers of the new patois. It was also the solemn language of the church and Bible. This arrangement no doubt seemed perfectly natural to all as the vernacular was considered to be a debased form of good Dutch.

The linguistic situation was complicated by the establishment in 1806 of an English colony at the Cape, which inaugurated a period of Anglicisation. This began at the top; English was imposed as the language of government, of the courts and the schools. English became the language of polite society at the Cape. In 1820 English settlers arrived in the Eastern Province. English continued to make headway in public and business life, but Afrikaans nevertheless generally remained the language of the home amongst 'Whites' and 'Coloureds'. In particular the Boers, who in the 1830s trekked northward to found the republics of the Orange Free State and the Transvaal, escaped politically inspired Anglicisation altogether. Their official language remained Dutch and their spoken language the African Dutch vernacular.

In the 1870s the question of the vernacular came to the fore as part of the political activity of the Afrikaners. Cut off for so long from Holland, they could by now rarely speak or write Dutch easily or correctly and the idea inevitably grew that the vernacular, Afrikaans, i.e. 'African', as it now began to be called, was the language of the future in South Africa. Publishing in Afrikaans began, in the face of the opposition of the supporters of literary Dutch and the contempt of the English section.

By the Treaty of Vereeniging in 1902 the republics of the

O.F.S. and Transvaal lost their political independence and became part of the British Empire, and a policy of Anglicisation began in these territories as well. But it was soon apparent that the old attitudes of imperialist administration were no longer possible. The opposition of the Afrikaners was too formidable and it was not long before their literary language, Dutch, won equal rights with English in all respects, as was laid down in 1910 in the Act of Union. But at the same time the inadequacy of Dutch was becoming ever more obvious. The movement for the official recognition of Afrikaans irresistibly gained strength and soon, for official purposes, 'Dutch' was being interpreted as 'Afrikaans'. By 1926, the latter had completely supplanted its rival in all official spheres, so that henceforth the official languages of South Africa were Afrikaans and English. The demise of Dutch led to an enormous increase in publishing in Afrikaans. As the language was now used in all spheres of modern culture and technology, its vocabulary developed apace and the language was handled with ability by creative writers. A translation of the whole Bible appeared in 1933.

Afrikaans is the home language of some 60% of the country's European population of rather more than 4 million. Some 90% of the more than 2 million 'Coloureds' and a very much smaller number of 'Natives' also speak Afrikaans as their mother tongue. Thus Afrikaans is the primary medium of well over 4½ million people in South Africa out of a total population of 25 million. English is spoken as the first language by about half as many as speak Afrikaans; the majority of the remainder of South Africa's 25 million inhabitants speak various Bantu languages, of whom an unknown number are able to express themselves, more or less, in Afrikaans and/or English.

Afrikaners today usually have a good knowledge of English, but it is much less usual for the English speakers to know Afrikaans well. The English speakers occupy a disproportionate number of the influential positions in the Union. They dominate, for instance, in the professions. A recent survey showed that 257 mine managers were English-speaking, only 49 were Afrikaans-speaking. Three-quarters of the doctors in South Africa are English-speaking. In the teaching profession, however, Afrikaans speakers predominate since children are, on principle, taught through the medium of the home language. But all learn the other official language as a subject. Inevitably there is considerable rivalry between English and Afrikaans in South Africa. English has the enormous prestige of a world language, but Afrikaans, as a uniquely African language, has a strong patriotic appeal. Present political trends are confirming and strengthening its position.

Dutch speakers have little difficulty in reading Afrikaans, but they need a little practice before they can easily follow the spoken word. Afrikaans is a bit of a joke among Dutchmen—it sounds to them something like pidgin English sounds to us. But this is, of course, purely subjective. Afrikaans sounds respectable enough to those whose mother tongue it is. In sober fact, Afrikaans is now as adequate as Dutch or any other modern literary language.

Outline of Afrikaans Grammar

SOUNDS AND SPELLING

In general, Afrikaans sounds are similar to Dutch and the spelling does not vary greatly. Notable differences, however, concern the loss of the Dutch short *i*, which has been replaced by the indistinct [ə]: *dik* [dək] thick, and the development of nasalisation: *ons* [ɔ̃:s] we, us. Du. *v*, when half-voiced, has fallen together with Du. *f*, but the Dutch spellings are retained, thus *vee* 'cattle' and *fee* 'fairy' are both pronounced [fe:]. Du. *v*, when fully voiced, has fallen together with Du. *w;* both are pronounced [v], uniformly written *w: liewer/liever* rather, Afr., Du. *wie* who. Du. *z* has become Afr. *s* in all positions: *suid/zuid* south, *huise/huizen* houses. Corresponding to Du. *sch* we have Afr. *sk*, presumably an archaism. Du. *ch* is spelt *g*, Du. *ij* is spelt *y: regtig/rechtig* real, *by/bij* near, at, by.

Owing to phonetic attrition, some Afrikaans words may look rather different from their Dutch ancestors. Typical examples are *wa* waggon, *vrug* fruit, *oor* over, Du. *wagen, vrucht, over.*

NOUNS

Plurals are most commonly formed by adding *-e* or *-s: stoel* chair, *oom* uncle, pl. *stoele, ooms.* Irregularities are often due to the phonetic attrition mentioned above: *wa* waggon, *vrug* fruit, pl. *waens*, *vrugte* (Du. *wagens*, *vruchten*).

Possession is indicated in two ways. 'Peter's key' is either *die sleutel van Pieter*, lit. the key of P., or *Pieter se sleutel* lit. P. his key, where *se* is a weakened (unstressed) form of the possessive *sy* (Du. *zijn*). This construction has spread to the feminine: *Anna se pop* Anne's doll.

ARTICLES

These are invariable: *die* the, *'n* [ə] a.

ADJECTIVES

These are usually invariable, but in the attributive position some take *-e*, which in certain words is associated with phonetic changes: *fris* fresh, *'n fris wind* a fresh wind; *blind* blind, *die blinde vrou; goed* good, *'n goeie daad* a good deed, *goeie dade* good deeds.

NUMERALS

1 *een*, 2 *twee*, 3 *drie*, 4 *vier*, 5 *vyf*, 6 *ses*, 7 *sewe*, 8 *ag(t)*, 9 *nege*, 10 *tien*, 11 *elf*, 12 *twaalf*, 13 *dertien*, 14 *veertien*, 15 *vyftien*, 16 *sestien*, 17 *sewentien*, 18 *ag(t)tien*, 19 *negen-*, *neëntien*, 20 *twintig*, 21 *een-en-twintig*, 30 *dertig*, 40 *veertig*, 50 *vyftig*, 60 *sestig*, 70 *sewentig*, 80 *tag(gen)tig*, 90 *negen-*, *neëntig*, 100 *honderd*, 1,000 *duisend*.

PRONOUNS

Some personal pronouns have an oblique form in the singular:

Sg.nom.	*ek* I	*jy,* (polite) *u* you	*hy* he	*sy* she	*dit* it
obl.	*my*	*jou*		*hom*	*haar*

Pl.   *ons* we, us, *julle,* (polite) *u* you, *hulle* they, them

The special reflexive is not usual: *sy was haar* she's washing herself.

The possessive adjectives are: sg. *my* my, *jou, u* your, *sy* his, its, *haar* her; pl. *ons* our, *julle, u* your, *hulle* their.

VERBS

The verbal forms in Afrikaans have been most drastically reduced. All distinctive personal endings have disappeared.

Except in the auxiliaries the preterite has been lost, leaving the perfect as the characteristic past tense. Apart from a few petrified phrases, inflexions survive only in the participles. The past part. is formed from the present stem, so that ablaut no longer plays any role. Thus the most typical feature of the Germanic verbal system, the division into strong and weak classes, has vanished from Afrikaans. This has occurred in no other Germanic language—Pidgin English excepted.

Infin. (*te*) *skryf* (to) write
Pres. *ek, ons* etc. *skryf* I, we etc. write.
Past *ek, ons het geskryf* I, we wrote, have written.
Imper. *skryf* Pres. part. *skrywende*
The future is expressed with *sal*, the passive with *word: ek sal skryf, die brief word geskryf.*

The auxiliaries 'TO BE' and 'TO HAVE' are as follows:

Infin. (*te*) *wees*, (*te*) *hê*, pres. *is, het*, past *was* or *het gewees*, had or *het gehad*, past part. *gewees, gehad.*

In spite of its formal simplicity, the Afrikaans verb is very expressive. It has developed continuous tenses, e.g. pres. *ek is aan die skryf* I am writing, lit. 'I am on the write', past *ek was aan die skryf*, fut. *ek sal aan die skryf wees*, fut.perf. *ek sal aan die skryf gewees het.*

Like *skryf: verloor* lose, *drink* drink, *neem* take, *lees* read, *graaf* dig; *maak* make, past part. *verloor, gedrink, geneem, gelees, gegraaf; gemaak.*

THE VOCABULARY AND SYNTAX OF AFRIKAANS

The traditional word stock is almost entirely of Dutch origin. It contains, however, a number of words which go back to Dutch dialect forms not found today in Standard Dutch. Examples are: *akker* acorn, *koei* cow, *mossie* sparrow, *seun* son (St.Du. *eikel, koe, mus, zoon*). The pronoun *hulle* has evolved from dialect Du. *hunlui* lit. 'them-people'. There have been various other special African developments of the Dutch element, like *moenie* don't, contracted from *moet niet* lit. must not. The diminutive is exceptionally frequent. It may express nuances of endearment or familiarity lost in English translation, e.g. *O liewe Heretjie*, meaning something like Ger. *O du lieber Gott*. Afrikaans, like Dutch, has its share of present-day international vocabulary in such words as *informeer* inform, *offisieel* official, *tuberkulose* tuberculosis, but it has, not unexpectedly, more loans from English than Dutch has, for instance *die motorkar*, but Du. *de auto*. The relatively few words taken over from African languages refer as a rule to purely African objects and conditions. An exception is *eina* ow!—an exclamation denoting pain; it is Hottentot. The common words *baie* 'much, many, very' and *soebat* 'plead' are of Malayan origin. A few features of syntax, too, are referred to Malayan influence, e.g. *dit reën so bietjie-bietjie* it keeps on raining a little bit, or *hy het rus-rus geloop* he walked and rested alternately. In essentials, Afrikaans syntax follows Dutch. A striking novelty is, however, the use of the double negative: *u moet hulle nie vertel nie* you mustn't tell them, *niemand is perfek nie* no one is perfect.

Specimen of Afrikaans

From the *Kulturgeskiedenis van die Afrikaner* (Cultural History of the Afrikaner), Part I, p. 115.

DIE DUITSERS IN SUID-AFRIKA

Reeds onder die bemanning van die drie skepe waarmee Jan van Riebeeck na die Kaap gekom het, was daar 'n paar Duitsers en in die loop van die 17de en die 18de eeu het 'n ononderbroke stroom Duitse immigrante na die Kaap gekom, 'n stroom wat tot by die einde van die Hollandse bewind (1814, Verdrag van Londen) tussen 14.000 en 15.000 Duitsers in die land gebring het. Ongunstige ekonomiese en maatskaplike toestande, armoede, werkloosheid, onderdrukking onder die destydse absolutistiese bewind het ongetwyfeld die meeste beweeg om hul geboorteland die rug toe te keer. Sommige is miskien voortgedryf deur die Duitse 'Wanderlust' om na die verre 'uithoek van Afrika' te verhuis, ander het seker ook tot die seksie van 'swarte skape' behoort wat dit om een of ander rede gerade geag het om hul heil in die buiteland te soek.

J. Hoge

(*hul* short form of *hulle*, *dit gerade ag* 'think it advisable', Du. *het geraden achten*)

GERMANS IN SOUTH AFRICA

'Even (lit. already) among the crew of the three ships with which J. v. R. came to the Cape were a few Germans and in the course of the 17th and 18th centuries an unbroken stream of German immigrants came to the Cape, a stream which by the end of Dutch rule (1814, Treaty of London) brought between 14,000 and 15,000 Germans into the country. Unfavourable economic and social conditions, poverty, unemployment, oppression under the then absolutist regime undoubtedly caused the great majority to turn their backs on their fatherland. Some were perhaps driven by German 'Wanderlust' to move to the 'remote corner of Africa', others certainly belonged to the section of 'black sheep' who for one reason or another thought it advisable to seek their salvation abroad.'

We conclude this brief account with an Afrikaans rendering of Matthew, x, 5–10. The reader may be interested to compare it with the Dutch version printed below the Afrikaans.

Afrikaans:

Jesus het hierdie twaalf uitgestuur en hulle bevel gegee en gesê: Moenie gaan op pad na die heidene nie, en moenie ingaan in 'n stad van die Samaritane nie; maar gaan liewer na die verlore skape van die huis van Israel. En gaan preek en sê: Die koninkryk van die hemele het naby gekom. Maak siekes gesond, reinig melaatse, wek dooies op, dryf duiwels uit. Julle het dit verniet ontvang, verniet moet julle dit gee. Moenie vir julle goud of silwer of koper in julle beurse aanskaf nie; geen reissak vir die pad of twee kledingstukke of skoene of 'n stok nie; want die arbeider is sy voedsel werd.

Dutch:

Deze twaalf heeft Jezus uitgezonden, en hun bevel gegeven, zeggende: Gij zult niet heengaan op den weg der Heidenen, en gij zult niet ingaan in eenige stad der Samaritanen; maar gaat veel meer heen tot de verlorene schapen van het huis Israëls. En heengaande predikt, zeggende: Het koninkrijk der hemelen is naarbij gekomen. Geneest de kranken, reinigt de melaatsen, wekt de dooden op, werpt de duivelen uit. Gij hebt het om niet ontvangen, geeft het om niet. Verkrijgt u noch goud, noch zilver, noch kopergeld in uwe gordels; noch male tot den weg, noch twee rokken, noch schoenen, noch staf; want de arbeider is zijn voedsel waardig.

BIBLIOGRAPHY

There is now no lack of dictionaries and manuals for the English speaker wishing to acquire Afrikaans, but all other serious philological work on Afrikaans is written either in that language itself or else in Dutch.

Authoritative essays on various aspects of Afrikaans linguistics form the first part of Vol. II of *Kulturgeskiedenis van die Afrikaner*, ed. by C. M. van den Heeven and P. de V. Pienaar, Cape Town, 1945–50, as follows (references to first pages):

p.1 D. B. Bosman 'Die ontstaan van Afrikaans', p. 23 S. A. Louw 'Die expansie van Afrikaans', p. 40 J. J. le Roux 'Die bou van die Afrikaanse taal', p. 73 S. P. E. Boshoff 'Die woordeskat van die Afrikaner', p. 96 P. de V. Pienaar ''n kulturhistoriese beskouwing van die klankbou van Afrikaans'.

Further, on the origin of Afrikaans: G. G. Kloeke, *Herkomst en Groei van het Afrikaans*, Leiden, 1950.

More information on the vocabulary of Afrikaans is contained in S. P. E. Boshoff, *Etimologiese Woordeboek van Afrikaans*, Cape Town, 1936. This book, however, does not aim at embracing all the words in the language. It concentrates only on those Afrikaans words which are significantly different from Dutch or which are not known in Dutch at all.

12

FRISIAN

According to the earliest testimonies (Pliny, Tacitus, Ptolomaeus) the territory of the *Frisii* stretched from the Rhine delta to the Ems. Their history in the following centuries is poorly documented. Unlike other Germanic tribes the Frisians did not move in a body at the time of the Migrations of the Peoples but remained in their old haunts. Later they became expansive; in particular they colonised the North Frisian Islands and the adjoining coastal strip. This northward movement is thought to have begun in the 9th century. The settlements east of the Jade will date from the 12th century. Since the beginning of the modern period at least, and especially since the 17th century, the Frisian-speaking area has been contracting (see Map 9).

In the conventional division of the Germanic languages into the genealogical groups North, East, and West, Frisian belongs to the West Germanic group. This concept of West Germanic is discussed elsewhere (pp. 4 ff.). In view of the many similarities Frisian shows with Anglo-Saxon it has been customary to postulate an Anglo-Frisian division within West Germanic contrasting with the other division consisting of Low and High German. This view is now contested. It is pointed out that Frisian shares no grammatical or phonetic features with Anglo-Saxon which are not found elsewhere. It is better to regard Frisian as a language drawn into the orbit of the surrounding Germanic dialects, preserving its identity, but participating in the general changes taking place around it. These surrounding dialects we may term North-West Germanic, to which Anglo-Saxon of course belongs. About the ultimate origin of the Frisians no more is known than about any of the other Germanic peoples.

The oldest sources for our knowledge of the Frisian language are almost exclusively legal writings dating from the 10th to the 16th centuries, though no ms. is older than the 13th century.

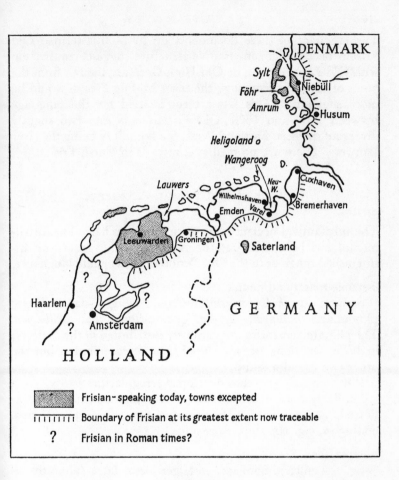

MAP 9

Greater Frisia

The language of these documents up to 1400 is termed Old Frisian because its conservative structure suggests comparison with Old Low German or Old High German, though from the point of view of chronology the term Middle Frisian would be more suggestive. This latter term is used for the language between 1400 and 1600. Old Frisian falls into two slightly divergent dialects, East and West, the boundary being the river Lauwers. There are no medieval records in North Frisian.

Outline of Old Frisian Accidence

NOUNS

The substantival declension is remarkably archaic. The instrumental has been lost, but the remaining four cases are distinguished much as in the Old Period of the cognate languages.

a-stems, masc. and neut.

Sg.nom.acc. *skilling* m. shilling, gen. *skillinges*, dat. *skillinge;* pl.nom.acc. *skillingar*, *-a*, *-an*, gen. *skillinga*, dat. *skillingum*. The pl. nom.acc. forms are variously distributed in the dialects; in WFr. *-an* alone occurs, in EFr. *-ar* predominates, but the other two are also found.

(OFr. *dei* (*dî*) 'day' has developed irregularities.)

Similarly *word* n. word, except that pl.nom.acc. are uninflected. As in OSax., a few neuters preserve a pl.nom.acc. ending *-u*, e.g. *skip* ship, *skipu* ships.

ð-stems, fem.

Sg. *ieve* gift; pl.nom.acc. *ieva*, gen. *ieva*, later (after the *n*-stems) *ievena*, dat. *ievum*.

i-stems, masc. and fem. Original endings have here been largely replaced by endings proper to *a*-, *ð*- and *n*-stems.

Sg.nom.acc. *iest* m. guest, gen. *iestes*, dat. *ieste;* pl.nom.acc. *ieste*, gen. *iesta* or *iestena*, dat. *iestum*.

Sg.nom.acc. *ferd* f. journey, gen.dat. *ferde;* pl.nom.acc.gen. *ferda*, dat. *ferdum*.

n-stems, all genders

Sg. *boda* m. messenger; pl.nom.acc. *boda*, gen. *bodena*, dat. *bodum*.

Sg.nom. *tunge* f. tongue, obl. *tunga;* pl.nom.acc. *tunga,* gen. *tungena,* dat. *tungum.*

Sg.nom.acc. *âge* n. eye, gen.dat. *âga;* pl.nom.acc. *âgon,* gen. *âgena,* dat. *âgum* (OFr. *herte* 'heart' has become feminine, inflecting like *tunge.*)

ADJECTIVES

The main division into strong and weak is maintained, though strong forms have penetrated the weak declension and the number of distinct inflexions is much reduced when compared with OLG or OHG. A notable feature is the replacement of the dat. **-um* by *-e* or *-a.* The paradigms of *sterk* 'strong' are as follows:

Strong forms: sg.nom. *sterk,* acc.m. *sterkne,* f. *sterkene,* n. *sterk,* gen.m.n. *sterkes,* f. *sterkre,* dat.m.n. *sterke* or *sterka,* f. *sterkre;* pl.nom.acc.dat. *sterke* or *sterka,* gen. *sterkera.* Weak forms: sg. *sterke* or *sterka;* pl.nom.acc.dat. *sterke* or *sterka,* gen. *sterkera.*

The adverb is formed by adding *-e* to the uninflected adjective: *sterke.*

The comparative and superlative of adjectives are formed by adding *-era,* *-esta* to the uninflected positive: *sterkera, sterkesta.* Irregular comparison occurs as in Old German, but some of the traditional words are lost: *gôd* good, *betera, best;* (*kwâd*) bad, *werra, werst;* (*grât*) big, *mâra, mâst; lîtik* or *littik* little, *lessera* or *minnera, lêrest* or *lêst.*

NUMERALS

As in OLG and OHG the first three numerals in Frisian are declined and distinguish the three genders. A trace of the prefix *ant-,* known from Old Saxon, sometimes occurs in the decades 70 to 90 as *t-,* and also by analogy in 60.

1 *ên* (inflects strong and weak, nom.m. also *ân*), 2 nom.acc.m. *twêne* or *twêr,* f.n. *twâ,* gen. *twira,* dat. *twâm,* 3 nom.m. *thrê,* f. *thria,* n. *thriu,* acc.m.f. *thria,* n. *thriu,* gen. *thri(r)a,* dat. *thri(u)m,* 4 *fiûwer,* 5 *fîf,* 6 *sex,* 7 *sigun, soven,* 8 *achta,* 9 *niugun,* 10 *tian,* 11 *andlova,* 12 *twelef,* 13 *thredtîne,* 14 *fiûwertîne,* 15 *fîftîne,* 16 *sextîne,* 17 *sigun-, soventîne,* 18 *achtatîne,* 19 *niuguntîne,* 20 *twintich,* 21 *ên ende twintich,* 30 *thrîtich,* 40 *fiûwertich,* 50 *fîftich,* 60 (*t*)*sextich,*

70 (*t*)*sigun-*, *soventich*, 80 (*t*)*achtich*, 90 (*t*)*niuguntich*, 100 *hundred*, 1,000 *thûsend*.

PRONOUNS

The personal pronouns are declined as follows:

Sg.nom.	*ik* I	*thû* you	*hî* he	*hiu, se* she	*hit* it
acc.	*mî*	*thî*	*hine*	*hia,* „	„
gen.	**mîn*	*thîn*	(*sîn*)	*hire*	(*sîn*), *es*
dat.	*mî*	*thî*	*him*	„	*him*
Pl.nom.	*wî* we	*î* you	*hia, se* they		
acc.	*ûs*	*iu*	„ „		
gen.	*ûser*	*iuwer*	*hira,* (OWFr.) *hiara*		
dat.	*ûs*	*iu*	*him*		

Although they are not met with in the surviving records, Old Frisian certainly possessed dual pronouns meaning 'we two' and 'you two', since such are known in the modern North Frisian dialects, q.v. As in Old Saxon there is no special reflexive pronoun.

ARTICLES

The declension of the definite article is as follows:

	m.	f.	n.		
Sg.nom.	*thî*	*thiu*	*thet*	Pl.	*thâ*
acc.	*thene*	*tha*	„		„
gen.	*thes*	*thêra*	*thes*		*thêra*
dat.	*thâ(m)*	*thêre*	*thâ(m)*		*thâm*

The indefinite article is identical with the numeral *ên* (*ân*) one.

VERBS

Strong verbs follow the normal Old Germanic pattern. The ablaut classes are easily identifiable, but there has been some loss of inflexions. In this respect Old Frisian closely resembles Old Saxon. It shows the characteristic North-West Germanic reduction of the separate plural endings to one single termination. But Frisian has gone further than Old Saxon in that it has replaced the old 2nd sg. pret.indic. (OS. *skrîƀi*) by an analogical form ending in *-est*. The subjunctive in Old Frisian is much decayed. Specimen paradigm:

Infin. *skríva* write

Indicative

Pres.sg.1 *skríve*	Pret.sg.1 *skréf*
2 *skrifst*	2 *skrévest*
3 *skrift(h)*	3 *skréf*
pl. *skrívat(h)*	pl. *skrivon*

Subjunctive: pres.sg. *skríve*, pl. *skríve(n)*; pret. *skrive*.
Imper.sg. *skríf*, pl. *skrívat(h)*
Pres. part. *skrívand*, past part. *skriven*. Gerund *to skrívanne*.

Principal parts (infin., 3rd pres.sg., pret.sg. and pl., past part.) of other ablaut classes: 2 *forliasa* lose, *forliast(h)*, *forlár*, *forleron*, *forleren;* 3 *drinka* drink, *drinkt(h)*, *drank*, *drunkon*, *drunken;* 4 *nema (nima)* take, *nimt(h)*, *nam (nôm)*, *nômon*, *nimen;* 5 *lesa* read, *lest(h)*, *les*, *léson*, *lesen;* 6 *grava* dig, *greft(h)*, *grôf*, *grôvon*, *greven*.

Weak verbs fall into two classes corresponding to the two main classes of Old Saxon, the infin. of the first ends in *-a*, the second in *-ia:*

Infin. *déla* divide, *makia* make

Indicative:

Pres.sg.1 *déle, makie*	Pret.sg.1 *délde, makade*
2 *délest, makast*	2 *déldest, makadest*
3 *délet(h), makat(h)*	3 *délde, makade*
pl. *délat(h), makiat(h)*	pl. *déldon, makadon*

Subjunctive: pres. *déle, makie;* pret. *délde, makade*
Imper.sg. *déle, maka;* pl. *délat(h), makiat(h)*
Pres. part. *déland, makand* Past part. *déled, makad*
Gerund *to délanne, makianne*

A few verbs have the preterite in *-ede*, e.g. *nera* nourish, pret. sg. 1,3 *nerede*.

The auxiliaries 'TO BE' and 'TO HAVE' inflect as follows:

Infin. *wesa*

Pres.sg.1 *bim* Pret.sg.1 *was* Imper.sg. *wese*, pl. *wesat*(*h*)
   2 *bist   2 *wêrst Pres.part. *wesand*
   3 *ist*   3 *was* Past part. (*e*)*wesen*
   pl. *sind* pl.   *wêron* Gerund *to wesanne*

Subjunctive: pres. *sê*; pret. *wêre*

The *e-* (also *i-*) prefix sometimes occurring in the past part. is a relic of *gi-*, a form also found occasionally in the earliest OEFr.

> Infin. (OEFr.) *hebba*, (OWFr.) *habba*
> Pres.sg.1 *hebbe*, *habbe*
>   2*hefst, *hast*
>   3 *heft*(*h*), *hat*(*h*)
>   pl.   *hebbat*(*h*), *habbat*(*h*)
> Pret.sg. *hêde*, *hade*; pl. *hêdon*, *hadden*
> Pres. part *hebband, *habband*
> Past part. *hêved*, *hawn*
> Gerund *to hebbanne*, *habbanne*

> (Other parts not attested.)

Compound tenses are formed after the same principles seen in the other medieval Germanic languages. In Frisian, too, the present may do duty for the future, but the usual construction is *skella* 'shall' with the infinitive.

Specimen of Old Frisian

The following recension of the Ten Commandments, in Old East Frisian, dates from the second half of the 13th century. It is edited from two mss. by W. Steller, *Abriß der altfriesischen Grammatik*, 1928, p. 91. In the following, however, quantity marks—which were not employed by Frisian copyists—have been added. Since the text is not otherwise normalised the forms occurring in it may conflict slightly with the normalised forms given in the notes below or elsewhere in this chapter.

Thet êrste bod: minna thînne god fore feder ende môder mith inlekere herta. Thet ôther bod: minna thînne eunkristena líke thî selwm. Thet thredde bod: fîra thene sunnandei end there hêlche degan. Thet fiârde bod: minna thîne feder end thîne môder, hû thû longe libbe. Thet fífte: thet thû thî nowet ne ower hôre. Thet sexte: thet thû nênne mon ne slê. Thet sogende: thet thû nowet ne stele. Thet achtende: thet thû thî nowet ne ûrsuere, ne nên falesk withskip ne drîue. Thet niugende: thet thû nênes thînes eunkristena wîues ne gereie. Thet tiânde: thet thû nênes thînes eunkristena gôdes ne ierie.

(*minnia* love, *inlek* intimate, *herte* f. heart, *evenkristena* fellow Christian, *fîria* celebrate, keep, *hêlich* holy, *nowet ne* not, *overhôria* commit adultery, *nên* no (adj.), *ûrswera* swear falsely, *wittskipe* witness, *geria, ieria* covet).

MODERN WEST FRISIAN

Frisian has maintained itself best in West Frisia. Certainly it has here too lost much ground since the Middle Ages, so that today it is substantially confined to the province of Friesland. Here it is spoken in most rural areas, but in the larger towns a compromise language, half-Dutch and half-Frisian, the so-called 'Town Frisian', is commonly used. It is estimated that between 250,000 and 300,000 persons use the Frisian language. But Frisian is not an official language in the full sense of the word, the language of the law and administration being Dutch. This has been the position since the first half of the 16th century. Prior to 1500 the Frisian tongue was not only the natural medium of the inhabitants of Friesland but also the usual language for official purposes. But particularly after the final establishment there of the alien House of Burgundy in 1524 a mass of Dutch-speaking officials entered the area and in a short time Frisian was ousted from official use. Established in the towns, the newcomers and their dependents were influential enough to modify the language there. 'Town Frisian' came into being very rapidly and even the Frisian-speaking countryside lay wide open to Dutch penetration, especially since the language of the Church now became Dutch.

Modern West Frisian literature begins with the work of a writer of distinction, Gysbert Japiks (1603–66), but the modern literary renaissance is not older than the 20s of the last century. Inspired by the Romantic movement of the early 19th century, Frisian intellectuals began to take a patriotic interest in their native language. Some dreamt of its being restored to its former position as the ordinary medium for all purposes. Their aspirations led to the formation of the 'Selskip for Fryske tael en skriftekennisse' (Society for Frisian Language and Literature) in 1844 which marks the beginning of the organised Frisian movement. But the path of the would-be restorers was not by any means a smooth one. Even though the Frisian language was a reality in the country districts, the people had got used to the closely related Dutch as the literary and official medium. Particularly the Church was most unsympathetic. The orthodox congregations felt that Frisian was not a fit language in which to call upon the name of God. Doubtless the conservative-minded leaders of the Church were also on their guard, because the leaders of the Frisian movement in the last century were chiefly free-thinking liberals. By now such prejudices have been mainly overcome, though it was not until 1943 that a Frisian version of the whole Bible appeared. The Frisian movement has registered other successes. In particular the language has recently become the medium of instruction during the first two years of primary school in many districts—this is of course sound pedagogy. Since the war it has been usual for village street names to be posted up in the local language and place names on sign boards are sometimes given in Frisian as well as Dutch, e.g. *Ljouwert—Leeuwarden.*

There is a considerable amount of publishing in Frisian, mostly of novels and poetry, plays and children's books and a modest number of periodicals are produced. But there is no daily newspaper in Frisian and Frisian speakers read infinitely more Dutch than Frisian. Nevertheless, in spite of disabilities, the language is maintaining itself. The rural areas where the language is spoken are prosperous and the Frisians obviously possess a degree of regional, if not national pride. As is usual in analogous situations the speakers of the major language, Dutch, do not as a rule bother to acquire Frisian, in the same way as English people living in Welsh-speaking parts of Wales rarely trouble to learn Welsh. But the speakers of the minor language are bilingual. Modern West Frisian has evolved under the close influence of Dutch and the spoken language especially is replete with Dutch words. The literary language however endeavours to escape from Dutch influence as far as possible. Unnecessary Hollandisms, even when current in popular speech, are replaced by genuine Frisian expressions. Anti-Dutch purism may even affect the choice of purely Frisian forms. For example, the following variants of the infinitive 'to have' occur in the dialects: *hebbe, habbe, hewwe, hawwe;* the literary language has adopted the last as the one most unlike Du. *hebben*. Tendencies similar to these are commonly found where-ever a minor language is struggling to preserve its identity.

It remains to be said that the literary language is well estab-lished. It is based upon the spoken dialects. It still admits a number of alternative forms so that it is not quite so standardised as, say, Dutch.

Outline of Modern West Frisian

SOUNDS AND SPELLING

West Frisian has a most complicated vowel system with a large number of diphthongs and some triphthongs, to which the present standard orthography is a somewhat imperfect guide. The consonants *p*, *t* and *k* are unaspirated as in Dutch. Accents are not printed over capitals.

NOUNS

As a rule case endings have been lost, apart from a limited use of the genitive terminations *-s* and *-e: syn wiifs heit* his wife's father (*wiif* wife), *memme hoed* mother's hat (*mem* mother). Possession is otherwise indicated periphrastically: *it gesang fan it fûgeltsje* the little bird's song, *ús beppe har hûs* our granny's house, lit. her house.

The usual plural endings are *-(e)n* or *-s* as in Dutch: *brêge* bridge, *wurd* word, pl. *brêgen, wurden; dochter* daughter, pl. *dochters*. Though the *-(e)n* ending is rather commoner in Frisian than in Dutch, the distribution of the two types of ending follows the Dutch closely. A score of words have quite irregular plurals, e.g. *kou* (m.!) cow, *skoech* shoe, *wei* way, pl. *kij, skuon,* *wegen;* two nouns show no change in the plural: *bern* child(ren), *skiep* sheep.

ARTICLES

The definite article is as follows: sg.m.f. *de* (*'e*), n. *it* (*'t*); pl. *de* (*'e*). The forms in brackets can only occur after prepositions: *doe krige de wolf de rook fan 'e woarst yn 'e noas* then the wolf got the smell of the sausage in his (lit. the) nose. The indefinite article *in* is invariable.

ADJECTIVES

These are uninflected when predicative: *it byld is moai* the picture is pretty, and also when attributive before a neuter noun ('strong'): *har nij boek* her new book. Otherwise the adjective nearly always takes the ending *-e: it âlde boek* the old book, *de greate beam* the big tree, *(de) moaie bylden* (the) pretty pictures.

NUMERALS

1 *ien*, 2 *twa*, 3 *trije*, 4 *fjouwer*, 5 *fiif*, 6 *seis*, 7 *sawn*, 8 *acht*, 9 *njoggen*, 10 *tsien*, 11 *alve*, 12 *tolve*, 13 *trettsjin*, 14 *fjirtsjin*, 15 *fyftsjin*, 16 *sechstsjin*, 17 *sawntsjin*, 18 *achttsjin*, 19 *njoggentsjin*, 20 *tweintich*, 21 *ien en tweintich*, 30 *tritich*, 40 *fjirtich*, 50 *fyftich*, 60 *sechstich*, 70 *sawntich*, 80 *tachtich*, 90 *njoggentich*, 100 *hûndert*, 1,000 *túzen*.

The ancient inflexion of 1—3 has been lost in the modern language.

PRONOUNS

The personal pronouns are:

Sg.nom.	*ik* I	*dou, -ou**; *jo* you	*hy, er** he	*hja, se** she	*it* it
obl.	*my*	*dy*	,,	*him*	*har, se*	,,
Pl.nom.	*wy* we	*jimme* you	*hja, se** they		
obl.	*ús*	,,	*har, se*		

*These forms are usual when following the verb, *-ou* being enclitic: *hastou?* have you?

The pronoun *jo* is polite and followed by a plural verb.

There is no special reflexive pronoun, hence *hja wasket har* she washes herself, contrasting with Du. *zij wast zich.*

The possessives are invariable: sg. *myn* my, *dyn*, (polite) *jou* your, *syn* his, its, *har* her; pl. *ús* our, *jimme* your, *har* their.

VERBS

The verbal forms of the old language have been somewhat reduced in number in Modern West Frisian. The subjunctive has disappeared and there is only one form for the imperative. But the gerund construction remains; it is treated as a second infinitive. OFr. *skrîva* appears in the modern language as follows:

Infin. *skriuwe, to skriuwen* write

Pres.sg.1 *skriuw*	Pret.sg.1 *skreau*	Imper. *skriuw*
2 *skriuwst*	2 *skreaust*	Pres. part. *skriuwend(e)*
3 *skriuwt*	3 *skreau*	Past part. *skreaun*
pl. *skriuwe*	pl. *skreauwen*	

Principal parts (infin., pret., past part.) of typical strong verbs: 2 *forlieze* lose, *forlear, forlern;* 3 *drinke* drink, *dronk, dronken;* 4 *nimme* take, *naem, nommen;* 5 *lêze* read, *lies, lêzen;* 6 *grave* dig, *groef, groeven.*

The weak conjugation resembles in essentials that of the parent language, though some details have been obscured by phonetic developments. OFr. *makia* appears in the modern language as follows:

Infin. *meitsje(n)* make

Pres.sg.1 *meitsje*	Pret.sg.1 *makke*	Imper. *meitsje*
2 *makkest*	2 *makkest*	Pres. part. *meitsjend(e)*
3 *makket*	3 *makke*	Past part. *makke*
pl. *meitsje*	pl. *makken*	

The auxiliaries 'TO BE' and 'TO HAVE' inflect as follows:

Infin. *wêze(n), hawwe(n)*

Pres.sg.1 *bin, ha(w)*	Pret.sg.1 *wie, hie*
2 *bist, hast*	2 *wiest, hiest*
3 *is, hat*	3 *wie, hie*
pl. *binne, ha(wwe)*	pl. *wiene, hiene*

Imper. *wês, ha(w)*
Pres. part. *wêzend(e), hawwend(e)*
Past part. *west, hawn*

Compound tenses are formed with the same auxiliaries as in Dutch: *ik sil skriuwe* I shall write (*sille* =Du. *zullen*), *it wurdt skreaun* it is (being) written (*wurde* = Du. *worden*); *ik ha skreaun* I have written, *ik bin bleaun* I have stayed (*bliuwe* stay).

Specimen of Modern West Frisian

From *Us Wurk* 'Our Work', April 1959.

OM IN NIJE STAVERING

Wy binne derfan útgien, dat in goede stavering safolle mooglik oanslute moat by it lûdsysteem fan de tael. Oan elk phoneem moat dus in apart teken bianderje en elk ûnderskaet teken fortsjintwurdiget in foneem. Dat systeem wurdt yn elke tinkbere stavering trochkrúst fan de regels fan de ôflieding, de analogy, de lykfoarmigens en de 'beschaafde uitspraak'. De ynfloed fan de ôflieding moat yn it frysk gâns ynperke wurde. Wol is it foar de kontinuïteit fan bilang en hâld safolle mooglik fêst oan de nou besteande tekens—as soks net yn striid komt mei it lûdsysteem—en dat is op himsels al in tradisjoneel elemint, mar foar de rest leau ik, dat inkeld in radikale oprúming fan de histoaryske eleminten ús fierder helpe kin.

Tony Feitsma

(*stavering* also *boek-,* cf. Ger. *Buchstabierung,* but Du. *spelling; wy* . . . *útgien* cf. Du. *wij zijn ervan uitgegaan,* Ger. *wir sind davon ausgegangen; oanslute* cf. Du. *aansluiten,* Ger. *anschließen; tael* language, cf. Du. *taal* do.; *elk* each, cf. Du. do.; *beanderje* a calque on Du. *beantwoorden; ûnderskaet* cf. Du. *onderscheiden* differentiated, different; *fortsjintwurdiget,* also *fortsjinwurdiget,* a calque on Du. *vertegenwoordigt,* for which concept German has *vertritt* rather than *vergegenwärtigt; trochkrúst* lit. crossed through, cf. Du. *doorkruist,* Ger. *durchkreuzt; ôflieding* cf. Du. *afleiding,* Ger. *Ableitung; lykfoarmigens,* i.e. with derivative termination *-ens,* more typically Frisian than *lykfoarmichheit,* reminiscent of Du. *gelijkvormigheid,* Ger. *Gleichförmigkeit;* 'beschaafde uitspraak' is Dutch; *ynperkje* cf. Du. *inperken; fan bilang* cf. the common Dutch expression *van belang,* also Ger. *von Belang; en hâld* lit. and keep, imper., a specifically Frisian construction having the force of 'in order to keep', an alternative wording being *om safolle mooglik oan de nou besteande tekens fêst to hâlden* with parallels in Dutch and German; *al* expletive, lit. already, cf. Du. do., or (for usage) Ger. *schon; oprúming* cf. Du. *opruiming,* Ger. *Aufräumung*)

TOWARDS A NEW ORTHOGRAPHY

'Our basic premise is that a good orthography must follow the phonetic system of the language as much as possible. A separate letter must thus correspond to each phoneme and each different letter stands for a phoneme. In any conceivable orthography this system is complicated by the rules of derivation, analogy, uniformity and cultured pronunciation. In Frisian the influence of derivation has to be very much restricted. Naturally it is of importance for continuity to keep as close as possible to the letters now existing—if such do not conflict with the phonetic system—and this is in itself a traditional element, but for the rest I believe that only a radical removal of the historical elements can help us forward.'

(A further specimen of West Frisian on p. 234.)

MODERN EAST FRISIAN

Frisian speech has now disappeared entirely from the traditional East Frisian area. It survived until recently on the small island of Wangeroog, where it became extinct in the 20s of this century, and in the colony from this island, Neu-Wangeroog, near Varel, where the last speakers died in the 30s. Sometime during the Middle Ages, perhaps in the 13th century, a colony of East Frisians was established south of the Frisian border in a remote part of Saterland and this enclave of East Frisian speech, though much diminished, has not yet entirely succumbed to the surrounding German. But since the language is now not used by more than about a thousand persons it is rapidly disintegrating. The few texts which have been published show that this last relic of East Frisian is so strongly Germanised that, to the superficial observer at any rate, it appears merely as an outlandish dialect of Low German. For example, the reflexive pronoun *sik*, which is absent from Frisian proper, has passed into ordinary use: *nu geen hi in sik, ûn quiid tou sik selwen* . . . then he pondered (cf. the German idiom *in sich gehen*) and said ('quoth') to himself . . . .

MODERN NORTH FRISIAN

Linguistic evidence suggests that North Frisia was colonised from East Frisia. For instance, corresponding to the OEFr. plural ending -*ar*, as in *skillingar*, the modern North Frisian island dialects have -*r̥*, while the mainland dialects have -*e* answering to OEFr. -*a* (*skillinga*). The OWFr. plural ending however was -*an* (*skillingan*). The North Frisian dialects are so diverse that mutual comprehension is not always easy. In particular the cleavage between the island and the mainland groups is both deep and ancient. Scholars are not agreed on the interpretation of the facts observed, but it seems likely that the islands and the coastal strip were colonised separately. What population already existed in the new territories and hence what part such a substratum may have played in the evolution of North Frisian is unknown.

It is however certain that in its new environment Frisian came into intimate contact with Danish both to the north and down the eastern side. Subsequently Frisians came under Danish rule. As a consequence a host of Danicisms—borrowings, loan translations, syntactical imitations, even phonetic habits—penetrated into all the North Frisian dialects, except that of Heligoland. It is this Danish element which makes North Frisian today so much different from East or West Frisian. Later, as the Danish in South Sleswig was gradually expelled by Low German, North Frisian became directly exposed to Low German influence. In the more recent period Standard German has made itself powerfully felt through the schools, the newspapers and the radio. German is, of course, the official language. All North Frisians know German and modern North Frisian abounds with words either from Low German dialect or from the High German Standard. Idioms from German pass easily into Frisian, so that even if the words themselves are Frisian, the spirit is often German. This applies of necessity to all terms relating to modern concepts. Just as in this respect West Frisian is deeply indebted to Dutch, so is North Frisian utterly dependent on German.

The Frisian movement in North Frisia has always been much weaker than in the West. Numbers have been very much smaller and these far from united, for the considerably differentiated dialects make for parochialism and hamper contact on a wider scale. Whereas West Frisian has developed a literary standard, North Frisian has not. The language lives on only in its dialects and hence all writing in North Frisian is of necessity dialect writing. Most of what little is printed appears nowadays in the West Moring dialect. This is the speech of the Niebüll (Naibel) area and only this form is quoted here. The future for North Frisian looks desperately black. Without official recognition or encouragement, its frontiers are rapidly receding. In parts of the remaining Frisian-speaking area its continued existence is threatened from inside by the presence of numbers of monoglot Germans who moved there after the war. At present not more than 5,000 know Frisian. Perhaps the last strongholds of the language will be the island of Föhr and the mainland area just south of Niebüll. Here there are villages where the child population is still nearly 100% Frisian-speaking.

Outline of Modern North Frisian

SOUNDS AND SPELLING

The vowel system of North Frisian is rather complex and only imperfectly represented by the orthography. Here it must suffice to say, as a rough guide only, that a short vowel is represented by a single letter: *hüs* house, and a long vowel by a double letter: *hüüs* hoarse. The spellings *dj, kj, lj, nj* and *tj* denote palatalised *d* etc.

NOUNS

In general, case endings are lost. There are just a few exceptions, notably an occasional genitive like *täätens koot* father's cottage (*tääte* father). An inflexional *-s* occurs in set expressions of the type *tu scheews* at table (*scheew* table) in imitation of Danish *til bords* (*bord* table). Possession is usually expressed periphrastically: *di däi foon et urdiil* the day of (the) judgement, *di böre sin håne* the farmer's hens, lit. the farmer his hens.

The great majority of nouns form the plural by adding *-e* to the singular, unless this already ends in *-e*, in which case there is no change: *fälj* field, pl. *fälje; åte* grandfather(s). A few relics of umlaut survive: *fötj* foot, *fätj* feet; half a dozen common words take -(*i*)*nge: iir* year, *knif* knife, pl. *iirnge, knivinge;* there are a small number of anomalous plurals like *schouf* shoe, *wäi* way, pl. *schuur, weege; stää* f. town, pl. *stääse*, but *stää* n. place, pl. *stäägne; schäip* 'sheep' does not change in the plural.

ARTICLES

The definite article is as follows: sg.m. *di* (*e*), f. *jü* (*e*), n. *dåt* (*et*); pl. *da* (*e*). The forms in brackets are common after prepositions: *weer as di kining foon e Jööse?* where is the king of the Jews?—but they may be found in other positions too, cf. specimen text below. After certain prepositions *et* may become -*t: amt* (for *am et*) *hüs* around the house. The indefinite article *en* is invariable.

ADJECTIVES

These are uninflected when predicative: *dåt bil as smuk* the picture is pretty, and also when attributive before a fem. and neut. sg.: *jü hiil wråål* the whole world, *en latj bjarn* a little child. Before a masc. sg. two endings, -*en* (strong) and -*e* (weak), are used: *en riken kriimer* a rich shopkeeper, *di grute buum* the big tree. The ending -*e* is also used before all plurals: (*da*) *smuke bile* (the) pretty pictures.

NUMERALS

A notable archaism is the separate forms of the numbers 1—3 before masculines: 1 *åån* m., *iinj* f.n., 2 *twäär* m., *tou* f.n., 3 *tra* m., *trii* f.n., 4 *fjouer*, 5 *fiiw*, 6 *seeks*, 7 *soowen*, 8 *oocht*, 9 *nüügen*, 10 *tin*, 11 *alwen*, 12 *tweelwen*, 13 *tratäin*, 14 *fjouertäin*, 15 *füftäin*, 16 *seekstäin*, 17 *soowentäin*, 18 *oochtäin*, 19 *nüügentäin*, 20 *twunti*, 21 *iinj än twunti*, 30 *dorti*, 40 *fäärti*, 50 *füfti*, 60 *süsti*, 70 *sööwenti*, 80 *tachtenti*, 90 *näägenti*, 100 *hunert*, 1,000 *duusend*.

PRONOUNS

The personal pronouns are:

Sg.nom.	*ik* I	*dü* you	*hi* he	*jü* she	*et* (*hat*) it
obl.	*me*	*de*	*ham*	*har*	*ham*
Pl.nom.	*we* we	*jam** you	*ja* they	(*also polite sg.)	
obl.	*üs*	,,	,,		

North Frisian preserves the dual forms *wat* we two, *jat* you two, the oblique cases being *unk, junk* respectively. They are followed by a plural verb. In the spoken language however these pronouns are now extinct, though they could be heard until very recently. In no other Germanic language has the dual as a separate grammatical category been kept so long.

There is no special reflexive pronoun, hence e.g. *ja måågeden ja aw e wäi*, contrasting with Ger. *sie machten sich auf den Weg*. The possessives mostly have special forms for the masc.sg.:

	(m.sg.)				(m.sg.)		
Sg.	*man*	*min*	my	Pl.	*üüsen*	*üüs*	our
	dan	*din*	your			*jarnge**	your
	san	*sin*	his, its			*jare*	their
	harn	*har*	her			(*also polite sg.)	

	(m.sg.)		
Du.	*unken*	*unk*	our two
	junken	*junk*	your two

Examples with *hün* m. dog: *man, üüsen hün* my, our dog; *min, üüs hüne* my, our dogs.

VERBS

As regards inflexion North Frisian is roughly at the same stage of evolution as the sister language in the west. The old subjunctive has gone, the imperative is reduced to a single form, the gerund construction remains as the second infinitive. But North Frisian has also lost the present participle as a functioning grammatical category. It survives only in set expressions like *laden giilj* savings, lit. lying money (*lade* lie). OFr. *skríva* appears in present-day North Frisian as follows:

Infin. *schriwe, tu schriwen* write

Pres.sg.1	*schriw*	Pret.sg.1	*schriif*
2	*schrafst*	2	*schriifst*
3	*schraft*	3	*schriif*
pl.	*schriwe*	pl.	*schriifen*

Imper. *schriw* Past part. *schraawen*.

Principal parts (infin., 3rd pres.sg., pret.sg., past part.) of typical strong verbs: 2 *ferliise* lose, *ferlüst, ferlüüs, ferlääsen;* 3 *dränke* drink, *dränkt, drunk, drunken;* 4 *naame* take, *namt, nüm, nümen;* 5 *leese* read, *leest, löis, lääsen;* 6 *greewe* dig, *greeft, grouf, grääwen.*

The weak verb (cf. OFr *makia*) inflects as follows:

Infin. *määge(n)* make

Pres.sg.	1	*määg*	Pret.sg.	1	*määged*
	2	*määgest*		2	*määgedst*
	3	*määget*		3	*määged*
pl.		*määge*	pl.		*määgeden*

Imper. *määg* Past part. *määged.*

The auxiliaries 'TO BE' and 'TO HAVE' inflect as follows:

Infin. *weese(n), heewe(n)*

Pres.sg.	1	*ban, hääw*	Pret.sg.	1	*wus, häi*
	2	*bast, hääst*		2	*wjarst, häist*
	3	*as, heet*		3	*wus, häi*
pl.		*san, hääwe*	pl.		*wjarn, häin*

Imper. *wees, hääw* Past part. *wään, hädj.*

Compound tenses are formed with the same auxiliaries as in German: *ik wårt schriwe* I shall write (*wårde* = Ger. *werden*), *et wårt schraawen* it is (being) written; *ik hääw schraawen* I have written, *ik ban blaawen* I have stayed (*bliwe* stay).

Specimen of North Frisian

From the magazine *Üüsen Äine Wäi* 'Our Own Way', Jan–Feb. 1959.

PADERSDÄI

Padersdäi wus di wichtiste däi önj di üülje frasche kaläner. Paders-däi gungt e wunter, än e uurs kamt.

Dåt iilj, wat di 21. (iinj än twuntiste) önj e biikenmoune am eenem oufbrånt wårt, wus önj üüljingstide en hiisen brük än schölj da dämoone ferdriwe. Karmene än wüste doonsden amt iilj än süngen deerbai jare iiljwise, uurde, wat we diling bål ai mör ferstönje koone.

Aw Padersdäi schölj åål dåt korn tjarsched weese, ouers füng di loie
tjarscher en fliigeklåp in önj e låås sman ma en latjen spootfjarsch 'rbai:

Padersdäi as nü forbai,
än N.N. heet nuch korn önjt strai.

Albrecht Johannsen

(*wichti* < NHG *wichtig; iilj* < Dan. *ild* fire; *schölj* cf. Ger. *sollte; biikenmoune* lit. beacon-month, *biiken* being the bonfire here referred to; *karmen*
man < Older Dan. *do.; wüset* woman < *wüfset* < OFr. *wüfshêd (wüfs-*
gen. of *wüf* wife, woman, -*hêd* -hood; originally an abstract noun like Engl.
womanhood); *diling* cf. *däi* day, and the adverbial ending -*ling* as also in
wääling this week (*wääg* week); *bål* < NHG *bald; ai* < Dan. *ej* not; *låås* an
old loan, cf. Dan. *lade* barn; *sman* past part. of *smite* throw; *'rbai* < *deerbai*)

(ST.) PETER'S DAY

'Peter's Day was the most important day in the old Frisian
calendar. On Peter's Day the winter goes and the spring comes.

The bonfire which was burnt on the evening of the 21st of
February was in ancient times a heathen custom and was
supposed to drive away the demons. Men and women danced
round the fire and sang their fire-song, the words of which we
can hardly understand today any more.

By Peter's Day all the corn was supposed to be threshed,
otherwise the dilatory thresher would receive a fly-swatter
thrown into the barn with a satirical little verse attached:

Peter's Day is now past,
and So-and-So still has his corn on the straw.'

We conclude this brief survey of Frisian with a parallel
passage (Matthew x, 5–10) in Modern North and Modern
West Frisian.

North Frisian:

De tweelven sånd Jesus üt än kånd ja aw än sää: Gung ai üt aw da
hiise jare weege än ai in önj e stääse foon da Samaritane. Gung liiwer
tu da farlääsene schäip foon Israels hüs. Aw jarnge fård schan jam
prätje än seede: Dåt hamelrik as näibai kiimen. Mååg krunke sün, mååg
düüdje wiikne, riinsch da ma ütslåch, driw hiinje geeste üt. Jam hääwe
dåt füngen for ninte, jeew et for ninte. Hääw niinj gölj unti silwer

unti koower önj jarnge riime; niinj tååsch tu e räis, unti twäär ruuntje, unti schuur, unti en stook; dan en årbesmansche as sin neering wjart.

West Frisian:

Dy tolve stjûrde Jezus der op út en hy sei harren syn bistel, sizzende: Gean net in wei op nei de heidenen, en gean gjin stêd yn fan Samaritanen; mar bijow jimme leaver nei de forlerne skiep fan it hûs Israël. En gean, en forkundigje, sizzende: It keninkryk der himelen is neiby. Genês siken, wekje deaden op, reinigje melaetsken, werp kweageasten út. Omdôch hawwe jimme it ûntfongen, jow it omdôch. Nim gjin goud, gjin sulver, gjin koper mei yn jimme rimen; noch in reissek foar ûnderweis, noch twa liifrokken, noch skoaijing, noch stêf, hwant de arbeider is syn lean weardich.

BIBLIOGRAPHY

B. Sjölin, *Einführung in das Friesische*, Stuttgart, 1969, provides a summary statement on Frisian in all its forms. Further, W. Krogmann, 'Die friesische Sprache' in W. Stammler, *Deutsche Philologie im Aufriß*, vol. I, 1952, cols. 1523–50.

Old Frisian:
W. Steller, *Abriß der altfriesischen Grammatik*, Halle, 1928.
F. Holthausen, *Altfriesisches Wörterbuch*, Heidelberg, 1925.

West Frisian:
A description has been given in English by P. Sipma, *Phonology and Grammar of Modern West Frisian*[2], Oxford, 1966. A shorter work, but in the present standard spelling, is K. Fokkema, *Beknopte Friese Spraakkunst*[2], Groningen 1967.

H. S. Buwalda et al., *Frysk Wurdboek*, Bolsward, vol. I (*Frysk-Nederlânsk*) 1956, vol. II (*Nederlânsk-Frysk*) 1952, is a comprehensive dictionary sponsored by the Frisian Academy (*Fryske Akademy*).

East Frisian:
A summary account of the Saterland Frisians with word lists and texts is available in J. Botke, *Sealterlân*, Bolsward, 1934.

North Frisian:
Grammars and dictionaries of several of the dialects have been published, see the bibliography to W. Krogmann's essay (above) cols. 1523–4, to which may be added a brief outline in English: J. Schmidt-Petersen and J. Craigie, *The North Frisian Dialect of Föhr and Amrum*, Edinburgh, 1928.

There is a dictionary in West Moring Frisian: V. T. Jörgensen, *Frasch-Tjüsch-Dånsch Uurdebök*, Husum, 1955, and a grammar by the same author, *Spräkeliir foon dåt Mooringer Frasch*, Bredstedt, 1968.

13

YIDDISH

The Jews in the diaspora have created several new languages. There are, for instance, Jewish varieties of Arabic and Persian. These developments have been favoured by the social exclusiveness of the Jews and by the many cultural differences between them and their non-Jewish neighbours. In Europe two such Jewish languages have become prominent; they have often been termed Judeo-Spanish and Judeo-German. Nowadays it is felt that such designations are inadequate, since the languages themselves are now so far removed from ordinary Spanish and German that they must be considered as independent languages. The Jewish variety of Spanish may be termed Judezmo, the Jewish development of German is best called Yiddish. Of all languages created by the Jews none has become so different from its source as Yiddish has.

Yiddish originated in the Middle Ages. Its history begins about the year 1,000 when Jewish settlers, apparently from France, made their homes in the German-speaking towns on the Middle Rhine. They brought with them their native language, a Jewish variety of Old French, though naturally they soon acquired German and eventually abandoned French. But in the German they used when talking among themselves they continued to use some words of Romance stock, for a number of these have survived. For instance *bentshn* bless, and *leyenen* read, ultimately from Latin *benedicere*, *legere*, are in use in Yiddish to this day. It is also certain that the new settlers used other foreign words; these were of Semitic origin, see the section 'Hebrew Component' below. Otherwise the German spoken by the Jews is not known to have been different from that of their Gentile neighbours and it evolved in the same way from the OHG to the MHG stage. But later on, especially after the Lateran Council of 1215, restrictions led to the closed ghetto and in the relative isolation of the ghetto, so it is supposed, Yiddish began to modify here and there its basic German element.

At the end of the 11th century there began a drift of German Jews eastward into Slavonic lands, chiefly to Poland, to become in the 13th century a mass movement which reached its height following the massacres after the Black Death (1348–9). This migration continued for quite two centuries more. Jews from South-East Germany and Jews from Central Germany met and mixed in the new territories. As a result there took place a unique fusion of South-Eastern and Central German dialects, which led to a new dialect, Eastern Yiddish. Inevitably this new dialect at once fell under the influence of Polish and other Slavonic languages and soon Eastern Yiddish became considerably differentiated from the older Western dialects which remained in contact with German and continued to be dominated by it. Yet all the same, Eastern Yiddish also remained in some contact with German. For centuries Germans were numerous and influential in the Polish towns and cities. In addition the Eastern Jews had, of course, connections with their Western co-religionists and there was always some movement between the two groups. Later on, in more modern times, Eastern Jews often acquired German; some used it as a literary medium in preference to Yiddish.

As a consequence of emancipation in the latter half of the 18th century the traditional life of Western Jewry largely dissolved and the Western Yiddish dialects declined. Within Germany they disappeared entirely, only in peripheral areas did Western Yiddish maintain itself until the present century, the most notable dialect being that of Alsace-Lorraine. But in the East, where more retarded conditions obtained generally, the old orthodox mode of Jewish life persisted almost unchanged since the Middle Ages right down to the second half of the last century. The Jews, though most often speaking the language of the country they lived in as well, were not assimilated. They lived together mostly in the towns in the recognised Jewish quarters. Hundreds, even thousands of families lived side by side and passed their whole social lives entirely within their community. In several large towns the Jewish population constituted half the total number of inhabitants or more. Before the First World War no less than 88% of the inhabitants of Berdichev were Yiddish-speaking Jews. In Pinsk the figure was 80%, in Odessa 57%, in Minsk 55%, in Kishinev and Warsaw 50%. Then there were the small Jewish townships—the *shtetlekh*—where the population would often be 100% Jewish or virtually so. In such cases one may almost think of Yiddish as having a territorial basis like other languages. In these conditions specifically Jewish culture was very strong and the number of speakers of Eastern Yiddish constantly increased as the communities grew larger. Beginning in the 1880s mass emigration to America and other places overseas carried the Yiddish language all over the world. It is estimated that in 1939 between ten and twelve million people spoke Yiddish, of whom more than two-thirds lived in Eastern Europe. But after the Catastrophe that overwhelmed Eastern Jewry in World War II these figures and the outlook for Yiddish have been radically changed. Of some six millions done to death, a good majority were Yiddish speakers, and the survivors have mostly left Eastern Europe. Brought almost to the verge of extinction in the areas that nurtured it as the primary medium, Yiddish now faces rapid decline, for linguistic assimilation is today nearly everywhere the rule. The largest Jewish populations are now in the Soviet Union and the United States. The Russian Jews seem to have largely abandoned Yiddish, while in America the younger generation has gone over to English either exclusively or as the main medium. In Israel only Hebrew is recognised as the official language, so that Yiddish seems destined to disappear there as well in a couple of generations or so.

But this time has yet to come. For the present there is still considerable literary activity in the Yiddish language and a vigorous popular press flourishes in America and Israel. A recognised literary standard exists, but a spoken standard has not been reached. Eastern Yiddish falls into three main dialects, a characteristic distinction between them concerning the pronunciation of certain vowels, so that when reading out the language, speakers normally follow their own dialect as far as the vowels go. Much Yiddish published nowadays appears in the orthography used by the Yiddish Scientific

Institute YIVO (*Yidisher Visnshaftlekher Institut*)—a sort of Yiddish Academy—founded in Vilna in 1925, since 1939 centred in New York, see 'Yiddish Script' below. In an attempt to standardise educated pronunciation YIVO has sponsored the pronunciation of North-Eastern Yiddish and has drawn up a standardised Roman transliteration based mainly on this dialect. This system of transliteration is used throughout the present account of Yiddish, which refers solely to the standard language (in the above sense), except where otherwise stated. It follows that several of the statements made below will, of necessity, not be valid for the whole of Yiddish. In particular, it could not be claimed that the pronunciation recommended by YIVO has yet been accepted by speakers of dialects other than N.E. Yiddish and it has not been adopted by the Yiddish Theatre.

THE GERMANIC COMPONENT

Compared with the Middle High German from which it sprang, Yiddish shows a number of innovations, particularly in its vocalism. A striking feature (though confined to N.E. Yiddish) is the loss of the distinction between long and short vowels (see 'Slavonic Component').

The main development of the MHG vowels in Yiddish is, in outline, as follows:

MHG *a* remains if it is short in NHG: *zak* (*Sack*, MHG *sac*), but becomes *o* where lengthened in NHG: *hon* (*Hahn*, MHG *hane*); MHG *â* becomes *o*: *nodl* (*Nadel*, MHG *nâdele*).

MHG *e*, of whatever origin, remains if it is short in NHG: *bet* (*Bett*, MHG *bet*), but where lengthened in NHG it may either remain: *redn* (*reden*) or become *ey*: *leygen* (*legen*); MHG *ê* becomes *ey*: *shney* (*Schnee*, MHG *snê*). MHG *ä* and *ö* fall together with *e*, *æ* and *œ* with *ê* and develop accordingly.

MHG *i* remains: *tsvishn* (*zwischen*); MHG *î* becomes *ay*: *ayz* (*Eis*, MHG *îs*). MHG *ü* falls together with *i*: *Yid* (MHG *jüde*, a dialectal variety of *jude*); MHG *iu* falls together with *î*: *layt* (*Leute*, MHG *liute*).

MHG *o* remains if it is short in NHG: *vokh* (*Woche*), but becomes *oy* where lengthened in NHG: *voynen* (*wohnen*, MHG *wonen*); MHG *ô* becomes *oy*: *groys* (*groß*, MHG *grôӡ*).

MHG *u* remains: *wunder* (*Wunder*); *û* becomes *oy*: *toyb* (*Taube*, MHG *tûbe*).

MHG *ei* remains (spelt *ey*): *neyn* (*nein*).

MHG *ou* becomes *oy*: *toyb* (*taub*, MHG *toup*); MHG *öu* becomes *ey*: *hey* (*Heu*, MHG *höu*).

The evolution of MHG *ie, uo, üe* is referred to below.

Yiddish contains a number of features traceable to Central or South-East German. Among Central features may be mentioned the monophthongisation of MHG *ie, uo, üe*: *shisn, shukh, grin* (MHG *schieʒen, schuoch, grüene*); this development is also characteristic of NHG: *schießen, Schuh, grün*. Other Central German features are unshifted *pp*: *kop*, NHG *Kopf*, initial *f* for usual HG *pf*: *fefer*, NHG *Pfeffer*, and initial *p* for *b* sporadically: *puter*, NHG *Butter*. Peculiar forms of words, or the words themselves, may point to Central Germany: *koyl* ball, MHG *kûle* (NHG *Kaul-*), a contraction of *kugele* (NHG *Kugel*); *fregn* ask, Central MHG *vregen* beside *vrâgen* (NHG *fragen*); *filn* feel, Central MHG *vüelen* as opposed to *spürn* the southern word (NHG *fühlen, spüren*, with differing regional usage); *zeyger* clock, Late MHG *seiger*, a word confined to East Central Germany; it still survives in local speech though often replaced by the unrelated word *Zeiger* with which it has been confused. South-Eastern or Bavarian features are, among others, the loss of final *e*: *kort* card, MHG *karte* (NHG *do.*), the change of *b* to *p* before *l*: *gopl* fork, NHG *Gabel*, the intrusive *d* between *n* and *l*: *shteyn* stone, diminutive *shteyndl*, etymological *u* in (*der*) *zun* son, (*di*) *zun* sun, whereas NHG has the Central German forms with change of *u* to *o*: *Sohn, Sonne*. Perhaps the velar pronunciation of *kh* in all positions, e.g. *ikh* I (iχ) is a southern trait; on the other hand it may be attributable to Slavonic influence. The use of the auxiliary *zayn* with verbs like *zitsn, shteyn*: *ikh bin gezesn, geshtanen* corresponds to southern usage: *ich bin gesessen, gestanden*, but elsewhere *ich habe gesessen, gestanden*. The loss of the preterite (see 'Outline of Grammar') may also be a southern feature, but that remains uncertain. Not all features of the Germanic element have as yet been explained. Puzzling, for instance, are the forms *land, kind* with final *d*, but *hant, gelt* with final *t*.

Sometimes the same words in Yiddish and Standard German have evolved in different directions so that their common origin is more or less obscured: *epes, etwas*, MHG *etewaʒ*; *arbes, Erbse*, MHG *araweiʒ*; *entfern, antworten*, MHG *ant-, entwürten*; *gikh* quick, *jäh* sudden, precipitous, MHG *gæhe*. In this last case the development of MHG *æ* in Yiddish is very irregular, the German form with initial *j* for *g*, first recorded in the 15th century, is dialectal; Luther has it. Where alternatives were present Yiddish and Standard German sometimes made different choices. Luther used a word *blotzling* suddenly; later on he adopted another variety of the same word *plötzlich*. In German *blotzling* has long been forgotten, but not so in Yiddish where it continues as *plutsling*. The NHG for palate *Gaumen* derives from MHG *goume*, while Yiddish *gumen* represents MHG *guome*. Both forms are ancient: OHG *goumo, guomo*, the difference being one of ablaut.

Yiddish uses a large number of words which are unknown in modern Standard German, being confined solely to certain dialects. The ordinary term *haynt* today, from MHG *hînt*, in full *hînaht* lit. this night, is paralleled in Bavarian dialect where *heint* is heard instead of Standard German *heute*. A similar semantic shift has led to *nekhtn* yesterday, from MHG *nehten* last night, and this again has a parallel in German dialect *nächten*. The Yiddish word for bed sheet is *laylekh*, but *Leilach* in German is only found in dialect and that to a very limited extent, it having been largely replaced by better known words like *Bettuch* or *Leintuch*. In *fatsheyle** handkerchief, Yiddish preserves what is probably the oldest word in German for this article. The word, first attested in German in 1482, derives from Italian *fazzoletto*. It was presumably introduced by Italian pedlars into Germany, but it is not now heard there much, though it survives in some southern dialects as *Fazzelet, Fazzenet(li)* etc. There are two verbs in Yiddish meaning 'to wash', *vashn* and *tsvogn*, the latter used of washing hair. This is a specialisation in sense of MHG *twahen*, the older verb for 'to wash'. The word also lives on in Germany, but only locally, in some places

---

* Non-Germanic words in Yiddish are stressed on the penultimate syllable except where otherwise indicated by an acute accent.

as *zwahen*, in others as *zwagen*. Yiddish has remained conservative in the names of certain relations, for example *shver*, *shviger*, *eydem*, *shnur* father-, mother-, son-, daughter-in-law. Older German used these words: *Schwäher*, *Schwieger*, *Eidam*, *Schnur*, but the modern standard language has *Schwiegervater*, *-mutter* etc., compounds which did not develop before the 17th century. The older words all survive sporadically in some German dialects, but the tendency is to replace them there as well by the standard terms.

But it would be wrong to think of Yiddish mainly as a repository of archaisms. Far from it; Yiddish has created a superabundance of innovations. German has traditionally one degree of diminution, expressed generally by the terminations *-chen* or *-lein*, but Yiddish nouns usually have two degrees of diminution. These are formed by the endings *-l* and *-ele* with umlaut of the root vowel where possible: *lokh* hole, *lekhl*, *lekhele*. Sometimes a diminutive has become the normal form of the word: *keml* comb (Ger. '*Kämmlein*', *Kamm*). Altogether the diminutive is a much more prominent feature of Yiddish than of German, or indeed of any Germanic language. In this Yiddish has undoubtedly received encouragement from Slavonic, see 'Synthesis of the Components'. Yiddish has also developed forms of words unknown in German. Poor is *orem* (Ger. *arm*), poverty is *oremkayt*, a neologism replacing MHG *armuot* (NHG *Armut*). Like Ger. *heutig* from *heute*, Yiddish forms *hayntik* from *haynt*. But Yiddish has further, in recent use, the near-synonym *haynttsaytik* to which there is no corresponding compound in German; you can't very well say **heutzeitig*.

In this section we have so far discussed only such basic elements of vocabulary as are of long standing in Yiddish. We may now recall that Yiddish has never really lost touch with its German parent; at times contact has been very close. As a consequence, German has, especially in recent times, been heavily drawn upon and its influence may be plentifully seen in the vocabulary of Yiddish. Thus *shtime* 'voice' and *shprakh* 'language' are seen to be recent acquisitions from NHG; traditional forms would be **shtim*, **shprokh*. In fact these Germanisms compete to some extent with the old-established Hebraisms *kol*, *loshn* (see below). Occasionally doublets occur through borrowing. Y. *kort* 'playing card' goes back to MHG, but *karte* 'map' is a neologism taken over from modern German.

Some idea of the radical changes in the morphology of Yiddish when compared with German may be gained from the 'Outline of Grammar'. Finally, there are innumerable innovations in syntax and idiom, often clearly traceable to Slavonic influence, sometimes also to Hebrew. All these give Yiddish its unmistakable flavour. Some indications of this may be conveyed in the following sections on the Slavonic and Hebrew components and in the specimen passages later on in this chapter.

THE SLAVONIC COMPONENT

Established in its Slavonic environment, the language of the Jewish immigrants underwent great changes which not only removed it much further from German proper, but also from the Yiddish spoken in the west. New Yiddish dialects now evolved in the east, sharing innovations unknown in the west. Henceforth Yiddish falls into two main dialect groupings: Western Yiddish and Eastern Yiddish. In the latter we distinguish three sub-divisions: Central, North-Eastern and South-Eastern Yiddish, spoken in areas which correspond basically to the areas of Polish, Belorussian and Ukrainian speech respectively. These are the Slavonic languages which have exerted the most fundamental influence upon Yiddish. The influence of Great Russian came much later, hardly before the last century. Great Russian gained currency in the above-mentioned areas as an official language. But it was a language imposed from outside, the everyday speech of the inhabitants continued to be Polish, Belorussian or Ukrainian— or Yiddish. Hence the effect of Great Russian on Yiddish has been superficial, affecting substandard speech rather than the literary language.

Slavonic influence is at once apparent in the phonetics of Eastern Yiddish. The occlusives *p, t, k* are widely pronounced without aspiration, *l* may be soft (mouillé) in palatalised surroundings, the consonant *zh* has entered the language, initial groups of *s* + consonant are possible. The glottal stop has disappeared, though this may be a German dialectal feature.

North-Eastern Yiddish has even abandoned the typical
Germanic distinction between long and short vowels in favour
of the medium-length vowel as in the surrounding Slavonic.

Equally apparent is the deep impress made by the Slavonic
languages on the vocabulary of Yiddish. Several names of
relations are taken from these sources : *mame* mother, *tate*
father, *bobe* grandmother, *zeyde* grandfather, all hypocoristic
terms usual in the Slavonic languages which have influenced
Yiddish, e.g. Polish *mama, tata, baba, dziad*. The names of farm
animals are often Slavonic, such as *baran* ram, *bik* bull, *tsap*
billy-goat, again terms widespread in the Slavonic languages,
cf. Pol. *baran, byk, cap*. Other everyday words are *kose* scythe,
pushke box, *smétene* cream, cf. Pol. *kosa, puszka, smetana*. There
are common adjectives like *proste* ordinary, *nudne* boring, Pol.
prosty, nudny. There are verbs like *khapn* to catch (Pol. *chapać*)
or *katshn* to roll (Beloruss. *kačić*). Many international terms
have entered Yiddish via Slavonic, such as *asimilatsye,
sotsyalizm*, cf. Pol. *asymilacja, socializm*, but Ger. *Assimilation,
Sozialismus*. Slavonic transmission explains the masculine
gender in such words as *klas* or *ideál*, where German has *die
Klasse, das Ideal*. Of Slavonic provenance are two common
particles, *tsi* and *zhe*. The former may be used in introducing a
question : *tsi hobn zey gekrogen dem oyto?* have they got the car ?
The latter is emphatic : *shlof zhe* do go to sleep.

It frequently happens that a Yiddish word is Germanic in
outward form but Slav in spirit. The verb *unterhern* means to
overhear. This sounds Germanic enough, but one could hardly
deduce its meaning from a comparison with German, since
there is no verb **unterhören*. But the Polish for to overhear is
podsłuchiwać, compounded of *pod* under, *-słuchiwać* to hear, with
analogous formations in other Slavonic languages. Certain
grammatical usages are also due to Slavonic influence. Double
and multiple negatives are a conspicuous feature of Yiddish :
er hot keyn lefl nit he hasn't a spoon, *zi hot im keyn mol nit geshribn
keyn briv* she hasn't once written him a letter. Though usual in
older German—and still found in some modern dialects—the
persistence of this feature in Yiddish will have been encouraged
by the neighbouring Slavonic languages where analogous
constructions are also the rule. But there are cases where there

is no doubt that Slavonic alone has inspired changes. For
instance, one says in German *die Jungen spielen* the boys are
playing, but the Yiddish version runs *di yinglekh shpiln zikh*, i.e
the verb is used reflexively. An explanation is provided by
reference to Slavonic sources where a reflexive verb is usual,
e.g. Polish *bawić się*. Incidentally the same construction occurs
in some German dialects and for the same reason; an Austrian
equivalent of the sentence would be *die Buben spielen sich*. But
Yiddish goes further; it extends the use of the reflexive pronoun
zikh to the first and second persons as well—after the analogy
of Slavonic. Compare *ikh ze zikh, du zest zikh in shpigl* with
German *ich sehe mich, du siehst dich im Spiegel* I see myself, you see
yourself in the mirror. The use of *fun* (= German *von*) after a
comparative: *er iz greser f u n dir* 'he is bigger than you' sounds
most un-German, where one must say *er ist grösser a l s d u*, but
the Yiddish construction is an imitation of Polish *od* from,
often found after comparatives in this sense. It should perhaps
be added that in Hebrew a somewhat similar construction is
used : *gódoyl mímkho* bigger than you, lit. big from-you; this may
have favoured developments in Yiddish. With this mention of
Hebrew, we may now consider the impact of Semitic on
Yiddish.

THE HEBREW COMPONENT

An inevitable component of any Jewish language is its Hebrew
element or, more exactly, its Hebrew-Aramaic element. A
knowledge of Hebrew remained general among the Jews even
after it had passed out of use as a vernacular. It was venerated
as a sacred tongue and the study of the Hebrew Bible was
enjoined upon all. Aramaic, a language closely allied to
Hebrew—one may almost speak of the two as closely related
dialects—is thought to have supplanted Hebrew as the ordinary
colloquial speech of the Jews by the second century B.C., if not
before, and much later literature, such as the Talmud, was
composed in Aramaic. Then in the 8th century Aramaic itself
yielded to Arabic as the colloquial speech of Palestine, but the
Jews continued to study and cultivate it side by side with
Hebrew. In fact, they did not always distinguish very exactly
between what was properly Hebrew and what Aramaic, and

eventually a strongly Aramaicised Hebrew emerged as the special literary language of the Jews. It is therefore not surprising that words of Hebrew or Aramaic origin should feature in a Jewish language and such a Semitic element was certainly in Yiddish from the beginning.

Doubtless numerous Semitic terms have persisted in Jewish speech since ancient times, particularly in the case of words appertaining to religion. We find in Yiddish such examples as *Shabes* Sabbath, Saturday, *Peysakh* Passover, *Sukes* Tabernacles, *Yom Kiper* Day of Atonement, *yontev* (Jewish) holiday—from *yom* day, *tov* good—*Toyre* (traditional Jewish) Law, *Khumesh* Pentateuch, *novi* prophet, *nevue* prophecy, *rov* rabbi, *khazn* cantor, *tfile* prayer, *luakh* calender, *malakh* angel, *gan-eydn* paradise, garden of Eden, *brokhe* blessing, *Mitsrayim* Egypt, *Moshiakh* Messiah, *matse* unleavened bread, *kosher* (ritually) clean—and its opposite *treyfe*. To these may be added traditional Hebrew names such as *Avróm*, *Dovid*, *Dvoyre* Debora, *Khane* Hannah, *Moyshe* Moses, *Rivke* Rebecca, *Rokhl* Rachel, *Shloyme* Solomon, *Sore* Sarah, *Yankev* Jacob, *Yitskhok* Isaac.

It is not improbable that other words came in through religious associations. The entry into Yiddish of such standard terms as *khoydesh* month and *levone* moon would be facilitated by the lunar aspects of Jewish worship. Even a word like *yam*, the ordinary term in Yiddish for sea, may fall into this category. At any rate the sea has made a great impression on the Jewish mind, for a special blessing—in Hebrew of course—is to be spoken by the pious whenever they catch sight of *ha-yam ha-gódoyl* the great sea. Religious influence would also account for such terms as *agole* hearse, *beys-oylem* (Jewish) cemetery, *keyver* grave, *levaye* funeral, *matseyve* gravestone, *orn* coffin. Many words connected with Jewish folkways are Semitic like the following terms relating to marriage : *shadkhn* matchmaker, *shidekh* match, *knas* engagement, *tnoyim* conditions of the engagement, *nadn* dowry, *kale* bride, *khosn* bridegroom, *ksube* marriage contract, *khupe* canopy, under which the bridal pair—*khosn-kale*—stand during the *khásene* wedding, surrounded by the *mekhutonim* in-laws.

But there are other groups of Hebrew loans in Yiddish, the presence of which is not so easily accounted for in detail. A strikingly large number of abstract terms, for instance, are Hebraisms; among everyday examples are *emes* truth, *eytse* advice, *khokhme* wisdom, *koyakh* strength, *moyre* fear, *nakhes* pleasure, *yedie* knowledge. Perhaps such words were first established in the language of the traditional schools where Bible and Talmud formed the main subjects of study. Here such words could have the status of technical terms in moralising or philosophical argumentation. Another group of borrowings may have a similar origin; it consists of words like *afile* even, *avade* certainly, *efsher* perhaps, *kedéy* in order to, *keseyder* continually, *kimát* almost, *tomid* always. All are commonly used words.

There still remain a great many words in everyday use which have no specifically religious or learned appearance, like *sakh* multitude, used with the indefinite article to mean 'many': *a sakh Yidn* many Jews, *khaye* animal, *khevre* group, society, *mishpokhe* family, 'clan', *sam* poison, *sod* secret, *shokhn* neighbour. There are opposites like *sholem* peace and *milkhome* war, or pairs like *meylekh* king and *malke* queen. There are adjectives such as *broygez* angry, *emes* true, *khoshev* respected, *poshet* simple. A number of Hebrew verbs have also been borrowed into Yiddish; examples of these are discussed in the section 'Synthesis of the various Components'. Furthermore, Yiddish has developed a periphrastic conjugation based on an invariable Hebrew participle (see the section 'Outline of Yiddish Grammar').

Sometimes the Hebrew terms are distinguished by some specialisation of usage. Hence *land* but *Erets Yisroel* Land of Israel, *bukh* but *seyfer* religious book. Hebrew words can occur as slang: donkey is *eyzl*, but *khamer* means only fool. In more literary usage, on the other hand, Hebrew terms may be introduced for stylistic purposes: *menader zayn* to vow (a periphrastic verb) is more formal than *tsuzogn* to promise (Ger. *zusagen*). It is, however, a fact that most Hebraisms which do not refer to purely Jewish customs can be replaced by a term from the Germanic or Slavonic component.

The extensive adoption of Hebrew words in Yiddish was facilitated by the fact that, in traditional Jewish society, a knowledge of Hebrew was exceptionally widespread. Pretty well everybody knew the rudiments of the sacred tongue, the men at any rate could read the prayers and the Torah, while the more educated, the men who set the tone in this studious community, could both read and write Hebrew fluently. The classical Yiddish writers all wrote Hebrew as well. Latterly, however, the weakening of orthodoxy has been accompanied by a decline in the knowledge of Hebrew. To reach as wide a reading public as possible, new editions of the Yiddish classics may contain a pronouncing glossary of the less usual Hebraisms.

THE SYNTHESIS OF THE COMPONENTS

The Slavonic and Hebrew components of Yiddish have become closely fused with the basic Germanic component, which on the whole has reshaped them in accordance with the general Germanic pattern. For instance, Slavonic verbs are assimilated into Yiddish by being provided with Germanic endings: *khropn* to snore (Pol. *chrapać*), *ikh khrop* (Pol. *chrapam*) etc. Similarly with Hebrew verbal roots: *shmadn* to baptise (Heb. root *šmd*), or with a Hebrew noun already in use in Yiddish: *kholem* dream, *khólemen* to dream. The infinitive ending also appears doubled, e.g. affixed to Hebrew roots: *gánvenen* to steal (*gnv*), *hárgenen* to kill (*hrg*). This formation occurs in the culturally important word *dávenen* to pray, supposedly of Eastern origin and regarded as having formed part of the lost language of the Slavonic Jews already present in Eastern Europe when the Yiddish-speaking immigrants from Germany arrived. The term contrasts with Western Y. *orn*, ultimately from Latin *orare*.

Pol. *błądzić* is naturalised in Yiddish as *blondzen* to stray; from this by the addition of the Germanic prefix *far-* (Ger. *ver-*): *farblondzen zikh* to go astray, lose one's way. Similarly with a simplex of Hebrew origin: *mishpetn* to judge, *farmishpetn* to condemn. The mode of formation in these examples runs parallel to Ger. (*sich ver*)*irren*, (*ver*)*urteilen*. Yiddish does not use the prefix *er-*, instead it has *der-* with excrescent *d*, as in Bavarian dialect: *dertseyln* to tell, cf. Ger. *erzählen*, dialect *derzählen*. It may extend to non-Germanic verbs: *derhárgenen* to kill, beside *hárgenen*. Likewise *ba-* (Ger. *be-*): *bagázlenen* to rob, beside *gázlenen*, a Hebraism, cf. *gazlen* robber. The first pair do not have an exact correspondence in German, but the second pair are related like *rauben* and *berauben*. In like manner other Germanic formative elements may be used with non-Germanic words. Heb. *beheyme* head of cattle (the behemoth of the Bible is the plural of this word) makes *beheymish* cattle-like, doltish, Heb. *almone* makes *almóneshaft* widowhood; Heb. *koved* honour makes *úmkoved* dishonour, where *um-* corresponds to Ger. *un-*, as in *Unehre*. The present participle of Yiddish verbs adds the Germanic termination *-ik: falndik* falling (Ger. *fallend*), see 'Outline of Grammar'. Then the final syllable *-dik* was felt to be an ending and became productive; it may be found with Hebrew words : *rakhmónesdik* pitiful, from *rakhmones* pity.

Yiddish continues the MHG feminine ending *-inne* (NHG *-in*) as *-n*: *kvatern* woman bringing child for circumcision (Ger. *Gevatterin* godmother), but also uses a termination *-te* proper to Aramaic : *khaver* (male) friend, *khāverte* (female) friend. This termination may be found with non-Hebrew words : *póyerte*† farmer's wife. Slavonic has a characteristic feminine ending *-ka*, e.g. Pol. *kaczka* duck, whence Y. *katshke*. This ending has spread to the other components : *shnáyderke* tailoress (*shnayder* = Ger. *Schneider*), *shóykhetke* wife of a *shoykhet* (Jewish) slaughterer.

Reference has already been made to the extensive use of diminutives in Yiddish. The Germanic endings *-l*, *-ele* are regularly found with non-Germanic words : *sod* orchard (older **sad*, cf. Pol. *do.*), dim. *sedl*; *sider* prayer book (a Hebraism), dim. *siderl*. The diminutive may be the normal form of the word : *bobl* bean, cf. Pol. *bób* do. Sometimes the diminutive may have a special or technical sense : *máysele* fairy story, from the commonly heard Heb. *mayse* story, yarn, cf. Ger. *Märchen* from the now archaic *Märe* story. The Slavonic languages have richly developed the principle of grammatical diminution. They employ a variety of suffixes which, as in other languages, may express endearment as well as smallness. Yiddish has taken over some of these : *mámenyu, mámeshi* mamma. The common Slavonic suffix *-inka* appears in Y. *-inke*. It is not only attached

† Basically Germanic words are marked with an accent when they contain a non-Germanic element.

to nouns : *zúninke* (dear) little son, but also to some adjectives :
náyinke new, and occasionally even to verbs : *ésinken* (nursery
talk) to eat. The diminutives of Yiddish are among its most
expressive assets with nuances which may be very difficult to
recapture in translation.   Here is a line from a lullaby : *di
eygelekh, di shvártsinke makh tsu*. This we may translate : close
your little eyes, the dear little black ones, but we can scarcely
reproduce in English the atmosphere conjured up by these
diminutive forms.

It goes without saying that in a language like Yiddish with its
basic Germanic pattern, compounds can be formed by simple
juxtaposition of words from the various components. One
example is *mame-loshn* mother tongue, esp. Yiddish (Slavonic +
Hebrew); others are *khupe-kleyd* wedding dress (Hebrew +
German), *elterzeyde* great grandfather (German + Slavonic).
In fact all three components can be present in a single word, as
follows. The common Hebraism *mazl* means (good) luck.
Combined with *shlim* (Ger. *schlimm*) we have *shlimazl* bad luck,
which, with a Slavonic suffix *-nik* m. or *-nitse* f. (e.g. Pol. *-nik*,
-nica) and an unexplained different pronunciation of the
Hebrew element, gives *shlimezalnik*, *shlimezálnitse* unlucky
person.

Outline of Yiddish Grammar

By comparison with New High German the case system of
Yiddish is much decayed; it is on a par with several modern
German dialects. The genitive survives only to a limited
extent, chiefly in the singular, and is formed by an inflexional
-s. Possession is most commonly expressed by *fun* (= Ger. *von*)
which, like all prepositions in Yiddish, governs the dative.
Proper names take an inflexional *-n* in the acc. dat. : *Moyshn*
from *Moyshe* Moses, and in a few similar words : *tatn* from *tate*
father.

Yiddish retains the traditional three grammatical genders,
though nouns often show a different gender from their equivalents in NHG. Yiddish inherited from German a considerable
diversity in the formation of the plural of nouns. The languages
still have much in common in this respect, but innovations, not

least on the Yiddish side, have led to many divergences. Two plural endings of Hebrew provenance, *-im* and *-(e)s*, are very significant.

Examples

No change in the plural, all genders : *der fish* fish, *di shvester* sister, *dos mol* time, occasion.

Plural indicated by umlaut, masc. and fem. : *der zun* son, *di hant* hand; pl. *zin, hent.*

Plural in *-n*, written *-en* after vowels and certain consonants, all genders : *der taykh* river, *di tir* door, *dos papír* paper; pl. *di taykhn, tirn, papírn; di froy* woman, *der tovl* board; pl. *froyen, tovlen.* A few Hebrew words have joined this class, e.g. *der yam* sea, *di sho* hour; pl. *yamen, shoen.*

Plural in *-er*, with umlaut where appropriate, all genders : *der shteyn* stone, *di vayb* wife, *dos kind* child; pl. *shteyner, vayber, kinder; der boym* tree, *di noz* nose, *dos hoyz* house; pl. *beymer, nezer, hayzer.* Here may be mentioned *ponim* face, from Hebrew where it is plural in form, but in meaning also singular. This awkward word is treated as a neut. sg. and has been given a Germanic pl. *pénimer.*

Plural in *-(e)kh*, diminutives in *-l, -(e)le* only, neuters : *meydl* girl, *neshómele* (dear) little soul (*neshome*), *eygele* 'Äuglein' (*oyg* eye); pl. *meydlekh, neshómelekh, eygelekh.* This ending, also a feature of certain German dialects, is a development of the MHG collective suffix *-ach.*

Plural in *-im*, the characteristic masc. pl. ending in Hebrew : *guf* body; pl. *gufim.* These nouns usually make some internal vowel change in accordance with Semitic practice, e.g. *meylekh* king, *khoydesh* month, *shokhn* neighbour, *novi* prophet; pl. *melokhim, khadoshim, shkheynim, neviim.* Occasionally non-Semitic words follow these principles : *poyer* farmer, *doktor* doctor; pl. *póyerim, doktoyrim.*

Plural in *-es* with internal vowel changes occurs in a small number of Hebrew masc. nouns : *kholem* dream; pl. *khaloymes.* This termination has spread to words of Slav origin : *der vorobeytshik* sparrow; pl. *vorobéytshikes.*

Plural in *-s*, which is characteristic of Hebrew feminine nouns in Yiddish : *almone* widow; pl. *almones.* Since the common

Slavonic feminine ending -a becomes -e in Yiddish, the plural in -s easily spread to such words too : *stelye* ceiling; pl. *stelyes*. The ending is also used with some words of Germanic origin : (*der*) *shrayber* writer; pl. *shraybers*.

Hebrew has only two genders, masculine and feminine, and Hebrew loans in Yiddish generally keep their original gender; a few, however, have become neuter : *kol* voice; pl. *koyles*.

ARTICLES AND ADJECTIVES

The indefinite article *a* does not decline; before vowels it becomes *an*. The declensional endings of the definite article and the adjective are as follows :

	m.	f.	n.
Sg. nom.	*der guter man*	*di gute froy*	*dos gute kind*
acc.	*dem gutn man*	„ „ „	„ „ „
gen.	*dem gutn mans*	*der guter froy*	*dem gutn kinds*
dat.	*dem gutn man*	„ „ „	*dem gutn kind*

Pl.nom.acc.dat.—*di gute mener, froyen, kinder*, gen.—*di gute meners* etc.

This is the only declension of adjectives current in Yiddish, except that in the neut.sg. uninflected forms may occur after the indefinite article :

nom.acc. *a gut kind*, gen. *a gut(n) kinds*, dat. *a gut(n) kind*. The uninflected nom.acc. form *gut* is an ancient feature, cf. MHG. *ein guot kint* besides secondary *ein guotez kint* > NHG *ein gutes Kind*. When used predicatively, however, an inflected form is used : *es iz a guts* it is a good (one), Ger. *es ist ein gutes*.

NUMERALS

1 *eyn(s)*, 2 *tsvey*, 3 *dray*, 4 *fir*, 5 *finf*, 6 *zeks*, 7 *zibn*, 8 *akht*, 9 *nayn*, 10 *tsen*, 11 *elf*, 12 *tsvelf*, 13 *draytsn*, 14 *fertsn*, 15 *fuftsn*, 16 *zekhtsn*, 17 *zibetsn*, 18 *akhtsn*, 19 *nayntsn*, 20 *tsvantsik*, 21 *eyn un tsvantsik*, 30 *draysik*, 40 *fertsik*, 50 *fuftsik*, 60 *zekhtsik*, 70 *zibetsik*, 80 *akhtsik*, 90 *nayntsik*, 100 *hundert*, 1000 *toyznt*.

The form *eyns* is used in counting, as in NHG.

PRONOUNS

The personal pronouns are :

Sg.nom.	*ikh* I,	*du, -u** you,	*er* he,	*zi* she,	*es* it
acc.	*mikh*	*dikh*	*im*	,,	,,
dat.	*mir*	*dir*	,,	*ir*	*im*
Pl.nom.	*mir* we,	*ir*† you,	*zey* they		
obl.	*undz*	*aykh*†	,,		

Reflexive pronoun all persons, sg. and pl. *zikh*.

mir < *wir* arose originally in the enclitic position by assimilation, the stages being e.g. *hoben wir* > *hobm wir* > *hobm mir*, then becoming generalised.

The possessives are :

Sg.*mayn* my, *dayn* your, *zayn* his, its, *ir* her; pl. *undzer* our, *ayer* your (also polite sg.), *zeyer* their. These are invariable in the singular, but add -*e* before plural nouns.

VERBS

The verb in Yiddish has become more analytical than in German. There is no subjunctive. The preterite has disappeared and as a result the difference between the strong and weak verbs is only manifested in the formation of the past participle. The function of the old preterite has been taken over by the perfect, as in many German dialects, and by a new periphrastic tense using as an auxiliary *flegn*.

The inflexions surviving in Yiddish may be seen from the following paradigm :

Infin. *shraybn* write

Pres.sg.1 *shrayb*, 2 *shraybst*, 3 *shraybt*; pl. 1,3 *shraybn*, 2 *shraybt*
Imper.sg. *shrayb*, pl. *shraybt* Pres. part. *shraybndik*
Past part. *geshribn*
Similarly the weak verb *makhn* make, apart from past part. *gemakht*

Examples of verbs with strong past participles : *farlirn* lose, *farloyrn*; *trinken* drink, *getrunken*; *nemen* take, *genumen*; *gebn* give, *gegebn*; *grobn* dig, *gegrobn*.

---

* Enclitic after the verb : *hostu?* have you ?   † Also polite sg.

The pres. participle with its -*ik* extension is a Yiddish innovation; formally one may compare Ger. *lebendig*.

The verbs 'TO BE' and 'TO HAVE' in Yiddish:

Infin. *zayn, hobn*
Pres.sg.1 *bin, hob*, 2 *bist, host*, 3 *iz, hot*; pl.1,3 *zaynen, hobn*, 2 *zayt, hot* Imper.sg. *zay, hob*; pl. *zayt, hot*
Pres. part. *zayendik, hobndik* Past part. *geven, gehat*

Compound tenses are formed with various auxiliaries; *ikh vel shraybn* I shall write (*veln* = Ger. *wollen*), the remaining forms being sg.2 *vest*, 3 *vet*; pl.1,3 *veln*, 2 *vet*. It will be noticed that the auxiliary here is a conflation of MHG *wellen* (NHG *wollen*) and *werden*, hence *vest, vet*, reduced forms corresponding to Ger. *wirst, wird* and *werdet*. When the meaning is 'want to' *veln* has these forms: sg.1,3 *vil*, 2 *vilst*; pl.1,3 *viln*, 2 *vilt*; past part. *gevolt*. Other compound tenses: *es vert geshribn* it is (being) written (*vern* = Ger. *werden*), *ikh hob geshribn* I have written, *ikh hob gehat geshribn* I had written, *ikh bin geblibn* I have stayed, *ikh bin geven geblibn* I had stayed (*blaybn* stay). Repeated action in the past is expressed by the auxiliary *flegn* (formally = Ger. *pflegen*): *ikh fleg shraybn* I used to write.

Yiddish has developed a periphrastic conjugation based on invariable nominal elements of Semitic origin, e.g. *mekaber* (*tsu*) *zayn* (to) bury, corresponding roughly in form to the construction '(to) be burying', though without the continuous sense implied by the English. Examples of tenses etc.:

Pres. *ikh bin mekaber*, past *ikh hob mekaber geven*, imper. *zay*(*t*) *mekaber*, pres. part. *mekaber zayendik*.
The object is inserted as follows: *zey hobn dem mentsh mekaber geven* they buried the man.
Similar combinations with *vern* are possible: *mekuyem vern* materialise. Such nominal elements only occur as an integral part of the conjugation; they have no independent existence.

THE YIDDISH SCRIPT

Like all Jewish languages Yiddish is written in Hebrew characters; these are read from right to left. The values given to the Yiddish letters are not, however, in every case identical with the values of the same letters in Hebrew, since the Yiddish alphabet is an adaptation of a Semitic alphabet to the needs of an Indo-European language.

The most obvious difference concerns the writing of vowels. The Hebrew alphabet originally contained consonants only, the structure of a Semitic language being such that this system sufficed for a tolerable degree of legibility. In the course of time, however, some of these consonants took on a second function. For example, the letters for w and y came to be employed as rough guides to vocalisation : w could suggest the vowels o or u, y could suggest e or i. With such and other approximate indications anyone who knew the language could read a text without hesitation, ambiguity being very largely excluded. At a much later date—perhaps during the 5th to 7th centuries A.D.—systems of complete vocalisation were evolved and one of these, the Tiberian, became the standard. It consists of a system of dots and dashes, the so-called points, usually added below the consonant to indicate the vowel following. The purpose of these points was to fix the pronunciation of a dead language and assure an indisputably accurate text of the Bible. But for other purposes Hebrew was, and is, normally written without pointing.

In using the Hebrew letters to write Yiddish, both of the above principles have been applied. For instance, Hebrew w and y stand in Yiddish for u and i respectively; the Hebrew glottal stop, transcribed ʔ, and the laryngal consonant ʕ, sounds which do not occur in Yiddish, are similarly used as vowels, the latter being e, the former a or o depending on the pointing. The Yiddish alphabet is as follows :

Letter	Name	Transcription
א	*shtumer alef*	–, in Heb. ʔ
אַ	*pasakh alef*	a
אָ	*komets alef*	o
ב	*beyz*	b
בֿ*	*veyz*	$\underline{b}$ pronounced as v
ג	*giml*	g

Letter	Name	Transcription
ד	*daled*	*d*
ה	*hey*	*h*
ו	*vov*	*u*, in Heb. *w*
ז	*zayen*	*z*
ח*	*khes*	*ḥ* pronounced as *kh*
ט	*tes*	*t*, in Heb. *ṭ*
י	*yud*	*i, y*, in Heb. *y*
כ*	*kof*	*k*
כ (ך)	*khof*	*kh* ('ch' in loch)
ל	*lamed*	*l*
מ (ם)	*mem*	*m*
נ (ן)	*nun*	*n*
ס	*samekh*	*s*
ע	*ayen*	*e*, in Heb. *ʕ*
פ	*pey*	*p*
פ (ף)	*fey*	*f*
צ (ץ)	*tsadik*	*ts*, in Heb. *ṣ*
ק	*kuf*	*k*, in Heb. *q*
ר	*reysh*	*r*
ש	*shin*	*sh*, in Heb. *š*
ש*	*sin*	*ś* pronounced as *s*
ת*	*tof*	*t*
ת*	*sof*	*t* pronounced as *s*

The forms in brackets are used when final.

* Asterisked letters occur in Hebraisms only (see below).

The remaining consonant sounds of Yiddish are represented by the combinations וו *v*, זש *zh* ('s' in pleasure), טש ('ch' in church). In the Yiddish pronunciation of Hebrew, ʔ and ʕ are only guides to vocalisation; this is usually the case with *w* (unless pronounced as *v*) and *y*, as also with final *h*; *ṭ* and *q* are pronounced as *t* and *k*.

י denotes *i* between consonants, *y* before and after vowels. Pointing may be used to avoid ambiguity : יִ *yi*, similarly וּו *vu*, וּו *uv*.

Silent *alef* is written at the beginning of a word before ו and י likewise before the diphthongs י־ *ey*, ײַ *ay*, וי *oy*.

Yiddish orthography is entirely phonetic except for Hebraisms. Here the spelling is that of normal unpointed Hebrew sometimes amplified by diacritical marks as illustrated in the alphabet above. Frequently however these marks are omitted, so that ב may be either *veyz* or *beyz* etc. Unless the reader already knows these words, he cannot pronounce them until he has referred to a dictionary where the pointing will be given. In the case of words containing a Hebrew component attached to non-Semitic elements the same rules apply : *shlimezalnik* 'unlucky chap' is written sh–l–i–m–z–l–n–i–k.

An exception to this is the Yiddish published in the Soviet Union, where Hebraisms are spelt phonetically like the rest of the language. For example, the common Hebraism m–l–w–k–h 'state, country' is pronounced *melukhe*, hence in Soviet spelling m–e–l–u–kh–e. The use of special forms for final letters was at first discontinued, but has since been restored. Apart from these modifications the Soviet orthography is virtually identical with the YIVO standard.

Older publications, especially newspapers, often appeared in an orthography bristling with redundant letters (in imitation of German) and copiously pointed. This orthography was the child of the Maskilim, the protagonists of the Jewish Enlightenment. Their system, or variations of it, dominated the press up to the First World War. The Soviet reform in the immediate post-revolutionary period was a radical realisation of calls for orthographical change which had already been urgently voiced. Elsewhere reform was slower and less drastic, but during the last 30 years a simpler, phonetic orthography, again with variations, has made great headway and is now usual.

Specimen of Yiddish

From *Three Gifts* by I. L. Peretz (1852–1915).

דרײַ מתנות.

1 אַ מאָל, מיט יאָרן און דורות צוריק, איז ערגעץ
ניפֿטר געוואָרן אַ ייד.

2 מילא! אַ ייד איז ניפֿטר געוואָרן–אייביק לעבן קען
מען ניט–טוט מען אים זיַין רעכט, ברענגט מען
אים צו קבֿורת ישראל.

3 נאָך סתימת הגולל–דער יתום זאָגט קדיש–פֿליט די
נשמה אַרויף צום מישפט, צום בית-דין של מעלה.

4 קומט זי אַרויף, הענגט שוין דאָרט פֿאַרן בית-דין
די וואָג, אויף וועלכער מען וועגט די עבֿרות און די
מיצוות.

5 קומט דעם בר-מנוס סניגור, זיַין געוועזענער יצר-
טובֿ, און שטעלט זיך, מיט אַ קלאָר וויַיס זעקל
ווי שניי אין דער האַנט, בײַ דער וואָגשאָל פֿון דער
רעכטער זיַיט.

6 קומט דעם בר־מננס קטיגור, זיין געוועזענער יצר־
הרע, און שטעלט זיך מיט אַ קריטיק זעקל אין דער
האַנט, בייַ דער וואָגשאָל אויף דער לינקער זייַט:

7 אין ווייַסן קלאָרן זעקל זענען מיצוות, אין ברודיק־
שוואַרצן זעקל עברות.

8 שיט דער סניגור פֿון שניי־ווייַסן זעקל אויף דער
וואָגשאָל פֿון דער רעכטער זייַט מיצוות, שמעקן זיי
ווי פֿאַרפֿומעס און לייַכטן ווי שטערנדלעק אין הימל.

9 שיט דער קטיגור פֿון ברודיקן זעקל אויף דער
וואָגשאָל פֿון דער לינקער האַנט עברות, זענען זיי
שוואַרץ ווי קויל און אַ ריח האָבן זיי – סאַמעראָדנע
פעך און סמאָלע.

10 די וואָגשאָלן הייבן זיך פֿאַמעלעך, אַרויף און
אַראָפ, אַ מאָל די, אַ מאָל יענע.

11 דער יצר־טוב, ווי דער יצר־הרע, דרייען אויס די
זעקלעך קאַפֿויר: ניטאָ מער!

12 און דעמלט גייט דער שמש צו צום צינגל זען,
ווי עס האָט זיך אָפּגעשטעלט: רעכטס צי לינקס.

13 קומט ער און קוקט אַזוי, און זעט אַזוינס, וואָס איז
נאָך ניט געשען זינט הימל און ערד זענען באַשאַפֿט
געוואָרן.

14 דאָס צינגל שטייט אין סאַמעראָדנע מיט–אויף–דער
האָר!

Transcription

The pronunciation of the Hebraisms is given below the text.
It may be noted that the Yiddish pronunciation of Hebrew is
very far removed from that of Biblical days and is also considerably different from the pronunciation of Israeli Hebrew.
    Asterisked words are of Slavonic origin.

DRAY MTNWT[1]

1 A mol, mit yorn un dwrwt[2] tsurik, iz ergets nyftr[3] gevorn
   a Yid.

2 Myl?[4]! a Yid iz nyftr[3] gevorn—eybik lebn ken men nit—
   tut men im zayn rekht, brengt men im tsu qbwrt yśr?l[5].

3 Nokh stymt hgwll[6]—der ytwm[7] zogt qdyš[8]—flit di
   nšmh[9] aroyf tsum myšpt[10], tsum byt-din šl mʕlh[11].

4 Kumt zi aroyf, hengt shoyn dort farn byt-din[11] di vog,
   oyf velkher men vegt di ʕbrwt[12] un di myṣwwt[13].

5 Kumt dem br-mnns snygwr[14], zayn gevezener yṣr-ṭwb[15], un
   shtelt zikh, mit a klor vays zekl vi shney in der hant,
   bay der vogshol fun der rekhter zayt.

6 Kumt dem br-mnns qtygwr[16], zayn gevezener yṣr-hrʕ[17],
   un shtelt zikh, mit a koytik zekl in der hant, bay der
   vogshol oyf der linker zayt.

7 In vaysn klorn zekl zenen myṣwwṯ[13], in brudik*-shvartsn zekl ʿḇrwṯ[12].

8 Shit der snygwr[14] fun shney-vaysn zekl oyf der vogshol fun der rekhter zayt myṣwwṯ[13], shmekn zey vi parfumes un laykhtn vi shterndlekh in himl.

9 Shit der qtygwr[16] fun brudikn* zekl oyf der vogshol fun der linker hant ʿḇrwṯ[12], zenen zey shvarts vi koyl un a ryḥ[18] hobn zey—samerodne* pekh un smole*.

10 Di vogsholn heybn zikh pamelekh*, aroyf un arop, a mol di, a mol yene.

11 Der yṣr-ṭwḇ[15], vi der yṣr-hrʿ[17], dreyen oys di zeklekh kapóyr: nitó mer!

12 Un demlt geyt der šmś[19] tsu tsum tsingl zen, vi es hot zikh opgeshtelt, rekhts tsi* links.

13 Kumt er un kukt azóy, un zet azóyns, vos iz nokh nit geshen zint himl un erd zenen bashaft gevorn.

14 Dos tsingl shteyt in samerodne* mit—oyf der hor!

1 *MATONES*, 2 *doyres*, 3 *nifter*, 4 *meyle*, 5 *kvures Yisroel*, 6 *stimes ha-goylel*, 7 *yosem*, 8 *kadish*, 9 *neshome*, 10 *mishpet*, 11 *bes-din (bezn) shel male*, 12 *aveyres*, 13 *mitsves*, 14 *bár-minens saneyger*, 15 *yeytser-tóv*, 16 *bár-minens kateyger*, 17 *yeytser-hore*, 18 *reyakh*, 19 *shames*.

Notes (numbers refer to sentences)

(1 *ergets* = Older NHG *irgends*, with change of *i* to *e* before *r* and loss of *n*; 2 *eybik* < MHG *êwic* (> NHG *ewig*), MHG *w* appearing sporadically as *b* in Yiddish as also in some words in NHG; *ken* reformed after the infin. *kenen* = Ger. *können*; *men* = Ger. *man*, with weakened vowel as in Dutch *men* do.; *brengen* Central German form; 3 *aroyf*, *a-* representing MHG *her-* (> NHG *do*.) as in some German dialects; 4 *farn* a contraction of *far dem*; 5 *gevezen*, a Germanism (*gewesen*); 6 *koytik* = Ger. *kotig* which in some districts has the same sense as the Yiddish; 7 *zenen*, alternative form to *zaynen*; *brudik* is Slav. *brud* dirt + the Germanic ending *-ik*; 8 *shitn* = Ger. *schütten*; *shmekn* = Ger. *schmecken*, the sense 'smell' being attested in MHG; 10 *pamelekh* is Pol. *pomału* 'gradually, slowly', contaminated by Ger. *allmählich*, cf. Silesian Ger. dial. *bemählich, beimählich*; 11 *kapóyr* < MHG *kein (gegen)* + *enbor (empor)*; *nitó* < *nit* not + *do* there, cf. the idiomatic expression *es iz nitó keyn* . . . there is no . . .; 12 *demlt* a secondary form of *demls*, Ger. *damals*; *tsingl* cf. Ger. *Zünglein* in the same sense; 13 *kukn* cf. Ger. *gucken* commonly pronounced like the Yiddish form, a pronunciation which arose through a crossing of *gucken* with its northern synonym *kiken* (cf. Du. *kijken* do.); *azóy* < MHG *alsô*; *azóyns* < *azóy* + *eyns* such a (thing); *zint* < MHG *sint*, with unexplained *n*, beside *sît* > NHG *seit*)

THREE GIFTS

1 Once, years and generations ago, somewhere, there died a Jew.

2 Alas! a Jew died—one can't live for ever—they do for him what is proper, they give him a Jewish burial.

3 After the grave has been filled in*—the orphan says *kaddish*—the soul flies up to the judgement, to the Court on High.

4 When it arrives, the scales on which the sins and the good deeds are weighed are already hanging there in front of the Court.

5 The dead man's advocate, his one-time good spirit, arrives and takes his stand on the right-hand side of the scales, in his hand a clean bag white as snow.

6 The dead man's prosecutor, his one-time evil spirit, arrives and takes his stand on the left-hand side of the scales, in his hand a dirty bag.

7 In the white, clean bag are good deeds, in the filthy-black bag sins.

8 When the advocate pours good deeds out of the snow-white bag on to the scale on the right-hand side, they smell like perfumes and shine like little stars in the sky.

9 When the prosecutor pours sins out of the dirty bag on to the scale on the left hand, they are as black as coal and have a smell exactly like pitch and tar.

10 The scales move slowly, up and down, now this one, now that one.

11 The good spirit, and the evil spirit too, turn their bags upside down : there is no more!

12 And then the usher goes up to the pointer to see how it is standing, to the right or to the left.

13 He comes and takes a look, and sees a thing which had not been seen since heaven and earth were created.

14 The pointer stands exactly in the middle—to a hair.

---

* Lit. after the placing of the stone (to block the entrance to the sepulchre).

Matthew x, 5–10:

די דאָזיקע צוועלף האָט יְשׁוּעַ פֿונאַנדערגעשיקט און

האָט זיי געבאָטן, אַזוי צו זאָגן: גייט ניט אויף קיין וועג

פֿון די גוײם, און קומט ניט אַרײַן אין אַ שטאָט פֿון

די שׁומרונים. נייערט גייט ליבערשט צו די פֿאַרלוירענע

שאָף פֿון דעם בית־ישראל. און בעת איר גייט, רופֿט

אויס, און זאָגט: דאָס מלכות־שמים איז נאָענט. הײלט

די קראַנקע, זײַט מחיה־מתים, רייניקט די מצורעים,

טרײַבט אַרויס די שדים. בחינם האָט איר מקבל

געווען, בחינם זאָלט איר געבן. נעמט ניט קיין גאָלד,

אָדער זילבער, אָדער קופּער אין אײַערע גאַרטלען;

ניט קיין רייזעזאַק אויפֿן וועג, ניט קיין צוויי רעק, ניט

קיין שיך, ניט קיין שטעקן; וואָרים דער אַרבעטאָרער

איז ווערט זײַן עסן.

Hebraisms: [1]*Yeshue*, [2]*goyim*, [3]*Shomroynim*, [4]*Bes-Yisroel*, [5]*beys*, [6]*malkhes-shomaim* [7]*mekhaye-meysim*, [8]*metsoroim*, [9]*sheydim*, [10]*bekhinem*, [11]*mekabl*.

THE INFLUENCE OF YIDDISH ON GERMAN

Yiddish, i.e. Western Yiddish, has had a certain lexical influence on German through the intermediary of *Rotwelsch*, the cant language of pedlars, thieves, vagabonds and the like. This language goes back to the Middle Ages, the term *Rotwelsch*, lit. Beggar's Welsh, being first attested in 1250. We now possess a very full work on this cant language : S. A. Wolf, *Wörterbuch des Rotwelschen*, Mannheim, 1956, page after page of which reads like a Hebrew dictionary where we may again meet the majority of the words already mentioned in this chapter. Jews were very prominent in long-distance trade in medieval Germany. They had only to interlard their German with Hebrew words to make it at once incomprehensible to the Gentiles. The advantages of such a jargon were not lost on other wayfaring elements and so the Hebrew component of Yiddish became a main source of *Rotwelsch*. In the course of time a number of originally cant words of Hebrew provenance passed into general use in German, though tending to remain at a more or less substandard level. Modern examples are colloquialisms like *acheln* eat, *Chuzpe* f. insolence, *Dalles* m. poverty, shortage of money, *meschugge* crazy, *mies* ugly, *Moos* n. money, *schicker* drunk, *schofel* trashy. These examples also occur in Standard Yiddish : *akhlen* (slang), *khutspe*, *dales*, *meshuge*, *mies*, *moes* (slang), *shiker*, *shofl*. Other cant words have penetrated certain German dialects without, however, becoming general, for instance *Doches* m. backside (St. Y. *toches*) or *Zores* m. confusion, mess (really a plural form, cf. St. Y. *tsore* trouble).

Though Yiddish died out in Germany during the latter half of the 18th century, the German Jews retained some relics of the old language. Some still survive like the typical Jewish expression of commiseration *nebbich* (St. Y. *nebekh*) : *ich hab' nebbich* (= *leider*) *kein Geld*, a term of Slavonic origin, cf. Czech *nebohý* wretched, which apparently entered Yiddish in the Middle Ages.

BIBLIOGRAPHY

The intending student of Yiddish may well begin with *College Yiddish* by U. Weinreich (YIVO, New York, 1949), an authoritative introduction to the proposed standard language. The essentials of the grammar are presented in graded lessons which include reading passages, exercises and vocabularies. The book gives an insight into Yiddish life and culture and is suitable for self-instruction. It would, however, have greatly assisted the learner in understanding the pronunciation of Hebraisms had these been given in the vocabularies fully pointed. As it is the student, unless he already knows Hebrew, really needs to refer to a Hebrew(-Aramaic) dictionary as well.

The Semitic component of Yiddish has been succinctly discussed by S. A. Birnbaum, *Das hebräische und aramäische Element in der jiddischen Sprache*, Leipzig, 1922.

A historical study of a dialect close to the form described above has been given by F. J. Beranek, *Das Pinsker Jiddisch*, Berlin, 1958. Examples in transcription.

S. A. Birnbaum, *Praktische Grammatik der jiddischen Sprache*[2], Hamburg, 1966. Concise grammar with a dictionary of commonly used words, particularly of such as are not found in German or are used differently; contains a long passage of Yiddish prose followed by a German translation.

U. Weinreich, *Modern English-Yiddish, Yiddish-English Dictionary*, New York, 1968.

N. Stutchkoff and M. Weinreich, *Der Oytser fun der Yidisher Shprakh*, New York, 1950. A thesaurus entirely in Yiddish.

M. Weinreich, *Geshikhte fun der Yidisher Shprakh*, 2 vols., New York, 1968.

For a general account of Yiddish linguistics see F. J. Beranek, 'Jiddisch' in W. Stammler, *Deutsche Philologie im Aufriß*, vol. I, 1952, cols. 1551–90.

HISTORY OF GERMAN: GENERAL BIBLIOGRAPHY

W. W. Chambers and J. R. Wilkie, *A Short History of the German Language*, 1970, gives an account of main trends.

R. Priebsch and W. E. Collinson, *The German Language*[6], London, 1968. A comprehensive handbook presenting a great deal of information on topics ranging from the Indo-European background to modern German handwriting. There are lengthy bibliographies and copious references to specialist literature.

A large number of histories of the German language have been written in German, for example, H. Moser, *Deutsche Sprachgeschichte*[6], Stuttgart, 1969, and F. Tschirch, *Geschichte der deutschen Sprache*[2], 2 vols., Berlin, 1971–75. A. Bach, *Geschichte der deutschen Sprache*[9], Heidelberg, 1970, is a valuable small-size handbook. E. Agricola *et al.*, *Die deutsche Sprache*, 2 vols., Leipzig, 1969–70, treats the subject after the manner of an encyclopedia.

The best known reference grammar on historical lines is H. Paul, *Deutsche Grammatik*; impression of 1958, Halle (5 vols). The author finished the third, definitive edition during the First World War. There is a shortened version in one volume: H. Paul—H. Stolte, *Kurze deutsche Grammatik*[3], Tübingen, 1962.

ETYMOLOGY

M. O'C. Walshe, *A Concise German Etymological Dictionary*, 1952.

The standard work in German is F. Kluge, *Etymologisches Wörterbuch der deutschen Sprache*. The author brought out ten editions, and after his death in 1926, various scholars have been responsible for keeping the work up to date. The 20th edition was published in 1967 (Berlin).

SYNTAX

The evolution of German syntax is admirably summarised by I. Dal, *Kurze deutsche Syntax*[3], Tübingen, 1966.

W. B. Lockwood, *Historical German Syntax*, Oxford, 1968.